THE HUMBLE AND
THE HEROIC

THE HUMBLE AND THE HEROIC

WARTIME ITALIAN AMERICANS

Salvatore J. LaGumina

CAMBRIA PRESS

YOUNGSTOWN, NEW YORK

This book has been registered with the Library of Congress.
LaGumina, Salvatore J.
         The Humble and The Heroic / Salvatore J. LaGumina
         p.   cm.
         Includes bibliographical references
         ISBN-10: 0-9773567-7-9
         ISBN-13: 978-0-9773567-7-5

Illustrations are from the author's personal collection as well as those graciously
provided by the following whom the author hereby gratefully thanks: Francesca
Magliochetti, Louis Pierini, Giuseppe DeLiguori, National Museum of the
United States Air Force, and the United States Army.

The background photograph on the cover illustrates the humble Italian American
garment factory workers who would make their contribution manufacturing
military uniforms. Superimposed is a photo of air ace Captain Don Gentile who
ascended from humble origins to the status of hero.

*For my children and
my dear wife, Julie*

CONTENTS

FOREWORD

In his latest book, *The Humble and the Heroic: Wartime Italian Americans*, Professor Salvatore LaGumina establishes himself as the preeminent chronicler of the Italian Immigrant experience. Laced with scholarly nostalgia and solid research, this is a timely "must read" for all Americans who are descended from immigrant forbears. Today's third and fourth generation Italian Americans are who we are because of the sacrifices of our forbears.

The author sets the stage for his manuscript by asking two basic questions: Was an extra measure of loyalty and patriotism required of Italian Immigrants because the country of their birth was a declared enemy of their adopted country; and, does their WW II experience offer meaningful insights as to how we should treat other immigrant groups in future conflicts?

While the answer to both questions is clearly "Yes," the long, hard road traveled by the early Italian immigrants is worthy of this scholarly study. That road was paved with sacrifice, bitter poverty, discrimination and, for many, the devastating indignity of being designated as "enemy aliens." Professor LaGumina's book presents a balanced and graphic description of an epic moment in one minority's fight for their right to assimilate.

The contributions of the immigrant Italian community to the war effort are legendary—13 Congressional Medal of Honor winners were of

Italian descent and this did not include Don Gentile who became the "highest-scoring fighter pilot in American history." Equally important was the "unfeigned patriotism" of the Home Front Italians perhaps best described by an immigrant Italian mother whose American GI son was captured : "We want America to win. We are over here since 1904, we've never been back ... We don't care about Italy anymore." Clearly, her ordeal was one of the many "required extra measures of loyalty and patriotism" on the road to assimilation.

The answer to the author's second question regarding immigrants whose native countries or co-religionists may be hostile to our security is not fully developed. Nevertheless, the author has artfully described a road map successfully employed by the Italian Immigrants ... At the end of the day, America is a welcoming homeland to those who are willing to work hard, assimilate and make sacrifices for the common good. In the oft repeated words of my sainted Mother: God Bless America.

Rear Admiral Andrew A. Giordano (Retired)
United States Navy

INTRODUCTION

After more than six decades, the mind still reels at that extraordinary transforming period in American history, albeit from the perspective of a young Italian American teenager. The outbreak of the Second World War was that interval in which the nation metamorphosed from a competing major power to the dominant arbiter of world affairs. It was within the life span of that generation that the United States marshaled together the most destructive engine of war in human history, a display of frightening power that was critical to the defeat of the monster Axis war machine that caused so much havoc and further threatened to harm the world. It was also the ultimate testing period for the nation's largest immigrant population—I was a product of this group, the Italian Americans—I was one of approximately 6 million Americans of Italian extraction, primarily first and second generation.

To those who question the rationale or necessity of an ethnic viewpoint, I simply aver that it is as legitimate as it is to refer to a John F. Kennedy as emanating from an Irish mold or an Adam C. Powell as speaking from an African American perspective. At particular periods in American history, certain ethnic groups have functioned on the periphery, as it were, wherein their views, feelings, and outlooks were either omitted or largely ignored by mainstream interpretations. To encounter this definitive turning point

of the twentieth century history from an ethnic group view point about
which there were misgivings owing to Italy's enemy nation status, will
help to shed light not only about Italian Americans, but also about the nation as a whole and others who would be in a similar position.

"Any war has two fronts." commented Tom Brokaw in his well-received
The Greatest Generation, wherein he cited exemplary performances of
ordinary Americans both on the battle front and the home front. Brokaw's
work is a very useful reminder that "The home front rarely gets equal
credit" for the commendable massive buildup of the sinews of war. "On
factory assembly lines or in shipbuilding yards, in government offices and
top secret laboratories, on farms and ranches, the men and women who
stayed behind were fully immersed in the war effort."[1] A.A. Hoehling,
in his volume on the topic, has made another sage observation revolving
around the impreciseness of the home front as a malleable term, one which
is not as readily definable as that which deals with the battlefront.[2] The
home front term encompasses a myriad of elements and frequently contradictory forces. To treat of the home front, is in other words, to deal with
diversity and restlessness, to deal with commonalties and discrepancies.
Nevertheless, in mining numerous and often overlooked threads of American life in this period, I am confident that it will substantially illuminate
this important chapter in American history.

It is revealing to note that although some works on the home front do
incorporate at least part of the Italian American experience, many others do
not. Notwithstanding Brokaw's superior effort in shedding light on what
ordinary Americans were doing at this time, with two exceptions—one a
reference to John Assenzio, apparently an Italian name, but not otherwise
identified as such in the text, and the other Brokaw's accolade of Congressional Medal of Honor winner Gino Merli in the introduction, no Italian
American is given major treatment that revolves around his ethnicity. Likewise, the convergence of major American historians in a 1989 symposium
to re-examine the topic of WWII, under the auspices of the Organization
of American Historians, found participants voice concern with legitimate

issues: the evil incarnated in German and Japanese characteristics, racism, segregation, Japanese American internment, anti-Semitism. Conspicuous by its absence was the Italian American wartime experience—it apparently was not even worthy of passing reference. This is not necessarily to infer a deliberate choice of omission, but rather a mindset and a reality that probably reflects a prevailing view—if that be the case, it is indeed disturbing.[3]

Until the recent generation, evasion and even avoidance can be used as adjectives that largely characterized Italian Americans participation. In his 1995 instructive article focusing on World War II, the late George Pozzetta, made a pertinent observation. "Most studies of America during World War II either ignore white ethnic groups altogether or approach their inquiries from limited perspectives ... few studies have looked within white ethnic groups to determine precisely how individuals responded to war condition and, equally important, how they influenced the larger society by their actions."[4] Writing from the viewpoint of surveying Italian American literary output, in 2002 Bill Tonelli echoed the sentiments of many regarding ethnic group evasion of the issue, when he wrote, "Scholars have yet to explore how deeply World War II drove Italian culture into hiding."[5]

In this endeavor, I hope to share my memories and feelings, as far as I can recall them, amply aided by contemporaries, especially my sister Madeline Sutera and brother Joseph LaGumina, whose collective memories help enlighten and inform about the impact of the war at that time. More than nostalgia, I am striving to interweave personal recollection and objective history, that is, to attempt to dovetail what was taking place on the home front on my block in Ridgewood/Bushwick in Brooklyn, New York with the wider ethnic community and with the mainstream society. My understanding of that earlier period has been reinforced by my professional career as a historian, and by research and study in the years since the war, always attuned to the particular role Italian Americans played in that tumultuous period and the effect it had upon them. In this regard, I have been fortunate to make the acquaintance of many individuals whose

xiv   THE HUMBLE AND THE HEROIC

wartime experience further embellishes the record. There is no claim that this is a universal perspective, rather it is a viewpoint shared by many in the Italian American ethnic community that will provide additional insight into this seminal period in our nation's history.

Hopefully a number of vital questions will be considered in the course of this journey, among which are: How does an ethnic minority deal with its near enemy status and conversely how does a nation deal with this minority? How did Italian Americans wrestle with a bi-furcated background? Was an extra measure of demonstrated loyalty required of the Italian ethnic group? Did expending themselves for American victory take its toll? Did native-born Americans really accept Italian Americans as full equal citizens? What were the political consequences of the ambiguous status? Does the wartime history of the Italian ethnic group offer meaningful insights for the treatment of other groups?

Pozzetta ended his essay on Italian Americans during World War II by correctly noting that the war's impact on the Italian ethnic group and the group's influence on mainstream society was a complex process that awaited further elucidation.[6] Hopefully this monograph will contribute to the search for an understanding of the dynamics that interacted between the larger culture and Italian identity in America.

CHAPTER I
ITALIAN AMERICANA
1920s–1930s

OVERVIEW

Post World War I America was confronted with a variety of perplexing issues that challenged its character as an open society wherein everyone, regardless of his or her background, was fully accepted. The republic had just engaged in a global contest that dwarfed other comparable wars in the scope of nations engaged and in the number of casualties suffered; it was justified as "a war to end all wars," a war "to make the world safe for democracy," in President Woodrow Wilson's felicitous phrase. However, it quickly led to disillusionment over the non-statesman-like grubby behavior of winning Allied powers that reverted to vindictiveness and revenge in dealing with enemies. A heightened form of nationalism infected the country expressing itself in such incidents as the Red Scare that sought to curb radicalism, socialism, and communism by harassing and expelling aliens connected with those ideologies. Domestic reaction that resolved to defend the American way with vigorous promotion of "one hundred percent Americanism" found the nation seething amidst an intensified unabashed nationalism intolerant of any "foreign" appearance in its core. To speak a non-English language, to participate in seemingly strange customs and devotions, to read foreign-language newspapers, and to refuse to shed ethnic backgrounds increasingly became unacceptable. In such a hostile atmosphere, it was manifestly assured that immigration would re-emerge as a controversial issue.

NATIVISTS

Nativists who had long sought to preserve the demographic (Anglo Saxon) purity of the nation via legislation like the 1917 Literacy Test that had met with only limited success in curtailing immigration, now became apprehensive about the resumption of full scale immigration immediately following the war. The rate of Italian immigration in 1920–1921, for example, approximating alarming levels of previous peak years in 1907 and 1913, served to convince the restriction-minded to take essential radical steps at ending or curbing the influx. The fact that Italians were considered the prime targets of the 1917 law, and that the forthcoming National Origin Quota Act of 1924 would have the most deleterious impact on Italians rendered it evident that Italy's immigrants faced a rather hostile environment. The Sacco-Vanzetti case may be adduced as the cause celebrè to illustrate how devastating the atmosphere could become. Beginning in 1920 and lasting until their execution in 1927 and even beyond, Italian American communities were roiled by the trial of two Italian immigrant anarchists, a shoemaker and a fish peddler. Convicted of murder during a payroll robbery on the basis of dubious testimony, including blatant disregard for the integrity of Italian immigrants as witnesses, this episode engendered turmoil both within and without Italian American communities. As anarchists, Nicola Sacco and Bartolomeo Vanzetti were convinced that their conviction was based not only on their ideology but also on account of their Italian nationality. (Significantly Massachusetts Governor Michael

Dukakis exonerated both of them posthumously 50 years later).

PROHIBITION

A heritage of World War I, Prohibition, that unique experiment to deprive Americans from imbibing in alcohol, was a distinctive sensational feature of the "Roaring Twenties" that also contributed to direct the spotlight on immigrant populations as it tended to focus on customs regarding drinking alcoholic beverages that were at variance with prevailing sobriety concepts. There was little appreciation for German beer-drinking customs or Italian wine-drinking practices, so graphically described by novelist John Fante in his memorable autobiography *The Wine of Youth* wherein he contrasted the pseudo wine used by the priest at mass with that of his father. "My father had swell red stuff in his cellar, ... you can down a whole barrel without it fazing you."[7] The notion that to imbibe in alcoholic beverages was to act against the law impacted many an Italian American household where homemade wine created in cellars had become a proud feature of life. The pride Italian Americans took in winemaking was a practice that flourished both during the "dry" period and also the "wet" period following the termination of Prohibition in the 1930s. Unfortunately, the prominence of Italian names among the more notorious Prohibition violators served to exacerbate the problem. It was my impression that perhaps half of the Italian Americans on my block made their own wine. Indeed even though this did not include my family, we had multiple opportunities to purchase the homemade product from neighbors, invariably opting for next door neighbor, volatile Mr. Nene Amodeo's creation that exuded his fierce personality and could readily produce a near bacchanal state.

INCREASED INFLUX

Despite these obstacles, Italian American enclaves in city after city increased significantly as Italian immigrants and their issue improved their lot by dint of hard work and sacrifice. Anticipating the influx, Alberto Pecorino, in an article published in 1911, captured the phenomenon, "The Italians are here; they are coming."[8] By the outbreak of the Second World War they had become residents in large enclaves in numerous New England metropolises such as New Haven, and Waterbury, Connecticut, Providence, Rhode Island, and Boston, Massachusetts. Italian Americans were likewise significant blocs in Pittsburgh, Chicago, Buffalo, Rochester and Syracuse. Their preponderance would continue for another generation with over one million (1,070,000) inhabitants of Italian heritage—15.5 % of New York City's population in 1930, they accounted for one in seven New Yorkers constituting the single largest nationality group.[9] To the several New York City Little Italies, including five in Brooklyn that Pecorino identified, more would be added within another generation. He described such neighborhoods as virtual transplants of small villages from which most Italian immigrants came, enabling one to find streets in Little Italy that in effect were replications of their villages. Pecorino also noted high rates of illiteracy in 1911—50% in the New York area thereby rendering them "a mass of faithful and honest workers—... these are the men who excavate the subways, clean the streets, work at cement foundations of the skyscrapers, and build the great subway stations."[10] My generation benefited from their industry and hard labor. It was not, however, a totally dismal picture for the first generation; thousands were not manual laborers, but worked instead in countless skilled fields: expert tailors, adroit seamstresses, skilled barbers, accomplished chefs, excellent electricians, capable carpenters, reliable mechanics and ingenious bricklayers.

LABOR STRUGGLES

By the 1920s, New York City's Italian American population, which consisted primarily of first and second generations, was essentially a proletarian people that sought employment in city manufacturing enterprises such as clothing, shoemaking or printing plants, as well as an assortment of small manufacturing operations. The need to work was answered not only by the men of the household, but also by many women who emanated from cultures where women customarily did not work outside of their homes, but were now driven into the workplace by the vicissitudes of a harsh and unforgiving depression. Notwithstanding the view that the underclass was accordingly susceptible to and did experience exploitation, it does not mean they did not respond to efforts to improve their lot. The prevailing perception that Italian Americans were tractable, obedient and subservient, and thus unreceptive to the burgeoning labor movement, was not accurate. Indeed, a closer look finds that there were more than a few instances that demonstrated their increased visibility and willingness to take up the cause of labor including strikes and walkouts. For example, controversial New Yorker Paul Vaccarelli, leader among Italian American longshoreman, utilized these weapons so successfully for years that it came to the attention and appreciation of the White House which called upon him to forego a strike in order to aid the struggle of a country at war, causing President Woodrow Wilson to commend him for not interrupting the war effort. In addition, Vaccarelli remained active as a labor leader in the postwar period.[11] By the 1930s, Italian Americans were an unmistakable presence in the garment industry, where under the leadership of people like Luigi Antonini, for example, they played an increasingly important role. Born in Vallata Irpini, Italy, in 1883, Antonini had emigrated in 1908, joined the International Ladies Garment Workers Union (ILGWU) in 1913, became vice-president of the union in 1914, and soon became editor of *L'Operaia*, an Italian language periodical that trumpeted the cause of unionization among Italian immigrants. By the 1930s, he had become a household byword in many an Italian American home via radio airwaves where his thunderous oratory gave fervid voice to Italian American aspirations. There were also striking instances of promoting the cause of labor by Italian Americans who had moved from the city to small Long Island enclaves where either as union members or on ad hoc basis, they struggled for wage and hour improvements even if it meant resorting to strikes.

EDUCATION

Although an overwhelming Catholic population, limited financial resources meant that a relative minority of Italian American children attended parochial schools, with large numbers enrolled in the public schools.
The prevailing system found children attending local public elementary
schools, followed by junior and senior high schools. During the Great
Depression, education for many Italian Americans, especially females,
terminated at age 16—the legal age before one could quit school to go
to work. Economic exigencies now comported with a peculiar mentality
about women. "To give a daughter more education than that required by
law was an extravagant waste of time and money," was the way novelist Jerre Mangione described it.[12] This pattern of sacrificing a female's
education in preference for males was not considered unusual; indeed, it
occurred in my family as my sister, although a more than able student,
departed from school to obtain a full time job in order to help the family
income. By contrast, notwithstanding our family's dependency on relief
and the child welfare program to get by, there was no pressure for me to
quit school.

Which type of New York City high school to attend was a decision of
great moment for Italian American youngsters in the 1920s and 1930s as
they were required to make a choice while still in eighth grade between
traditional academic institutions or vocational high schools? The vocational school movement was based on the premise that these institutions
were desirable alternatives for students presumably unable or uninterested
in competing successfully in academic programs. It is not by accident that
vocational schools were deliberately located in poor, immigrant neighborhoods; it comported with the prevailing stereotyped belief that these
people were not desirable academic material.[13] This negative attitude was
reinforced by extensive use of the Binet Test that was widely used during
the First World War which purportedly measured natural intelligence and

seemed to indicate an inferiority complex among first and second generation Italian Americans since so many did not score very high. However,
as educator Leonard Covello points out, no allowance was made for the
absence of home support of the child brought up in slum areas where
parents' poor expressions of English served as a model. Thus the child
"usually did not have the vocabulary to express himself and had not the
opportunity to absorb the fundamentals of education as thoroughly as a
student from a better economic environment."[14] Other scholars of education and its impact of Italian American youngsters were similarly critical
of the system for making little effort to relate to the parents of the children
and their culture. Sr. Mary Matthews who studied the impact of public
school education on Italian Americans in New York City concluded, "That
the schools had little contact with the parents and that nothing was done to
bring the parents into the educational process so far as their children were
concerned are now clearly recognized as defects of the system."[15]

It was a comparable story in other Italian American enclaves outside of
New York City. Irvin Child's study of Italian American life in New Haven,
Connecticut, during this era indicates a similar disposition on the part of
the educational establishment to disparage Italian culture while becoming
preoccupied with full-scale assimilation.

> ... but there can be no doubt that the general policy of the
> school system is oriented toward developing American
> citizens and that very little is done in school that would
> tend directly to increase individual adherence to the Italian
> group ... The child is brought into contact at school with
> teachers who are for the most part not of Italian descent.
> He is forced to observe how non-Italians talk and act,
> whereas he may not have had any previous opportunity
> to observe them except at a distance. He is treated by his
> teachers in the way they have learned as participants in
> American culture, not in the way his parents have learned
> as participants in Italian culture.[16]

Although I considered myself fortunate in having fine teachers, I was aware there was a relative paucity of Italian American teachers in my school; I cannot recall any teacher in my elementary school with an Italian name to serve as a role model. Formal guidance, as I remember, left much to be desired—rather than an exercise tailored to individual aptitudes, it was closer to the practice of funneling students into presumed predictable patterns that frequently meant encouraging enrollment in vocational schools in poorer immigrant neighborhoods. Thus, although possessing a superior academic elementary school record including skipping a grade for proven proficiency, I opted for a vocational school. My thinking was that since I would most likely end up working in the trades, as was the case with the overwhelming majority of young people in my neighborhood, it would be useful to learn a trade in a vocational school. Neither elementary school personnel nor family dissuaded me since in fact it was an unalterable fact that most of my acquaintances, including those who went to academic high schools, earned a living working in factories. Accordingly, I did learn the basic rudiments of machine shop in high school, and for a few years worked in that field; however, the vocational high school curriculum was bereft of language study, advanced English literature, higher mathematics and advanced science. In the early grades of secondary school, the physical education program was also disappointing—basically, it consisted of taking showers—undoubtedly the influence of the Americanization emphasis that characterized that era which placed a priority on sanitary conditions and cleanliness. Fortunately, physical education courses improved in the later grades. I cannot help but consider that it most surely would have been a different experience for me in a traditional high school where I might have studied Italian, for example. Study of Italian in high school, long resisted by the educational establishment, apparently was of relatively recent vintage having only been introduced in the 1920s. Ironically, many years later, I was to establish a close relationship with Leonard Covello who was a pioneer in the educational field in the immediate post-World

War I period, and who tersely described the effort to establish a conformist school curriculum.

> The war had strengthened the idea of conformity. Americanization meant the casting off of everything that was "alien," especially the language and culture of national origin. Yet the amazing paradox lay in the fact that it was perfectly all right for the Italo-American boy to study Latin or French, German or Spanish.[17]

There was something ironic in the educational package offered to Italian American youngsters during the inter-war years. While commendable efforts were taken to provide education for immigrant children, thereby enabling them not only to become better educated, but also prepared for better jobs, the system also discouraged formal study of the rich Italian heritage. Remigio Pane, a young Italian immigrant in the 1930s, who later established one of the nation's foremost graduate Italian language programs at Rutgers University, recalled with dismay the disinterest in studying Italian.

> The reluctance to study Italian on the part of the first generation was indeed due to a sense of discrimination. I remember when I was first hired as an instructor that during the freshmen registration many students would freeze when they saw "Italian" and move towards Spanish, French and other languages. The chairman of the department, who was anxious to develop the Italian course, would see students with Italian names and express his surprise at the way they would avoid taking the language.[18]

As Luciano Iorizzo and Salvatore Mondello explain, "Most educators tried to teach Italian-American children American traditions while overlooking their Italian heritage. A great educational opportunity to integrate both cultures was lost in the years of mass immigration."[19] The hard reality was that there seemed to be a lack of appreciation for Italian culture on the part of the educational establishment.

THE CHURCH

The Catholic parish church was a fixture in effectively every New York Italian enclave. "The church, of course, was always a restraining and guiding force. From the earliest days in Brooklyn, it bound the Italian people together. It would be impossible to overestimate its importance as a social influence."[20] Frequently, the result of efforts by the Italian immigrants in the neighborhood parishes reflected the regions of Italy of the majority residents in the area. For instance, the Neapolitan background of immigrants in the Williamsburgh, Brooklyn neighborhood was reflected in the establishment of Our Lady of Mount Carmel, and remarkably more than century later, it continues to manifest itself in the celebration of the Giglio, one of the foremost feasts in the northeast. There were at least three Catholic parishes within easy walking distance to where I lived—St. Barbara, originally of Germanic background, St. Brigid of Irish background and ours, St. Joseph Patron of the Universal Church that was conspicuously Italian. Newly-arrived Italian immigrants readily felt a distinctive ethnic ambiance in the Italian parish that put them at ease as Mario Macaluso's autobiography affirms,

> Saint Joseph Patron Roman Catholic Church in Ridgewood, Brooklyn, was my first parish when I emigrated to America. The church was the heart of all Italian immigrants who lived in the neighborhood ... Italian immigrants married and baptized their children in this church where artistic décor, atmosphere and liturgical services, held in the ethnic tongue, reminded them of the land they left behind. First and second generation Italians worshipped in Saint Joseph, and came to the rectory to seek spiritual guidance, comfort and also help to secure a job to earn honestly a livelihood in the new world."[21]

The church, built in 1921 largely with Italian American support, permeated with the sense of Italianitá that was readily evident in the persons of Abruzzi-born Monsignor Ottavio Silvestri, founding pastor and assistant pastors who were either Italian Americans or priests recruited directly from Italy. Sermons, confessions, and missions were frequently in Italian, while the parish highlight—the celebration of the Feast of St. Joseph, reflected an ethnic character and Italian-language Catholic media like *Il Crociato* and Italian language prayer cards were available in the church vestibule. Just as they did in Italy, congregants were likely to talk animatedly to friends and neighbors during services, a custom that provoked occasional rebukes by the pastor, but did not stop the practice. In addition to regular Mass and confession, one afternoon a week, I also studied religion by attending Confraternity classes in the classrooms of St. Joseph. To go to St. Joseph's Church on Sunday meant to walk six blocks through a heavily Italian neighborhood dotted with thriving mom-and-pop grocery stores, fruit stores, tailor shops, barber shops, Italian bakeries, and pastry shops. On the way home, one could always stop for items that were not bought on Saturday, the main shopping day. That Monsignor Silvestri was in fact more than an ordinary cleric was acknowledged decades after his passing in an informative *New York Times* article on the exceptional number of Sicilian American judges and lawyers from the vicinity over whom he had sway. "It was there that Msgr. Ottavio Silvestri, an ambitious and political-ly well-connected Roman Catholic pastor, cast his influence over a group of bright, young Italian children, who in turn would inspire others."[22]

As a priest and public figure whose influence extended beyond our neighborhood, some controversy surrounded Silvestri. This was in part due to the insensitivity he sometimes displayed—on one occasion, he rep-rimanded my mother when she took one of the chairs from the altar, believ-ing he had placed them there for parishioner use during an overcrowded Good Friday service.[23] While local rumor as I recall it stressed his private wealth, to others it was his political leanings that attracted attention. Dedi-cated anti-fascist Gaetano Salvemini maintained that because Silvestri spoke at a Fascist-organized function in 1936, that rendered him, in effect, a supporter of the foreign ideology.[24] I was too young to be aware of such inclinations in 1936; however, other than his presumed wealth, even when

I became more mature by the early 1940s, I can truly say neither I nor other contemporaries recall any intimation about his purported association with Fascism. Rather his strong voice on behalf of Italy reflected the prevailing view of upholding Italy primarily on nationalistic grounds.

The Block

The block was the place, the spatial entity that virtually encompassed the community and served as the catalyst for a mindset regarding second generation Italian Americans in the pre-World War II era in the nation's big eastern cities. The block, encompassed a rectangular expanse of soil with houses that "were like boxes stuck together, and we ourselves, the tenants called them 'railroad flats' because the rooms were lined up, one behind the other."[25] On my block, these railroad rooms were what we called home—dwellings for approximately 1,000 souls—that in some respect, mirrored the small villages from which most of the Italians came, and represented the circumscribed but amicable vantage from which one viewed and judged world events.

Himrod St., in Ridgewood / Bushwick, Brooklyn, USA, between Irving and Knickerbocker Avenues was the place where I became especially conscious that my parents, relatives, friends, and neighbors shared a common nationality. Even more pronounced was the Sicilian connection. Within a few minutes walk from our house, we children trailed our mother as we visited close or distant relatives or a variety of paisani from Pioppo, her home village in Sicily. While we were proud of our American identity, we also strongly identified with our Italian legacy, perhaps in part to bolster our self-respect. The street in which one lived held a special meaning; it became our unvarying compass, one that provided readily recognizable credentials, one that was the basis upon which to differentiate among other blocks in the immediate vicinity and it constituted a necessary foundation with which to interact with the wider world. It was difficult to conceive of meaning without the block as a reference point. I can never forget how vehemently my sister, brother and I opposed my mother's intention of moving to a flat only a few blocks distant, regarding the suggestion as the equivalent of calling upon us to abandon our ancestral home and village, to move away from everything that held meaning for us. My mother acquiesced to our concern and agreed to move across the street. The mindset was local and provincial, an outlook that could be found in other Italian enclaves as a study of Italian Greenwich Village confirms.

> Since the tenement flat was too congested for much else besides sleeping and eating, especially in the case of large families, the street became the social stage. Groups of men collected on street corners and in candy stores. Housewives turned shops and doorways into meeting places ... Watching such goings-on in the street from a window perch was a form of entertainment ... Locals were not able to sever themselves from the comforting routine and ambience of neighborhood life for any length of time."[26]

Because of sometimes oppressive summer heat and humidity, much of life in this ethnic venue was lived outdoors where one became accustomed to predictable neighbor scrutiny. Block residents learned to cope with the uncomfortable weather conditions in the pre-air condition era when on those especially hot days and nights landlords hosed down sidewalks in front of their houses to cool the sidewalks—originally slabs of slate or bluestone—and then opened cellar doors to bring out makeshift benches and kitchen chairs, creating one row against the cast iron railings in front of the tenements and another row along the curb. Tenants on the first and second floor would sit at the window facing the street, using bed pillows on the window sill to lean on. Pitchers of ice water would be passed around, and children would play games like ringolevio, punch ball, or searchlight on the street or ride on Chicago roller skates that they got free, thanks to a promotion from a newly opened Miles Shoe Store. This left a narrow path for block residents to pass by and exchange greetings or merely acknowledge each other as they came and went from their houses, thereby providing ample opportunity for sidewalk sitters and window observers to comment about the work habits, clothing, health, love life, idiosyncrasies, etc. of the passers by. It could be intimidating for those unaccustomed to the atmosphere; however, while to those of us who grew up in the environment, it may have been a nuisance at times, it otherwise was regarded a natural and inevitable circumstance of life on the block. As I look back at this setting, I can better understand the immigrant's strength of attachment to the village of one's youth in the old country and of one's longing either to return home to visit or to see, hear and talk with someone from the old country. The reality was that pre-Pearl Harbor America was not a melting pot, it was instead a society "marked by important ethnic divisions and tensions," a society in which immigrant groups highly valued ethnic "churches and schools, lodges and mutual aid societies, shops and festivals, foreign-language newspapers and radio stations, and group intermarriage."[27]

GERMAN BACKGROUND

Although by the time I became a teenager, there were perhaps only two or three buildings on the block that housed non-Italians, mostly Germans, there were multiple palpable reminders of a Germanic background in the immediate neighborhood. There were many German delicatessen stores, bakeries, and beer parlors that attracted family gatherings on Sundays and the Wagner, a movie house that featured German-language films. German heritage was manifest in the faded, but still visible Myrtle Avenue elevated line station sign, heralding the Hamburg Avenue station that had been obviously been supplanted after the First World War by Wilson Avenue. It was also evident in the German language newspapers that competed with Italian newspapers that could be purchased daily. On occasion, I would go on an errand to purchase a German newspaper for an elderly German woman who lived in our building. Proximity, not surprisingly, led to friendship with German youngsters. In one case, my brother had a friend on the block whose family was known for its pro-German sentiments, and although I did not witness this personally, another block resident swore that when he went to the house of the young German friend, he saw a poster of Hitler on the wall of the apartment.[28] For a time in the 1930s, I was friendly with Willy, a German boy who lived down the corner and whose home I occasionally visited until his family moved back to Germany. I always wondered what ever became of him because he would have been of draft age during the war.

So prevalent was the Germanic characteristic in the area that some students of Italian descent who attended parochial school were required to study the Teutonic language. For example, Sicilian-born Alex Pisciotta, future New York City Magistrate and Army officer in World Wars I and II, was taught by German nuns and studied that language in elementary level grades. Although the acculturation process would eventually erode the Teutonic flavor, Germanic customs were still in evidence in Ridgewood throughout the 1940s and even beyond.[29]

Together with other young neighborhood boys and my brother, it was to the German bakery on Wyckoff Ave. and Bleeker St. that I went on Saturday mornings, with the ten cents my mother somehow managed to squirrel away, to buy twenty pretzels at a cost of two for a penny. Fresh out of the basement oven that threw off a warm, wonderful aroma of dough being baked, the baker tossed in a warm, golden brown extra pretzel for me. Then I would place the pretzels in my makeshift former fruit basket, cover them with a towel to keep them warm, and try to sell twenty of them for one cent a pretzel—the amount required for my brother and I to go to Saturday afternoon movies. These movies usually consisted of a cartoon, chapters from serials like "Buck Rogers" with implausible conclusions, and a double feature including a B grade or unmemorable A grade film.

GROWING UP ITALIAN

To grow up in the Ridgewood / Bushwick section of Brooklyn, New York, in the 1930s was to acquire a sense of identity and pride that one was part of communal lifestyle characteristic of Italian immigrants and their descendants, one that was in marked contrast to much of the world beyond. It served also for the development of a provincial outlook, in which youngsters boasted that the kids on their block could defeat neighboring blocks in sports contests or in plain street brawls. This ethnocentric perspective ill-prepared us for those times when boys from other blocks attacked ours, sending us scampering to the safety of our homes or trying to hide in neighbors' cellars and hallways. To my adolescent mind, it was perfectly natural to look at the world from my street and my neighborhood; a viewpoint shared by Nat Scammacca.

> "During my adolescence, two cities of New York existed for me—one fascinating, mysterious, panoramic—the world permitted only to adults; the other, the corner of the street where I was permitted to play ... I knew nothing of the world that existed beyond the East River which separated Brooklyn from the long "peninsula" of Manhattan ... I did not know that there was an extensive section of Brooklyn called Williamsburgh between us and the river where hundreds of thousands of human beings even poorer than I lived. I did not know that, in that part of the city, whole gangs, the sons of immigrants, fought for space in this or that zone."[30]

Physically, the block comprised primarily of 18 three-story wood frame tenement houses on both sides of the street, most of which housed six families in railroad rooms. These were flats of either four or five consecutive contiguous and modest cubicles bereft of separate hallway access and incapable of providing minimum privacy. In the absence of central heat, at first a coal-burning then an oil-burning cast iron stove in the kitchen supplied heat in decreasing intensity to the distance of rooms from the source, that meant the parlor was always cold in the cold winter months. The stove also served as the medium to cook meals. Built originally for a proletarian German population in the early 1900s, closet space was exiguous able only to accommodate the sparest of wardrobes. There were also a few extant dumbwaiters. Flats contained neither bath and shower facilities nor separate bathrooms. The lucky ones were those able to bathe in the kitchen laundry tub when the apartment was otherwise empty or to visit community bathing houses several streets away once a week; these constituted the only sanative options. Two families on each floor shared a hall bathroom, which naturally meant a degree of intimacy that demanded extraordinary patience, decorum, and forbearance as neighboring families extended themselves to maintain sanitary conditions. Remarkably, neighbors usually accepted their mutual responsibility amicably and conscientiously. In the mid-1930s, under city mandate, each apartment was to have its own bathroom and either shower stall or bathtub.

A TRANSPLANTED VILLAGE

In an extraordinary example of Old World ancestral transplantation that was frequently replicated in Little Italies, whole families, immediate and sometimes extended, from small towns in Italy, clustered in particular buildings or streets. A veteran reporter alluded to the tenacity of Old World culture that was clearly illustrated by Calabrians and Sicilians in Brooklyn.

> Each street in which Italians settled became a community of old Italy in the literal sense, filled with transplanted neighbors and kinsfolk. No streets in Brooklyn were given over to unrestrained life. None were so exuberant, and none so spontaneous. The first generation Italians lived as they had been accustomed to live under the azure Italian skies, which were much of the day's functions and the intimate affairs of life were carried on in the open village piazzas. Little Italy was natural and unashamed.

> On fine summer days, young mothers sat on doorsteps, babies at their breasts; children swarmed the streets, neighbors sought the sunshine and exchanged confidences. Everything possible was done out-of-doors and in the companionship of neighbors and friends.[31]

Four married Rizzo brothers and their families lived in four of the six flats in the house next door to me, for example, thereby preserving the integrity of the family—the first and foremost social group to which anyone belonged. It was natural to observe the Rizzo families doing things together, and to assemble seated on stoops or homemade wooden benches on the sidewalk until late evening on hot summer nights when the oppressively sweltering and humid flats left tenants flaccid and exhausted. Congregating outdoors in the summertime was something virtually all the Italian Americans on the block did whether or not related, in contrast to non-Italians who were less visible. The next level of relationship was extended to paisani, that is, those individuals who came from the same village or town in Sicily. We were taught to relate to them with a level of respect approximating that of close relatives, and always addressed them in formal, respectable ways such as "Donna" and "Signora." We also utilized the Sicilian term "Vosia," etc. This filial phenomenon could be found extending beyond the block as, for example, in the Chicago area where one leader described his neighborhood as a place "where as many people know each other as they do in our district. We have to a very great extent the same kind of warmth, friendliness and intimacy in our community life that was to be found in the small towns of Sicily from whence our parents came."[32]

The block in which I lived harbored an Italian grocery / meat store replete with familiar and pungent foods. Liberally extending credit, the congenial grocer, Mr. Canzoneri, mastered a primitive form of bookkeeping, wielding a coarse lead pencil that he periodically whittled to a sharp point with his intimidating butcher knife, to maintain records of groceries bought on credit in a large ledger book. Although a few customers were able to pay cash daily, most paid their bills weekly or monthly. On the block, there was also a barbershop, a hot dog and sandwich store, an ice stall manned by Frank Stallone, an immigrant from Bari, and a garment factory where immigrant women worked as finishers, button-hole makers or sewers of linings. Shoe repair shops were readily available, if not on the block, right around the corner. It was astonishing to see a mature Italian shoemaker working in dark basement or, as in the case of our back yard neighbor, on the first floor store that pulsated with running motors and slapping belts of leather trimmers and buffing wheels, who managed to conduct business speaking broken English.

One cellar on our block accommodated an Italian bakery, operated by the Leggio family where one saw men covered with white dust delivering large bags of flour, followed by inhaling the warm, soothing aroma of freshly-baked bread, rendering it difficult not to buy the freshest baked product daily for evening meal. On special occasions such as Thanksgiving, for a small fee block residents could have their large meats or turkey baked in the Leggio ovens. The purchase of fruits and vegetables was an artful enterprise in which all Italian American mothers took justifiable pride in the skill required to discern between overripe produce and that which was ripe and ready. The choices were to walk along Knickerbocker Ave. where there were a number of fruit and vegetable shops originally Jewish-owned, but which gradually became an entry point for Italian American entrepreneurs. When the weather was favorable, Italian Americans waited for the itinerant pushcart peddler whose horse-drawn cart was stocked with crates featuring fresh items and prices crudely marked on brown paper bags. Employing a singsong manner, the peddler would shout with conspicuous accent his features of the day "scarola (escarole), lattuga (lettuce), melone (watermelon)" etc. He made periodic stops to cater to women who sometimes shouted their orders from their windows and either came out into the street themselves or sent one of their children with the requisite cash.

BROOKLYN'S LITTLE ITALIES

To say that one grew up in an Italian area in Brooklyn in the generation preceding World War II is somewhat misleading. There were, in fact, several Italian "Little Italies"—Red Hook, The Navy Yard, East New York, Gravesend, Greenpoint, Williamsburgh, and Ridgewood—ethnic enclaves that rendered Brooklyn arguably the county that housed more residents of Italian heritage than any other; however, these enclaves were, in reality, more accurately known as Napolitano, Abruzzese, Calabrese, Sicilian, etc.[33] Formation of ethnic neighborhoods in Brooklyn was part of a familiar pattern repeated extensively as Italian immigrants settled in numerous cities and towns in the northeast. Following a chain migration pattern, namely the well-worn tendency to move near friends and relatives who shared similar backgrounds, languages or dialects, and familiar mores, meant that people transplanted their regional characteristics to specific neighborhoods.

While there was some interaction with children of non-Italian background, the overwhelming number of relationships was those whose parents were of Italian birth; but the sense of ethnic heritage was more than that of being Italian—on my block, it meant to be of Sicilian ancestry. So conspicuous was the sense of being Sicilian that the first question asked by mothers upon learning about the prospective marriage of a neighbor's daughter was whether the future groom was Sicilian. If the answer was affirmative, it almost automatically conferred approval. If not, then in descending order the next best preference was that he be Italian, Catholic, or finally an American. Sicilian was obviously the preferred socio-psychological lineage; it was almost as if connection with the Mediterranean Island of Sicily possessed those intrinsic, inherent choice qualities that alone could provide sheltered sustenance and true fulfillment of life.

Most of the Sicilian immigrants on the block called their Brooklyn neighborhood "Bruculinu", as recalled by Vincent Schiavelli in his delightful book, *Bruculinu, America*, and it was on the block that they sought to maintain their Sicilian culture for the most part unconsciously and informally.

> If the weather was fair, the streets themselves would be teeming with life. Women would be haggling with push-cart vendors in Sicilian and broken English over prices of fruits and vegetables. Other vendors in horse-drawn wagons would be chanting their wares, amid the sound of the ragman" bell and the iceman" bellows ... Growing up in

this place was like having one foot in mid-twentieth-century United States and the other in mid-century Sicily.[34]

THE FEASTS

The ongoing struggle for survival in factory and home was interspersed by a traditional array of holidays such as Christmas, New Year's Day, and Easter, uniquely affected, however, by lusty foods, delicious desserts, and quaint customs of Italian/Sicilian heritage. In addition, there were special feast days appropriate to our Sicilian background, chief of which was the Feast of St. Joseph. Our "Italian" parish, St. Joseph, Patron of the Universal Church, sponsored a community celebration that was memorable to all, especially the young. We thrilled at the sight of glorious bright and colorful lights strung across the street not only in front of the church but also for blocks around. We marveled at the young children dressed as angels who seemed to be floating in mid-air as they were hoisted in holders strung on heavy wire from one side of the street to the other. The total experience was exhilarating: "Our ears were filled with a symphony of voices, pierced by the sound of spinning wheels of fortune and the screams and groans of players. Mothers called after lost children, amid the pop of shooting galleries. Great gales of laughter rose from strolling groups of families and friends." The great church celebration for the community was supplemented by private celebrations of St. Joseph's Table, a festivity that was held in private homes in which furniture was removed in favor of tiers of lavishly prepared food surrounded by lovely colorful and aromatic flowers. On the highest tier, a homemade altar held statues of the Blessed Virgin and St. Joseph holding the infant Jesus. On March 19, three orphan (or semi orphaned) children, once played by my sister, my brother and myself, were dressed in biblical clothing. We were instructed to knock on the door three times before gaining admission and then were seated at a table of honor where we were treated to the most wonderful food prepared by the hostess and neighbors. Friends, relatives and acquaintances from the block and nearby were invited to partake of the repast.[35]

SICILIAN PREDOMINANCE

Although of 80 to 90 percent of block residents were of Sicilian background, there were small segments of Neapolitans, Abruzzese and others descended from northern Italy whose dialects were so different from those of southern Italy that many of the latter could not easily understand them. The successful local merchants were those who, although non-Sicilian, quickly learned enough to communicate. The mix of regional dialects would stump outsiders, but almost as second nature, was comprehensible to inhabitants of the block. The phenomenon of regional settlement meant that the Italian colony was divided into almost as many groups as there were sections of Italy, with each group manifesting its singular institutions and customs that reflected its background in the form of mutual aid societies, newspapers, religious feasts, regional dishes, etc.

LIVING WITH POVERTY

Poverty was more likely to be endemic rather than a stranger on the block during the Great Depression—more than a few relied on government relief and welfare assistance, in the daily struggle for economic survival. Our neighborhood was quite familiar with the harsh struggle to earn a living and the travail of families coping with the deaths of breadwinners, as in the case of my father, whose three year bout with cancer cost him his life in 1938. For those who could afford it, wakes were conducted in formal funeral parlors; however, for those who could not, as in our case, wakes were conducted at home where a casket surrounded by floral displays was set up in the parlor. Friends and relatives who came to pay condolences were greeted by a floral arrangement on the front door of the house, by women who were close survivors dressed in black and immediate male members of the family who wore a black arm band. Normally mourners who were siblings of the widow would stay perhaps through the night; however, since no member of my mother's immediate family lived in this country, that task was left to cousins. At night time my sister, brother and I were put to bed where before we fell asleep ,we could still hear their low voices trying to comfort my sobbing mother. Thus, this encounter with poverty and death struck my family as it left my mother destitute and alone to deal with the formidable challenge of bringing up three small children ranging in ages from seven to ten. It seemed an enormously bleak and intimidating prospect for my immigrant non-citizen mother who was bereft of savings and income, and had no close family members to help out. My Sicilian mother, however, was of the old school—a woman of implacable courage and remarkable fortitude. She was a small woman, who although possessing only three years of formal nineteenth-century Italian education, had deep faith in God, was through years of deprivation experienced in the world of survival, and inured by years of hard work and forfeiture of non-essentials—experiences that well-prepared her to make the sacrifices necessary to carry on. We followed her lead. Although we had roller skates, thanks to a promotion launched by a newly-opened shoe store nearby, no one in my family enjoyed the experience of owning a two wheel bicycle. Among the things we could undertake as a family was to assume the chore of being janitors of our building, a task that could save several scarce dollars a month on rent. Thus my mother would have to deal with tasks that challenged grown men such as struggling to put out for sanitation collection the heavy corrugated metal pails laden with ashes. Saturdays found my brother, sister, and I, not yet teenagers, sweeping and cleaning the interior of the building, rolling up and taking the course green and red twenty-foot long (burlap type) hall rugs out onto the sidewalk to sweep, and polishing the brass mail box and hallway door knobs. In addition, we would carry the garbage pails out of the cellar onto the street after ascertaining that the ubiquitous mice had jumped out of the pails following their foraging.

AT HOME IN LITTLE ITALY

Growing up Italian in Brooklyn in the 1930s meant also to be part of the wider New York City colony—in many respects, a world unto itself. It was to imbibe in a subculture wherein a young Italian American conscious of his ethnic background, could venture into other Little Italies where the accustomed language and even recognizable dialects could be heard and where stores sold familiar foods. These were enclaves that housed accustomed institutions—churches, mutual aid societies, and feasts—they shared in common, where they were accepted and not made to feel ill at ease or out of place.[36] Many Italian enclaves were tiny, but cohesive, as for example, Corona, Queens, New York, that made headlines in the 1960s when it was threatened with destruction because of a decision to construct a high school and athletic field. This was described as a crime-free oasis, resembling a close knit community where the heavily Italian American inhabitants shared memories and festivities, worshipped together, and interacted as if they lived in small village in Italy.[37]

ITALIAN IDENTITY

Going to school and to work in New York during the 1930's meant interacting with other nationalities, religions and races, of course. Accordingly, friendships with other ethnic groups developed, although on my block, the majority of relationships were with those of Italian ancestry. Italian identity was manifest even in the games we played. A faint prompting of memory recalls a game called "War." It summoned players to partition with chalk a 2' x 2' segment of the sidewalk or street, selecting and writing the name of a country in the square (no country could be duplicated) and "defending" it against a player holding a spalding or tennis ball in the center of the country designated. The ball holder would then chant "I declare war on" and try to hit a player defending and standing within one of the countries. As one could imagine, Italy was usually was one of the first to be chosen, and if one did not get his bid in immediately, he would have to settle for a less desirable nation.

MILITARY MATTERS

However meager our knowledge of military matters previously, the gap was being filled in; months before the attack on Pearl Harbor and United States entry into the war, the Italian ethnic press published an increased number of articles emphasizing the Italian American role in defending the United States. In September 1941, for instance, *Il Progresso Italo-Americano* provided extensive coverage of the World War I heroics of Brooklyn's Anthony Peronace who won battlefield honors alongside of the famous hero Sergeant Alvin York. The following month, the newspaper's editorial praised the exceptionally large number of Italian American youth as a demonstration that they were "among the finest of the Great Army which is now being formed for a more secure defense of the vital interests of the nations."[38]

My knowledge of military matters as a youngster in the 1930s was at first limited to war stories of the older generation and to watching the labored walk of the local mailman who continued to suffer from the effects of being gassed during the First World War. There were also snatches of a few stories told to me by my father who had served in the Italian Army during that conflict. That participation by Italian Americans in the Great War both within and outside my area was rather extensive was a subject I was to learn in the course of time. For example, Alex Pisciotta, a young neighborhood product, who had served as an officer in the United States Cavalry became a founder of the George Caccioppo American Legion Post in the post-war period, chairman of the fund-raising committee that led to the Italian parish of St. Joseph Patron Universal Church, and campaigner for Italian American candidates for public office, including LaGuardia. Italian American World War I veterans were active in veterans' organizations elsewhere. For instance, in East Harlem, the father of future

Congressional Medal of Honor winner, Anthony Casamento, was instrumental in establishing the Thomas Jefferson American Legion Club whose members were predominantly of Italian background. Furthermore, future New York City mayors Fiorello H. LaGuardia and Vincent Impellitteri, who volunteered to serve in the Army and Navy respectively, were active members of veterans' organizations.

On another level, the Civilian Conservation Corps (CCC) program of the New Deal that utilized unemployed young men dressed in khaki uniforms for a range of worthy conservation projects, conveyed a military-like presence. Still another local warlike reminder was evident in a small triangular park only two blocks from Himrod St., at nearby Greene and Myrtle Avenues, that featured a bronze statue of a larger-than-life muscular American doughboy soldier. The besieged soldier whose helmet had fallen off and who was surrounded by the enemy conveyed a heroic image of raw strength, indomitable courage and a firm resolve to sacrifice. It was an inspiring sight to young and old.

SABELLI

Almost as if to counter the image of poor performance in combat that subjected them to ridicule, proud Italian Americans sought solace in instances of heroic performances that were attributed to those of their ancestry. One such illustration revolved around the career of Italian-born

Italian Americans supported the efforts of Cesare Sabelli (sixth from left) who sought to become the first to fly from New York to Rome. Giuseppe Bellance (fifth from left) was the designer of the airplane "Roma".

Cesare Sabelli, who became an Italian air "ace" during the First World War, and had immigrated to the United States in 1920, harboring a goal to become the first to fly non-stop from New York to Rome. Occupied for several years with the necessity of earning a livelihood first as a barnstorming pilot and then as a real estate entrepreneur, he succeeded in selling property in Brooklyn to immigrants from Bari. After accumulating some capital, he sought and succeeded in winning additional financial support from prominent Italian Americans, including opera luminaries Beniamino Gigli and Claudio Muzio. In competition with Charles Lindbergh, Sabelli was determined that his flight be an all-Italian enterprise, including a crew of Italian Americans and financing by Italian Americans as a demonstration of what Italians were able to accomplish. Sicilian-born and Brooklyn resident Giuseppe Bellanca designed the sesqui-plane "Roma" that was forced to abort after a troubled take off in 1928. Not discouraged, after a few more years, in 1934, Sabelli, together with co-pilot George Pond, successfully flew from Brooklyn's Floyd Bennett Field across the Atlantic Ocean in the "Leonardo DaVinci" airplane.[39]

BALBO

Another airplane feat that was to excite Italian Americans occurred in July 1933, at a time when piloting a plane safely over the ocean was still considered a highly risky proposition. This achievement was the stunning and historic flight of a squadron of twenty-four Italian seaplanes from Rome to Chicago then celebrating a Century of Progress Fair. Led by dashing and charismatic Italian Aviation Minister, General Italo Balbo. This extraordinary voyage of military planes established the feasibility of the Atlantic as a commercial aviation route and demonstrated Italy's aviation prowess in a major bid to take its place with world powers in the realm of air power. The outpouring of Chicago area Italian Americans and civic officials was astounding as tens of thousands lined the city streets in jubilation to watch him unveil a statue of Columbus and acknowledge the street named in his honor. Balbo and his armada proceeded to New York City where they were treated to a hearty reception at Brooklyn's Floyd Bennett Field, an enormous ticker-tape parade in Manhattan, and then enjoyed lunch at the invitation of President Roosevelt. Surely such acclaim could not fail to warm the cockles of Italian American hearts that responded enthusiastically to the honors bestowed upon Balbo as a way validating their presence and contribution. One example of the exuberance occurred in Far Rockaway near Jamaica Bay where the Italian planes were to depart for their return trip to Italy. Judge Frank Giorgio was then presiding over a trial when according to a newspaper account, "As the planes approached the courthouse, Magistrate Giorgio, himself an Italian, ordered the recess and the throng of people hurried from the courthouse and stood outside waving to General Balbo's fliers." Judge Giorgio determined to get even closer to the intrepid airmen by ascending the courthouse roof where he "waved vigorously to witness personally the departure of the squadron."[40] Closer to my home, Italian-born Monsignor Silvestri, our pastor, accompanied by friends and relatives, went by boat to Jamaica Bay to view the seaplanes and greet Balbo.[41] Many years later, 90-year-old Saverio Rizzo, a sensitive and thoughtful immigrant, offered still another example of the response to the Balbo expedition.

> I was in the elevated train on my way to New York and it had reached Eastern Parkway when all the passengers rushed out of the train to look at the distant sky. I ran out and there were 10 airplanes in a V formation. It was a grand spectacle which, after so many years lingers in my mind. Twenty-three Italian aviators had arrived to bring glory to Italian aviation, and to our country.
>
> The following day there was a parade on lower Broadway and a reception at City Hall where General Balbo received the keys to the city from the Mayor. The park and the surrounding spaces were crowded to capacity by Italians and admirers from other nationalities. I, and many others from Jamaica, participated in honoring our national heroes. It was a grand spectacle of admiration.[42]

DEPRESSION HITS HOME

With one out of four Americans unemployed and even higher rates in some neighborhoods, it was evident that the nation was continuing to reel from the tenacious economic depression during the second half of the 1930s. Like my father who was an experienced plasterer, many were skilled craftsmen who remained unemployed, but nevertheless constantly showed up at shape-up halls to see whether employment was available, only to be disappointed. While still a youngster, I once accompanied my father to a union hall where, along with dozens of others, Italian and non-Italian, he looked in vain for signs of employment. It marked the first time I heard him referred to as "Jack", rather than Giacomo, his birth name—an ironic indication of acceptance and assimilation precipitated by dire economic circumstances.

The Great Depression impacted everyone of course, but it was particularly devastating to minorities and immigrants, of which Italians were among the most prominent. An important study of Jews, Irish, German and Italians in New York in early twentieth century found that Italians were conspicuously lower in occupational hierarchy than many other ethnic groups. They were the city's largest single nationality group by 1930, at which time 31% worked as unskilled laborers—the highest of the four groups. Compared to the other groups, fathers of Italian American youth were almost twice as likely to be unskilled labor.[43] Those employed, moreover, were primarily in the skilled, semi-skilled, and unskilled occupations, with very small percentages in managerial and employer roles. Italian American youth had the highest proportion of unemployment as well as relief rolls. In a nutshell, they were more conspicuous in negative statistics than other white ethnic groups who saw them increasingly as competitors for scarce jobs.

Given their high non-citizenship rates, New York's Italian Americans received little sympathy as most Americans subscribed to the view that in hard times citizens should have first call on jobs and benefits. Simply put, the prevailing atmosphere that would be reflected in Congressional attitudes intensified an unfriendly attitude, if not outright hostility, towards immigrants as it strove to restrict such government employment to American citizens. Because of their recent arrival, their preoccupation with economic survival, and other basic concerns, many Italian Americans had not yet obtained citizenship and thus were ineligible for Works Progress Administration (WPA)—a government-funded program to provide temporary employment at jobs deemed useful to the community. The seriousness of the atmosphere is reflected in proposed legislation sponsored by dozens of congressmen that would have solved the problem of unemployment by ridding the country of aliens. The dubious reasoning was that since the number of unemployed approximated the number of non-citizens, the unemployment problem would be solved—a simplistic solution that defied economic coherence and was pregnant with inhumane elements. For example, there were numerous instances in which an Italian father may have lacked citizenship, yet the welfare of his American-born wife and children were jeopardized. "Starve the father and you starve his American child," were the stark words of the talented and controversial New York Congressman Vito Marcantonio whose impassioned pleas in behalf of Italian immigrants went unheeded.[44] In the years just preceding World War II, Marcantonio and other spokesmen like Edward Corsi joined with the Italian Committee for the Defense of Immigrants in an effort to protect Italian immigrants who were subject to discrimination and in danger of deportation. Corsi, former Commissioner of Immigration, rendered a somber observation regarding the impact of discrimination he experienced while serving as commissioner, including witnessing the arrival of newcomers who enthusiastically and courageously went to work; however, "More lately I see their children attracted to unlawful activities because of the brutality of social negligence and because they have been deprived of the more elementary necessities of life."[45] Corsi attributed the large numbers of Italian Americans on relief roles to this background. "It is sufficient to read the newspaper want ads to be convinced of this; the employment advertisements exclude Italians and Negroes."

For many, finding government-sponsored WPA work was the only option as few jobs were available in the private sector. Although some critics labeled working for the government project as "boondoggles"—highly inefficient and wasteful—the WPA fabrication of post offices, school playgrounds, roads, and parks in neighborhoods were visible manifestations of the type of positive construction that was accomplished. Knickerbocker Park, a few blocks away from my block, served to remind us of this type of effort. Until he became too ill, my father worked on the WPA; however, after three years of illness and much of the time lingering in the hospital, he died in February 1938.

Bereft of assets and with no close relatives to assist us financially, my mother was forced to turn to the city's Child Welfare program that provided a scant amount of dollars monthly for dependent children in the family, but made no provision for my mother. If authorities discovered that my mother did earn money, that amount would be deducted from the given allowance designated for the children, rendering it a dispiriting situation. My brother, sister, and I, as children of the depression, learned to be resourceful. We assisted her to perform "homework" by regularly wheeling an old baby carriage to a factory several blocks away, where clothing was loaded onto it and taken home to my mother who sewed on buttons for a miserly amount. Every member of our family had to be very alert for the visitation of the detested inspector, the welfare program agent who visited homes of welfare recipients to see that the regulations were adhered to. When we heard that such a person was seen on the block—a task not too difficult since everyone knew when a stranger was present on the street—we hurriedly hid the clothing under the bed to frustrate the prying eyes of the inspector as he checked the rooms. A humiliating experience, its memory seared so deeply into my mind that it solidified a determination that, if at all possible, I would avoid government handouts for the rest of my life.

1939 DIVERSIONS

I turned eleven in the fate-full year of 1939 that began so auspiciously with the April 30 opening of the World's Fair in Flushing, Queens, that revolved around the theme of "The World of Tomorrow". It was hoped that the bold modern architecture and the miracles of inventions and industrial efficiency that were the embodiment of the American dream would generate sufficient interest and crowds to help end the depression as well as offer a glimpse into the fabulous future. To the attainment of that end, there were constant references to the exhibit that not only brought people from afar, but also became a topic of interest in local newspapers and schools. We rapidly became familiar with and attempted to copy or draw facsimiles of the Trylon and Perisphere, the fair's easily recognized symbol that was so ubiquitously replicated on cards and banners, and we badgered our parents to take us to the fair. I considered it fortunate to visit it once where I stood in wonderment at the huge gleaming white symbols: the Trylon— an obelisk-like edifice and the Perisphere—a great globe. I was fascinated with the many flags and banners at various national pavilions, and was particularly impressed with the General Motors exhibit the imaginative and futuristic "World of Tomorrow," that was pegged to come to fruition in 1960, a time that seemed too impossibly distant to a young person. The Italian pavilion, which featured a large tower and water flowing down steps, was one of the fair's largest and most impressive exhibits. It seemed to herald Italy's modern-day renaissance. "For Brooklynites the lesson of this exhibit was that a part of Italy's great cultural treasure was deposited permanently in the borough, in the memories and skills and genius of its Italian citizens."[46] However, by the end of the Fair's first year, international events had deteriorated so dangerously that the Fair no longer attracted large numbers. Meanwhile, the neutrality provisions of United States underwent their severest test as future allies became engaged in burgeoning conflict with aggressor nations that had become more emboldened to the degree that neutrality legislation proved to be totally inadequate. Although we in the United States were not fully aware of the gravity of the situation, Germany's invasion of Poland, which marked the official beginning of the Second World War, was about to force the nation to re-examine its posture.

RADIO

Radio, which came of age during my youth, and was a must in every household, had evolved into a medium of entertainment that brought much-needed diversion. Programs like, "The Make Believe Ballroom," was a virtual prerequisite for followers of popular music, while schedules that featured Jack Benny, Fred Allen, Bob Hope, Edgar Bergen and Charlie McCarthy, and George Burns and Gracie Allen provided tremendous humor. For thrills and excitement, few programs could match "The Lone Ranger," "Gang Busters," "Sherlock Holmes," and "The Shadow Knows."

Over and beyond the importance of radio to the general public was its significance to ethnic groups, such as Italian Americans. The "radio days," of 1930s and 1940s as so fascinatingly described by Emelise Aleandri, demonstrated that that electric medium served to reinforce ethnic theater when Italian food companies realized that utilizing the airwaves was a boon to their businesses.[47] One recalls advertisers such as Paramount Foods, Caffe Medaglia D'Oro, and Roma Macaroni, among others, as sponsors of a number of programs. At one point, some fifteen New York radio stations offered many hours of Italian language broadcasting, with WOV and WEVD among the most well-known. The radio was a staple of entertainment in other cities that housed large numbers of Italian Americans. One notable case in point was the Prince Macaroni-sponsored "All Italian" amateur hour that began to be heard in Boston in 1935 as a means of bringing to the fore the talent of people of Italian background. WOV in New York City produced a number of dramatic programs that were regularly aired. There were, in fact, more than a few radio stations that featured Italian-language news, soap operas, and music wafting through the street when windows were open during summertime. Among the more frequent operatic voices were those of Tito Schipa and Gino Becchi, who frequently sang arias from opera favorites while Carlo Buti, the Italian with a sweet tenor voice, competed for popularity with Bing Crosby in my locale. Another favorite radio show of the day was "Orlando il Furioso," in which Emma Barbato played the hilarious and assertive Sicilian house-wife. One could see Italian films in local movie houses as well as Italian ethnic theater. I went to at least one show at the nearby Starr Theater that I found entertaining, although I did not entirely understand the language.

Participants in Italian radio regarded the subject matter of the programs as unrefined and simple. The description of Joseph Zappulla, respected and serious poet, journalist, and radio program writer, who worked with an Italian actor is revealing.

> During that time I also had some experience with Italian radio programs. When Giuseppe Sterni, one of the best actors in the United States, established "Il Teatro d'Arte Italiano" I attended and reviewed his monthly perfor-mances ... He admired my poetry so much that he often recited it on the radio and once or twice printed my poems in the playbill he had distributed in the theater of each performance.

> At the conclusion of his series of performances he was engaged by a macaroni manufacturing company to give plays, in daily episodes, over the Italian radio station WOV. Each play was adapted for the radio, with a re-duced number of actors, to about 20 minute episodes. Once a play took more than thirty days to be broadcast in its entirety. It seems that the listeners enjoyed these bits of acting and never lost track of characters and events.

> When my collaboration with Sterni came to an end I was asked by other heads of similar dramatic companies to write episodes for them. I remember one long series of episodes written from a popular (and absurd) novel ... The

series was being produced by another macaroni manufacturer. When I asked the actor why he had chosen that
novel, he told me that the manufacturer's wife had read it
and had insisted that it be given on the radio ...

It was then that I fully realized what most of the Italian
programs were. Only a few were interesting and well
done. There were some good radio announcers who not
only talked well, but used the language correctly. There
were some announcers, however, whose only qualification
was a pleasant voice. They had no culture and mistreated
the language. Because this was noticed by many cultured
Italians who strove to preserve the language of Dante, I
published an article on this subject in *Il Carroccio*. Later I
wrote a satire in verse castigating the culprits.[48]

Julian Miranda, another participant in Italian radio, recalled that in
their heyday, New York Italian radio stations broadcast from 9:00 a.m. to
6:00 p.m., presenting some programs half an hour in length while others
were of fifteen-minute duration. They employed many Italian actors, some
of whom were not memorable, and others who elicited such interest that
listeners would then go to the theater to see the same radio personalities
appear on stage. After some of these performances, the response on the
part of the audience could, on occasion, be extraordinary. "There were
occasions when mounted police had to be called out to control the crowds.
They would mob the actors afterwards because they were so realistic.
Once in New York I remember seeing a man called Gino Caini playing St.
Francis and people rushed backstage to kiss the hem of his robe."[49]

MUSIC AND OTHER ENTERTAINMENT

Youngsters of my generation and acquaintance enjoyed the swing
music made popular by instrumentalists of that era—Benny Goodman,
Artie Shaw, Tommy Dorsey, Glenn Miller, Gene Krupa, Count Basie, and
Louis Armstrong. It was near the end of the 1930s that I began to shine

shoes to earn money. On Saturdays, the most popular day of the week, I
carried my homemade but serviceable shoe shine kit to the social club
in the late afternoon to polish shoes of neighborhood young men in their
late teens anxious to look natty and chipper in their shark skin wide lapel
fashion suits and neat shirts topped off with ties knotted in the mandatory "V" fashion for a night out dancing. While performing my chores in
the clubhouse, I was treated to the latest band music emanating from the
phonograph machine and learned the lyrics to many a favorite song. So
popular were these bands that it was not uncommon for young people to
play hooky from school to see a favorite band and or singer appearing at
a big band mecca like the New York Paramount. I also enjoyed reading,
especially boy's adventure books such as Jack London's *Call of The Wild*,
while the taste of the older generation seemed inclined to prefer escapism
in books like *The Good Earth*, *Northwest Passage*, and *Gone With the
Wind*. Most of these became popular motion pictures that my friends and
I devoured in that wonderful land of celluloid make-believe. Of course,
reality was never distant and would encroach with thunder by the end of
the decade.

CHAPTER II
FASCISM AND
ANTI-FASCISM

IDEOLOGY

The decades between the two World Wars spawned dictatorships and totalitarian social systems that would severely try the mettle of democracy. One of the most prominent of these systems was Fascism, a political system that became ascendant in Italy under the dictatorial rule of Benito Mussolini, a former Socialist who emerged as the world's pre-eminent exponent of Fascist philosophy. In its initial period, Fascism was given qualified support because it had not yet emerged as a fully developed system and seemed to strike responsive chords by utilizing the rhetoric of revolution and social leveling, while simultaneously touting a national revival. As it advanced in Italy in the 1920s and 1930s, Fascism became a system of government based on a one-party dictatorship, one that suppressed opposing political parties and one that promoted a centralized economic system. Mussolini also extolled the virtues of the glorious Italian heritage from the days of ancient Rome and celebrated Italian nationality in an undisguised effort to claim Italy's place in the sun among the world's leading powers.

Theoretically and in practice, while private enterprise was permitted, it was heavily fettered by government control that played a major role in the interplay between labor and management. That Mussolini's determination to advance Fascism rested on aggressive, even brutal, actions by his followers is underscored by the violent death of Giacomo Matteotti, member of the Italian Parliament in 1924, following the Socialist deputy's courageous denunciation of the illegal tactics used by the fascists to assume power. In the wake of the harsh face of Fascism, a number of anti-fascist Italians fled Italy for America, where they were to play important roles in the ethnic community. Thus, notwithstanding Mussolini's cruel conduct, the apparent success of his early tenure was destined to have international reverberations.

In her incisive analysis of totalitarianism, Hannah Arendt informs us that what was transpiring was the decline of Italian constitutional parliaments and the multi-party system in favor of "one party above parties." She also indicates that although a budding nationalist dictatorship, Fascism did not became truly totalitarian until 1938.[50] Famed Italian journalist Luigi Barzini provides the perspective of a sagacious observer from within when he wrote "Then came fascism and no one knew what to think. Many wore the black shirts (out of conviction, or a sense of discipline) and shouted the same slogans—fascism had many forms and seemed the answer to each person's particular worries."[51] The Fascist state arose not simply because a mesmerizing leader seized state power in unsettled times, but also because the democratic institutions that might have opposed him had rotted away.

AMERICAN REACTION TO FASCISM

The probing question as to what Americans thought about this development is best answered by noting that in the 1920s public opinion was split with Mussolini's actions eliciting as much praise as condemnation.

The bifurcation reflected the lack of clarity about Italy's political system that was, in fact, still evolving and not yet fully lucid to the outside world. Many commentators concluded that given the fragility of Italy's embryonic experience with democracy, exacerbated by the chaotic conditions in the post-war period, including huge wartime manpower losses, a reeling economy, and bitter disappointment at the peace settlement, that the nation was ripe for a strong man rule. Simply put, the frailty of Italian democracy did not seem capable of satisfying an increasingly disillusioned populace, thereby setting the backdrop for the rise of Fascism.

Among American observers who espoused this view was popular writer Kenneth L. Roberts. In his discerning study on the topic, John Diggins shows that Roberts was effusive in his adulation of Fascism as the cure for an Italy beset with all kinds of competing and debilitating internal forces.[52] While Roberts' views may be attributed to his illiberal and rabid anti-immigrant outlook, it is curious to learn that at the time those of traditional liberal persuasion found Fascism appealing because of "its experimental nature, anti-dogmatic temper, and moral élan."[53] In addition to Americans, during its early stages respectable world-renowned leaders like Great Britain's Winston Churchill, Irish playwright George Bernard Shaw, and Columbia University President Nicholas M. Butler, also sang the praises of Mussolini. Regarding Mussolini as open to reason, Churchill contacted him more than once in the second half of the1930s, and even rebuked the British government for chastising the Italian conquest of Ethiopia. "Today all Abyssinia is irrevocably, fully, and finally Italian alone." He accordingly labeled as "imprudent" Great Britain's protestations. "By estranging Italy, they had upset the whole balance of Europe and gained nothing for Abyssinia."[54] There is even a bizarre and unsubstantiated account that, notwithstanding the commencement of war in 1939, the British Prime Minister carried on substantial correspondence with the Italian dictator in an effort to bring about an early end to the conflict.[55] Among those who admired Mussolini in the early 1930s was Breckinridge Long, President Franklin D. Roosevelt's ambassador to Rome, who described what was transpiring in Italy as "the most interesting experiment in government to come on the horizon since the formulation of our Constitution 150 years ago."[56] Roosevelt himself demonstrated a genuine interest for Mussolini in a letter he wrote about the Italian leader in 1933. "There seems no question that he is really interested in what we are doing and I am much interested and deeply impressed by what he has accomplished and by his evidenced honest purpose of restoring Italy and seeking to prevent general European trouble."[57]

During its honeymoon period, Italian Fascism seemed to enjoy favor among the corps of New York City reporters for some of the most notable newspapers. Four out of five *New York Times* reporters who covered Fascism and Mussolini in this period wrote approvingly of Italy as did reporters from other major city dailies. These approbatory views were to be found elsewhere as in the *Cleveland Plain Dealer* that commended Mussolini for saving democracy in Italy, while others referred to him as a kind of redeemer for that nation. Newspapers like the *Washington Post* that did not otherwise support Fascism proffered endorsement of Mussolini's prescription of order, discipline and work as a viable solution to Italy's problems.[58] Undoubtedly, while a vehement concern over the spread of international communism lay behind these expressions, favorable comments also have to be read in the light of a heightened domestic nationalism and growing apprehension that the United States might be vulnerable to unwelcome ideologies.

Until the mid-1930s, Mussolini's apparent success in rescuing Italy's economic system evoked attention in the United States as it began to enter its own tribulation of the Great Depression. It has been noted that the highly touted 1933 New Deal program, the National Industrial Recovery Act that sought to regulate industry by fostering extensive cooperation between business and labor, and in the process bring economic recovery, possessed similarities to Fascism. The legislation called for a government agency, the National Recovery Administration (NRA), to facilitate the establishment of codes that were to govern trade associations with regard to wages, hours, and production. Commenting on Mussolini's 1934 economic program, one editorial astutely perceived:

> It was then he officially installed the Council of Corporations, on which labor and capital are equally represented, to control the economic life of Italy. The scheme is not an Italian NRA, though it bears some resemblance through the nature of duties undertaken. It is also a recovery scheme by which Italy proposed to stimulate consumption through higher standards of living to balance the production of the country. We do not have to embrace Fascism to pick out points in Mussolini's administration which are admirable. He has long fascinated us because he appears more human, more just and infinitely more capable that any other dictator of Europe."[59]

While describing his reaction in watching a huge NRA-sponsored parade in New York City, NRA head Hugh Johnson unintentionally acknowledged comparison in the public mind between his agency and the system led by Mussolini.

> I stood in the reviewing stand in that parade and there were hundreds of people I knew who waved as they went past. Down below were massed batteries of cameras and I knew if I raised my hand higher than my shoulders, it would seem and be publicized as a "Fascist salute." So I did not raise it higher, I just stuck my arm out straight and wiggled my hand around. But that didn't help me—*Time* came out saying I had constantly saluted *au Mussolini* ... [60]

ITALIAN AMERICANS REACT TO HOSTILITY

For a time, Italian Americans as a whole looked favorably upon Mussolini —an attraction that has to be understood against a background of negligence, disrespect, and outright discrimination. From the onset of mass immigration, Italian newcomers were ambivalently received; on the one hand, there was grudging acceptance because this nation needed cheap labor, while on the other hand, they were subject to outright hostility particularly during times of economic stress. Italian Americans were well aware that their co-nationals were the principal targets of immigration restriction laws enacted in this era, and that the public readily accepted the constant association of Italian Americans with organized crime. In the New York area, they became major targets of the "Americanization" program that discouraged immigrants from being too conspicuous about their ethnicity and their religion. The ugly and intolerant attitude manifest itself in Patchogue, Long Island, for example, when a Ku Klux Klan leader deprecated Catholics and then waxed venomously when speaking about a "dago" Pope.[61] It is not to be wondered that some regarded Americanization an ugly word

> In short, by threat and rhetoric 100 per cent American-
> izers opened a frontal assault on foreign influence in
> American life. They set about to stampede immigrants
> into citizenship, into adoption of the English language,
> and into an unquestioning reverence for existing Ameri-
> can institutions. They bade them abandon entirely their
> Old World loyalties, customs, and memories. They used
> high-pressure, steamroller tactics. They cajoled and they
> commanded.[62]

Thus conscious of the low esteem in which they had been held for so long, the elevation of Mussolini to worldwide prominence seemed a welcome counterbalance. An active participant in New York's Italian American radio and theater mediums, Julian Miranda graphically but perceptively captures the prevailing mentality among Americans of Italian descent in the 1930s. His critique offers food for thought.

> The Italian American population was not split at all re-
> garding Mussolini. They upheld support for the Italian
> government, regardless of who was ruling. It could have
> been Attila the Hun, or it could have been the Pope. This

was the first time that they seen Italy as a nation achieve something which, in their view was commensurate with what other governments were achieving. Almost all the Italians I knew supported the government. Most of them were probably monarchists. All the people I knew in Italian radio seemed to be. My grandmother gave her gold ring and I think she no more had an idea about fascism than she did of any other political system. The popular view of fascism was a naïve one. Finally someone had come along to make Italians do what they were supposed to do and the English world seemed to respect them ...

The degree to which Italians identified with fascism was a function of two things. One was their sense of homesickness and loyalty to the ethnic group. Second was the function of their poor self-image in this country. Except for doctrinaire nuts, and there were very few in this country, I think most fascists were created by American prejudice and bigotry.[63]

NOSTALGIA

From a psychological perspective, historian Stanislao Pugliese cautions that in supporting fascism Italian Americans indulged in a "culture of nostalgia"; that is it involved something more fundamental than nationhood, indeed it involved one's connection to his village, his place of birth. It was to a considerable extent a selective memory, an ideology of compensation.[64] That Italian American support for Mussolini's Italy was largely an expression of patriotism to the land of their birth, rather than one of embracing a transparent political ideology, certainly seems to have been the case in my neighborhood where pro-Mussolini voices could easily be found, especially among the less educated old-timers like Mr. Lentini, who lived in our building and who was wont to boast facilely about Italy's greatness whenever Mussolini became a subject of discussion. It was rather evident that my neighbor's praise of Mussolini rested on a sense that Italy was making headlines that compelled other countries to take notice. My boyhood recollection is that few, if any, Italian Americans in my neighborhood could truly articulate the philosophical intricacies of Fascism, being content rather with commenting on the dictator's success in forcing powerful nations finally to take Italy into account. In our innocence, even we youngsters less than ten years old and second generation Italian Americans, evinced something akin to pride when referring to Italy vis-à-vis other countries. In lauding Mussolini's accomplishments, little was heard about the high cost they extracted from Italians or others. The essence of this attitude was captured in a 1938 study, "It is this nationalism of the blood rather than of citizenship which makes the second generation Italians frequently sympathetic to the international aims of the old country's present administration and to its struggle for supremacy in the Mediterranean world."[65]

Early Italian American Fascists

It is interesting to note that some of Fascism's staunchest proponents, chief among which was Italian-born Agostino De Biasi, actually began promoting the ideology prior to Mussolini's ascent to power in Italy. Emigrating to New York in 1900, and editor of various Italian American publications, De Biasi, described as "the founding father of American Fascism," was deeply affected by "prejudice and a sense of inferiority that many Italian immigrants encountered."[66] It is to be noted that one of the journals De Biasi edited, *Il Carroccio*, was considered to have literary value, the fascist political connection notwithstanding. In the opinion of contemporary poet, writer and journalist Joseph Zappulla "*Il Carroccio*, [was] a good monthly magazine which supported fascism … I had contributed very little to it with an occasional poem and non-political article I never wrote about politics. *Il Carroccio* dedicated its August issue each year to literature and most of its content was quite good including the local contributions."[67]

Giovanni Di Silvestro, who had various careers including that of Grand

Venerable of the Order Sons of Italy in America, was another early defender of Fascism who utilized his leadership post to try to steer the largest Italian fraternal ethnic organization into the center of the fascist orbit. Undoubtedly, the most rabid of Italian American pro-fascists was Domenico Trombetta whose Italian-language newspaper *Il Grido del Stirpe*, described as a perverse publication, constantly and unwaveringly commended Mussolini. A social worker described Trombetta as a pitiable man who ironically had to beg mercy for freedom after war broke out and his internment began at Ellis Island.[68]

GENEROSO POPE

Few Italian Americans had as much influence within New York's ethnic community as did Generoso Pope. A sixteen-year-old semi-illiterate immigrant in 1917, he quickly climbed the ladder of economic success in an exceptional "rags to riches" Horatio Alger fashion, through ownership of the largest construction materials company in the world and a media empire that included ownership of *Corriere d'America*, and *Il Progresso Italo-Americano*. The local candy / newspaper store on my block probably sold as many copies of these papers as it did English-language newspapers. The parents of most of my friends, as did my father, for example, read *Il Progresso Italo-Americano* religiously and formed their opinions about public issues from its pages. There is evidence that Pope was able to acquire his newspaper empire

Generoso Pope, humble immigrant turned highly successful entrepreneur. At first a supporter of Mussolini, with the outbreak of war, he became a staunch advocate of victory for Americans and was instrumental in mobilizing support among home front Italian Americans for war bond drives.

through the influence of the Italian Fascist officials who with minor mis-givings saw in Pope "someone absolutely faithful to Italy."[69] Throughout most of the 1930s, Pope's newspaper sang the praises of Mussolini miss-ing few opportunities to feature positive comments registered about the dictator by influential public figures. Notwithstanding Pope's unambigu-ous pro-Mussolini stance in this era, it was not one of blind subservience, as indicated by his willingness to part with the Italian Fascist leader over passage of Italian anti-Semitic laws in 1938. Mincing no words, he at-tacked the Italian decrees on constitutional and humanitarian grounds, and further warned the Fascist government against alienating the friendship of the six million Italians and four million Jews in the United State. Diggins concluded that, "Pope's editorials opposing anti-Semitism at least served to inform Italian-Americans that some things in Italy were undeniably rot-ten. Pope was not a hopeless reactionary."[70]

Further confirmation that Pope was beginning to alter his pro-Fascist views in 1939 by condemning Mussolini's anti-Semitic policies is offered by Vanni B. Montana who commented that the publisher was ready to put some distance between his former position and his place in America now because, " ... his affairs were in America, his Colonial Sand and Stone Company dominated by the building construction industry. Did not his friend President Roosevelt say to him, 'Your duce was mistaken, don't make the same mistake yourself.'"[71] In spite of the fact that fascist or-ganizations operated rather autonomously Mussolini welcomed their existence as a means of countering anti-fascist influence while simulta-neously promoting a favorable attitude toward his government among Italian immigrants in the United States, even subsidizing some of them. The Fascist League of North America (FLNA) was created initially by Italian Americans, ostensibly to sponsor cultural and athletic events in Italian American communities, but was surrounded by a distinctive fascist coloration. When the FLNA was reactivated in 1924, the role of the Ital-ian government was even more prominent as it appointed Italians, rather than Italian Americans, to direct FLNA activities. Interestingly, Agostino

De Biasi, the so-called pioneer of American Fascism, and possessed of a prickly personality, broke with this official Italian arm of the movement, maintaining his independence to be a critic while continuing to identify himself as an Italian and a Fascist.[72] Although the league flourished for a few years, criticism mounted to such an extent over its avowed intention of promoting Fascism that it was dissolved in 1929; however, alternate Italian American-generated fascist organizations continued to promote activities, extolling the Italian ideological system. In the famed "Little Italy" of the Bronx, for example, one of these organizations sponsored Italian language classes that expected Italian American youngsters to not only study language, but also to march in parades in black-shirt uniforms.[73]

ANTI-FASCISM

The anti-Fascist movement among Italian Americans began slowly, and at first seemed to be concentrated in the labor movement led by socialist-oriented individuals like Luigi Antonini, Giuseppe Catalanotti, Frank Bellanca, Arturo Giovannitti, and Carlo Tresca. Each one of these possessed special qualities that made an impact on New York's Italian American community. Antonini would have a long and productive career as the preeminent Italian American labor leader, orator, and factor in New York City politics, while Catalonnotti and Bellanca were effective union organizers within the ethnic group. Oratory and poetry were the strong points of Giovannitti, while Tresca enjoyed a career as a colorful anarcho-syndicalist. Tresca had arrived in New York in 1904, having run afoul of the law for radical activities. An eclectic and flamboyant individual, and a man of fierce temper, he continued his revolutionary work through his immoderate public political

Luigi Antonini, labor leader and radio speaker, utilized his powerful oratorical skills among home front Italian Americans to promote the war effort and urge the downfall of Mussolini.

positions and via his newspaper *Il Martello* that attacked traditional Italian institutions, including Fascism.[74]

ROLE OF EXILES

The "fuorusciti"—Italian anti-Fascists who were either driven into exile or who voluntarily left the detested Mussolini regime, were among the most vociferous voices to denounce the dictatorial Italian system. They included some who were only moderately well-known such as Cesare Corvo as well as those who were very well-known such as Giuseppe Lupis, Massimo Salvadori, Girolamo Valenti, and especially Gaetano Salvemini. A Sicilian journalist who opposed Mussolini, in the 1920s, Corvo joined his family in Middletown, Connecticut, where he began to publish the Italian language newspaper *Bolletino* that later became the Middletown *Bulletin* kept its readers abreast of fascist and anti-fascist political activities in Italy and the United States. (His son Biagio (Max) would come to play a meaningful military role in the liberation of Italy.)

Born 1873, Salvemini was a brilliant historian and an outspoken critic of Mussolini. He was arrested and forced to depart from the land of his birth in 1927. After a stay in France and England, he came to the United States in 1934 where, in addition to teaching Italian history at Harvard University, he also published extensively on the topic. A harsh and persistent Mussolini censurer, he founded the anti-Fascist Mazzini Society in 1939 that was very influential in continuing to inform intellectuals and the general public about the corruption and depravity of Fascism. Among other intellectual fuorusciti (exiles) who joined Salvemini was the prominent Max Ascoli, who helped the Mazzini Society to publish its own newspaper *Nazioni Unite*, where it articulated its views.[75] Regrettably for the anti-Fascists, their impact on rank and file Italian Americans was limited largely because "their elitism along with their intellectual approach earned them comparatively little backing and circumscribed their efforts in advance."[76]

ETHIOPIAN WAR

In a move to establish an empire, in October 1935, Mussolini's Italy launched an invasion of the African country of Ethiopia that roiled Italian American colonies. Although the response by major powers, including the United States, was swift in condemning the action of a modern nation taking advantage of its military superiority against a poor and backward nation, no genuinely effectual steps were taken that might have successfully stopped or slowed down the action. Indeed, in the judgment of many, the realistic result was an appeasement that served to whet the appetite of aggressors.[77] Italy's invasion of Ethiopia marked an important turning point not only with respect to most Americans' view of Italy, but also with regard to the reaction within the Italian American community. This belligerent engagement, the latest evidence that the emanation of unbridled totalitarianism, posed a serious challenge to the League of Nations. It also began to elicit growing apprehension amongst American public opinion that intensified when Italy invaded the African nation on October 3, 1935. Americans became much more sympathetic to Ethiopian Emperor Haile Selassie. After the League of Nations denounced Italy as an aggressor nation, pressure mounted in the United States—not a League member—to impose economic sanctions as a way of registering its disapproval of the Mussolini invasion. Although an embargo list that included a number of items that might be regarded as war material was developed, the embargo failed to include oil exports, rendering the ban "not as drastic and as extensive as some statesmen had wished."[78] Though far from indicating they were pro-Fascists, most Italian Americans did not appreciate Roosevelt's action.

As for the ethnic media, it is estimated that the majority of one hundred twenty nine Italian-language newspapers in the United States were either Fascist or sympathetic to Mussolini, including pro-Fascist spokesman Generoso Pope's Il *Progresso Italo Americano* and *Corriere d'America*.[79] Experienced American journalists were quick to condemn the Italian ethnic press for using journalistic deceptions to advance the Fascist philosophy.

The Italian press of New York, it was asserted, possessed "a temperamental inability to let pass any news, no matter how slight, without pro-Italian editorial comment."[80] In myopic fashion, Mussolini supporters emphasized the "civilizing mission" in which Italy was engaged, while denouncing Great Britain's sanctimonious anti-Italian position as hypocrisy in view of the fact that England was the principal imperialist nation in the world. This view was acknowledged even by non-Italian political leaders such as Brooklyn Congressman Emanuel Cellar, who maintained that Italy "in dismembering Ethiopia, may be no more guilty than England in dismembering the Boer Republic and India."[81]

When the Roosevelt administration concluded that public opinion would not support stronger steps, it confined its criticism of Italy's aggressive action to verbal condemnation that amounted to little more than a moral embargo.[82] Undeterred by the criticism, Italian American pro-Mussolini supporters in various Italian American organizations sought to muster strong support for the Italian dictator's grab of an African colony. One example was that of the Italian War Veterans of Waterbury, Connecticut, and described by journalist Sando Bologna. Caught up in the euphoria of nationalism, the organization lent its support to "Italy in its adventure in Ethiopia, marching with the Italian salute in Columbus Day parade, and contributing to the Pro Patria Committee Campaign for $15,000 for the Italian Red Cross. Many felt that Pro Patria was really for Fascism."[83] The Italian American press provided extensive coverage to Mussolini's efforts to recruit thousands of Italians living abroad to return to Italy to fight in Ethiopia. When, however, the United States government strongly discouraged this policy, the Italian government moderated its plan and had to content itself with perhaps as few as only several hundred Italians who left this country to fight in his army. Italy was more successful in obtaining financial assistance from Italian Americans, highlighted by the extraordinary action of hundreds of Italian American women donating their gold wedding bands for the Italian cause. Italy's completion of its conquest of Ethiopia in May 1936 was hailed as such a major victory that some celebrated by marching through the streets of Harlem, exulting that "The Eagles of Rome have devoured the Lion of Judah," while a marching band played the Fascist anthem.[84]

ITALIAN AMERICANS
RESPOND TO ETHIOPIAN WAR

The Ethiopian War also became an issue within the context of considerations over neutrality legislation when Roosevelt requested presidential discretion regarding exercising embargo of war materials and other products to belligerent nations. Fearing this putative expanded power would be used against Italy, Italian Americans lambasted the legislation; ironically, the crisis served to promote a degree of unity within the Italian American community. New York Supreme Court Justice Salvatore A. Cotillo, a respected East Harlem product, submitted a legal brief on neutrality to every member of the House and Senate, while influential publisher Generoso Pope met with President Roosevelt and other government leaders to present the ethnic group's position.[85] Evidently, such cohesion enabled Italian Americans to exercise political clout within the American political establishment. Thus while the government received 3,000 letters endorsing its so-called "moral embargo" policy designed to discourage United States trade with Italy, in ten days Italian Americans responded with 2,500 form letters attacking the policy prompting one historian to state, "Whether as a result of this pressure or not, Congress rejected the section of the Neutrality bill that enlarged the President's embargo powers."[86]

Italian Americans contributed to the Italian Red Cross at the time of the Italian invasion of Ethiopia.

Another student of the subject is equally discerning. "Since the great majority of Italians were members of the Democratic Party, these protests had considerable weight." Until this incident, the exercise of Italian American influence on American foreign policy was rare. By contrast, the exercise of African American political influence remained much less effective.[87]

Undoubtedly, the Ethiopian War had enormous impact in Italian American communities such as mine in Brooklyn; however, I was really too young to remember the contemporary impact vividly, except for the boast of certain old-timers about Italy's military prowess and the frequent refrains of the Fascist national anthem —La Giovanezza. I joined with others in singing some of the lyrics including "la faccetta nera," completely oblivious to its literal translation "black faces"—a reference to the conquest of African Ethiopians. To my generation, the bouncing, martial melody was enjoyed in a celebratory mood, devoid of other connotations and consequences. History informs us, however, that war had much graver repercussions.

AFRICAN AMERICANS VS. ITALIAN AMERICAN

It was in the large Little Italy of East Harlem, adjacent to heavily African American Harlem, that tension was most severe and erupted in violence. In the decades prior to the 1930s, the Harlem and East Harlem ethnic entities had evolved alongside each other with seemingly little violent behavior toward one another. This is not to suggest that there was close harmony or no contrary manifestation or discord—indeed, there had been alternating periods of peaceful distrust, co-existence, and strain. By the 1930s, however, with the onset of the Great Depression, African Americans again saw Italians as competitors for jobs, as well as a threat to black neighborhoods where Italians rented apartments. Italian Americans, it seemed, were purchasing residences in black neighborhoods and displacing them. [88]

Because black Americans had all but embraced Ethiopia as their country, the intense accommodation between New York's African Americans and Italian Americans collapsed when Italy invaded Ethiopia. On the afternoon of October 3, 1935, racial disorder commenced in Harlem when a group of African Americans waving a banner bearing the message, "Let's get Italians out of Harlem," began to picket a Jewish-owned emporium in which Italian butchers and vegetable venders rented stalls.[89] Since this action dissuaded potential shoppers from entering the market for most of the afternoon, store employees responded by going outside to remonstrate with the pickets. The incident led to a gathering of 150 Italians and African Americans hurling insults at each other and on the verge of coming to blows. Consequently, authorities ordered the deployment of 1,000 policemen and 200 to 300 detectives to defuse the emerging riot. These forces were to remain deployed on a daily basis so long as the danger of local violence attributed to the Italian-Ethiopian crisis remained.[90] The Harlem riot was not an isolated situation as simultaneous fistfights broke out between black and Italian students and adults at a large Brooklyn public high school, necessitating deployment of emergency police forces. Altogether approximately ten percent of the city's entire police force was mobilized to deal with a potentially frightening situation in Brooklyn and Harlem. In addition, there were reports of similar racial problems in other cities, with police forces called out to stop a disturbance outside the Italian consulate in San Francisco, while in Chicago three hundred demonstrators were arrested.[91]

Although Italy's belligerent attitude toward Ethiopia served as the immediate catalyst to the riots, there were, in addition, economic grievances that revolved around the issue of African American demands that neighborhood merchants hire blacks as sales clerks, rather than only as janitors and porters.[92] Dr. Adam Clayton Powell, Jr., energetic Assistant Pastor of the Abyssinian Baptist Church in Harlem, along with other local clergy, elicited considerable support within the community with the slogan "Don't Buy Where You Can't get Work."[93] With justification, Harlem residents had complained for decades that they were virtually excluded from most employment opportunities, even in their own neighborhood. Accordingly, they were conscious and resentful of whites working in their core neighborhood earning livelihoods by selling products to Harlemites.

CARNERA VS. LOUIS

While relations between the two ethnic groups were generally devoid of antagonism before the 1930s, Italy's belligerent attitude toward Ethiopia in the months prior to the invasion now elicited growing apprehension. In part, this reflected a turn in American public opinion that, prior to 1935, did not voice great alarm over Italy's African adventure—indeed, there were more than a few voices raised in support of the venture. However, as tension between Italy and Ethiopia mounted in the early months of 1935, public opinion became sympathetic toward Emperor Haile Selassie, particularly in black communities. Anxiety between the two groups also manifested itself in sports activity, specifically a 1935 heavyweight boxing match in Yankee Stadium between African American Joe Louis and a giant Italian 6'7', 260-pound Primo Carnera. Dubbed "Mussolini's Muscleman," Carnera had fought most of his major bouts in America where he had become Italy's first World Heavyweight Boxing Champion by virtue of his defeat of Jack Sharkey in 1933. Unsurprisingly, the New York Italian American community hailed him with great enthusiasm as the primary world heavyweight boxer. The pending Louis-Carnera bout offered another opportunity for Fascists to brag about people of Italian blood that one of their own could command such attention and merit lavish coverage in the press. Notwithstanding the opinion of American boxing experts that Carnera possessed very modest boxing skills, pro-fascists emphasized his size and exceptional skills as "the best representation of our ancestral heredity." By contrast, African American leaders, aware that Ethiopia was only one of two African independent nations that had not fallen to a colonial power, viewed the African nation's stance as a symbol of racial pride.

The pending pugilistic event offered a classic rivalry between two underdog ethnic groups in America, as Fascists in particular and Italian Americans in general basked in the glow of Carnera, while African Americans saw their affirmation in superior ability of Louis. The inevitable stereotypes abounded among the sparring groups as Italian-language newspapers commented that Louis like all Negroes was vulnerable to blow in the stomach, but not in the head, while for their part African Americans adumbrated the certain connection of Carnera with gangsters.[94] "Circulating through the tense crowd were 1,500 policemen, the largest detachment ever assigned to a prize fight. Outside the stadium, emergency squads stood by with riot equipment."[95] Joe Louis knocked Carnera in six rounds prompting jubilation in the African American community, even inspiring a song, "He's in the Ring Doin' the Same Old Thing." In contrast, some angry Italian Americans reacted by engaging in street brawls during which they taunted African Americans with predictions that the Italian army would route Ethiopia in the anticipated conflict. Other clashes occurred when a crowd of 400 African Americans, just returning from a pro-Ethiopia rally, smashed windows of Italian store-owners in Harlem, despite the large numbers of police who were assigned to patrol the Italian neighborhood.

As the war came to a conclusion, Italian Americans strove to obtain better treatment for Italy, as indicated at this Madison Square Garden protest meeting.

REPERCUSSIONS

There were, of course, strident critics of the Fascist policy within Italian American communities, and soon the two opposing forces engaged in accusations against each other. Italy's action in Africa also wrought division within the Italian American community by intensifying the ongoing pro- and anti-Fascist strife. Some politicians, such as East Harlem Congressman Vito Marcantonio, who was the most progressive and radical congressman of his time, came to pay a heavy price for his conspicuous denunciations of Fascism. In August 1935, as tension over Ethiopia mounted, he was one of only a few leading Italian American spokesman to participate in an anti-Fascist rally in Madison Square Garden, an action that led to the burning in effigy of Haile Selassie in front of his house.[96] It also contributed to Marcantonio's defeat when he ran for re-election in 1936 as *Il Progresso Italo Americano* along with other influential Italian Americans supported his opponent; and it caused Marcantonio to temper his anti-Fascism for several years afterwards.[97] Even LaGuardia learned to mute his attacks on Mussolini in this period. In the aftermath of the invasion and riots, the relations between African American and Italian American, though suffering some violent incidents, did not succumb to extremism. More than one responsible African American leader reminded his people that they should not indict all Italian Americans for the belligerent actions of Italy. Congressman Mitchell, the only African American then serving in Congress, called upon blacks not to take out their frustrations against all Italian Americans. Likewise Adam Clayton Powell noted that it was just as wrong to consider all Italian Americans as followers of Mussolini as it was to consider all Southerners as lynchers. He also reminded them that there were many Italian Americans who opposed Mussolini's policies.[98]

For their part, responsible Italian American leaders refrained from using the occasion to aggravate relations. Thus LaGuardia and Marcantonio, while circumspect in how they dealt with Italy, refrained from using the event for political purposes at the expense of exacerbating racial relations.

The esteemed East Harlem educator and community leader Leonard Covello made the astute observation that the presumed deterioration of Italian American / African American relations tended to be exaggerated by the media. He cited an occasion wherein a newspaper reporter went to Benjamin Franklin High School on the heels of Italy's invasion of Ethiopia, in the belief that the international incident was reflected in clashes between Italian American and African American students. Covello vehemently denied the existence of significant hostility between his Italian American and African American students, and sought to bolster his contention by asking students from the two different ethnic groups whether the Ethiopian War adversely affected their regard for each other. Their simple and forthright rejection of the notion left the reporter without his story.[99]

The Ethiopian episode that led to the dismemberment of the African nation exposed the critical feebleness of the League of Nations as well as the irrelevance of the United States. In November 1936, Mussolini showed his contempt by withdrawing from the league.

THE GATHERING STORM

"The bells are tolling for democracy," intoned Ernest Hemingway in his classic 1940 novel *For Whom the Bells Toll*. Although a story about the demise of democracy in Spain, it was also an approximation of what was occurring throughout much of Europe and elsewhere during the late 1930s. Emboldened by early successes, Mussolini flattered himself into believing Adolph Hitler would follow his lead, whereas in reality the German dictator would soon have Mussolini at his beck and call. In the process, Mussolini thrust his nation further into the camp of military antagonists by agreeing to a Rome-Berlin Axis. Both nations, furthermore, provided substantial help to the Spanish fascist forces led by General Francisco Franco, who led the nationalists and had rebelled against the leftist republican government in the long and bloody Spanish Civil War (1936-1939), while Spanish Republicans received aid from Soviet Russia. Although the response of the American public was mostly one of apathy, a number of American Catholic leaders hailed the United States neutrality posture because of the reprehensible anti-clerical policies of the republican government. Thus many laymen of Italian descent favored the nationalists. On the other hand, approximately 2,800 Americans—some committed Communists and others an assortment of socialists and left-wingers—joined the Abraham Lincoln Battalion that took up arms against Franco's fascist forces. The impression is that although few volunteers were New York Italian Americans, one such candidate was picturesque Ralph Fasanella from East Harlem's Little Italy, a non-doctrinaire supporter of American leftist causes. An active union organizer early in his career, by the time I made his acquaintance in the 1960s, Fasanella was enjoying a belated but remarkable career as an artist whose works frequently depicted life in his East Harlem ethnic neighborhood that earned him comparison with Grandma Moses.

In a further demonstration of its aggressive stance on April 7, 1939, Mussolini's Italy invaded the backward nation of Albania, thereby adding another irritant to United States-Italy relations. By osmosis, America's growing criticism of Italy's behavior negatively impacted Italian Americans, as illustrated in a November 1939 public opinion poll that "suggested that Americans gave first place to Italians as undesirable citizens."[100]

POLITICAL SCENE

The years between the two world wars constituted the entry phase for Italian Americans in the realm of elective politics, especially in New York. Functioning essentially on the periphery of the political world until the 1920s, and thus effectively shut out of more prestigious political posts, they were now ready to strive for more powerful offices. Whereas previously, with a singular exception, they could not hope to achieve positions higher than assistant commissioner in city government, they now were prepared to run for the highest offices in city government as well as other important posts. During the striving phase, Italian Americans in various parts of the country vigorously contended for and attained more prestigious political posts. For example, Angelo Rossi, recognized leader within San Francisco's Italian community was elected mayor of San Francisco in 1931, while Robert Maestri became mayor of New Orleans, and Baltimore's "Little Italy," elected Vincent Palmisano and Thomas J. D'Alessandro, Jr. to Congress. It must be emphasized that Americans of Italian descent represented significant voting blocs in all these cities and that therefore the candidacies of the aforementioned were direct expressions of ethnic considerations. Simply put, the ethnic neighborhoods were becoming such vital springboards in the direction of political participation that shrewd political bosses, even when otherwise scornful of the Italian element, found it expedient to cultivate them.

To organize the ethnic group into a cohesive political bloc was a prerequisite to a major role in political life in New York. Accordingly, it was after Italian Americans became involved in and took control of important local political clubs that they became a force with which to contend because the clubs provided important economic assistance and simultaneously served as cohesive political forces. Efforts at political organization intensified in the 1930s, with Italian American political clubs comprising the largest number of nationality associations in the city.[101] One example of this development occurred when Jerome Ambro contested and finally toppled a German American club leader in 1932. This set in motion steps to achieve the highest political ambitions. A Brooklyn Democrat Assemblyman, Ambro now had his sights on the mayoralty. Although he commanded support in Brooklyn, he lost the 1933 Democratic nomination to John P. O'Brien who promptly lost to LaGuardia. That German Americans had long presented obstacles to Brooklyn's Italian Americans is confirmed in the pages of L'Aurora, a Brooklyn based ethnic journal, that cited as an example the 19th Assembly District "which for many years has waved the Democratic flag under the leadership chiefly of Americans of German descent." The journal estimated that in 1921, over 700,000 Italians and their descendents lived in the Greater New York, including 300,000 living in Brooklyn, of whom 30,000 were voters.[102]   Thus while Ambro's effort proved to be premature, given the prevailing ethnic and political realities within the Democratic party at the time, it nevertheless served as an indication that it would not be too long before the growing Italian American city population would prevail in this regard. Indeed, it came with ringing finality with Fiorello H. LaGuardia's election as mayor.

The preeminent New York political figure in the striving stage, LaGuardia, born of an Italian father and an Italian-Jewish mother, was brought up as a Protestant in western army camps, and became the hybrid politician par excellence. Firmly embracing an Italian identity, which struck responsive chords within his heavily Italian district in New York City's Lower East Side, LaGuardia won public office as a congressman in 1916, and in 1919 as President of New York City's Board of Aldermen. Subsequently, he was elected to Congress repeatedly from East Harlem, in its time the nation's largest "Little Italy." More than all those of his nationality who rose to prominence in the nineteenth century, LaGuardia could be considered an authentic ethnic representative who reflected the emergence of the group and voiced their aspirations. Throughout his long career in public life, he served with distinction in the United States Congress, speaking on behalf of Italy's international aspirations and authoring laws vital to the rights of organized labor such as the Norris-LaGuardia Act. Ascending the mayoralty of New York City in 1933 and winning re-election

twice, he established a merited reputation as a progressive, caring government official who worked steadfastly on behalf of constituents, confronting the nation's worst depression. Among other accomplishments during his

Wartime Mayor of New York City, Fiorello H. LaGuardia had been a major in the American Air Force stationed in Italy during World War I.

tenure was an unrelenting attack on corruption and gambling, expansive relief and welfare programs, economic promotion of the city with exhibits like the World's Fair and the opening of New York's first commercial airport in 1939, (originally called New York City Municipal Airport)—it was renamed in his honor shortly after it began to operate. He is generally regarded as New York City's greatest twentieth-century mayor.

One of the most powerful factors in politics in his time was Generoso Pope, who, although never holder of a public office, nevertheless became a major power broker through his ownership of *Il Progresso Italo-Americano*, the largest Italian language paper in the country, as its 200,000 daily circulation rendered it a major force, especially within the Democratic Party throughout the 1930's, 1940s, and 1950s. So commanding was the regard for *Il Progresso Italo-Americano* that even President Franklin D. Roosevelt, when running for re-election in a particularly tight race, importuned Pope to intercede on his behalf before the Italian electorate.

1940 ELECTION

The 1940 presidential election offers an insight into the interaction between ethnicity and politics. Running for a third term, incumbent President Roosevelt normally would have been expected to garner New York City's important Italian American vote since it had been part of the great coalition that had supported Roosevelt previously, and it was then heavily Democratic in registration. Unfortunately, Roosevelt's intemperate remarks in a Charlotte, North Carolina speech describing Italy's invasion of France as, "the hand that held the dagger has plunged it deep into his neighbor's side" put a heavy strain on relations between the President and the ethnic group. Roosevelt's stiff denunciation of Italy was a calculated risk. On the one hand, his advisors warned that the stab-in-the-back metaphor was so inflammatory it would hurt him with Italian American voters; on the other hand, the President, in a determination to speak candidly, went ahead with the remark satisfied that it would affirm United States policy to aid victims of Nazi aggression—an assumption that

excluded Italian Americans.[103] Simply put, the vilifying depiction helped
fan the flames of anti-Italian prejudice with the Italian American media,
uniformly denouncing it as defamatory. That it presented difficulties is evidenced in research that showed complaints by Democratic workers in Italian American enclaves were hampered in promoting Roosevelt's candidacy
"without police escort because of local resident's anger at Roosevelt."[104]

In an effort to minimize the political damage, the Roosevelt administration called upon any figure likely to serve as an intermediary, even one who
did not occupy major office. A case in point was Vincent R. Impellitteri, not
yet holder of an important public office, but nevertheless active as president
of the Rapallo Lawyers Association, which boasted of a membership that
included virtually all the prominent Italian American lawyers and elected
political figures in New York state. Accordingly, he figured prominently in
Tammany Hall's effort to promote Italian American candidates. Impellitteri likewise attracted the attention of the President's campaign managers
concerned that Roosevelt's comparison of Italy's invasion of France as being the equivalent of a "stab in the back" rendered him vulnerable among
New York City Italian Americans in the critical 1940 presidential election.
Whatever else was conveyed in the Roosevelt message, it was considered
unusually offensive to New York's Italian community which had labored
for years to shed a negative stereotype as "stiletto wielders."[105] Although
Roosevelt's statement heightened fears that New York's Italian Americans
might resort to demonstrations did not materialize, it did intensify anxiety
and confusion especially among aliens who had not attained citizenship.

> Suddenly signs of anti-Italianism were heightened in the
> United States: "dago," and "wop" and similar insults were
> heard more frequently ... in many American cities and the
> Italo-American members of several "Italian" clubs in the
> country changed the names of their social organizations
> to "Columbus" clubs seeking to link their Mediterranean
> roots to the laurels of the fifteenth century sea captain from
> Genoa.[106]

There was little question that suspicion about Italian Americans was on the increase. "Both the Italian attack [in France] and the President's criticism of it spurred American suspicions of Italians, as well as Italian trepidations about their place in American society."[107] With the passage of the Smith Act which required registration of aliens occurring shortly afterwards, apprehension among the huge number of Italian immigrants increased.

LITTLE ITALY 1940 REACTION TO INVASION OF FRANCE

Italy's declaration of war versus France and England on June 10, 1940, had a disturbing effect on New York's Little Italy. According to a keen observation, "Everybody was unusually quiet ... The neighborhood iceman sat on the shoe repairer's doorstep, but they were not arguing as was their custom. Men and women in front of stores and tenements looked about furtively, as though they were suddenly being watched." Veteran neighborhood dwellers in this country for a generation were somewhat confused as to what the meaning of Italy's invasion of France meant for them. Some tried to defend Italy with vague generalities, while others were generally distressed. "Most of them expressed shame and apprehension. Roosevelt was right; only maybe he should not have said it for our sake. We voted for him in '32 and '36. But what can we do?" The observer also provided a trenchant glimpse into the mentality of young Italian Americans in the New York of that period.

> The young Italian Americans, as a rule, are nowhere culturally. Nice kids, some of them; but really, neither Italians nor Americans. They have little notion of democracy. Many are without jobs, without any perceptible future. They are "wops" and "dagoes" when they get outside the neighborhood. They are up against a vague difficulty in relation to America. Are they part of the country or aren't they? ... They do not understand Hitlerism and Mussolini's fascism. They don't give a damn, or so they say if you ask

them. But they are carried forth in the grip of something
in the air. A force. Something is happening in this world.
It is affecting America. Them. Us. In case of a real crisis
in this country, I think, the young Italian Americans will
respond if the government and the leaders will know how
to appeal to them. The crux of the problem is not that they
are "Italians," for they are not, but that they are, as I say,
nowhere, in a cultural no man's land.[108]

Clearly Mussolini's invasion of France "greatly complicated life for
Italian Americans, and exacerbated their sense of insecurity and margin-
ality."[109] Even while they voiced criticism of Mussolini, few renounced
Italy as they proclaimed loyalty to America. That Roosevelt's campaign
managers had something serious to worry about was evident in a race for
the State Assembly in my Ridgewood/Bushwick neighborhood. A largely
Democratic bailiwick with a sizeable Italian American population, in 1940
the community voted against an Italian American incumbent Democrat
candidate for the office, opting instead to vote for a German American Republican. It was not so much a fear that Italian American voters might vote
for Wendell Willkie, the Republican presidential candidate, but rather that
they might sit out the election, depriving Roosevelt a major element in his
coalition. Under these circumstances, it was necessary for ethnic power
brokers such as Mayor LaGuardia, Generoso Pope, and Luigi Antonini
to mend Roosevelt's political fences. The results did indeed demonstrate
the seriousness of the situation in that New York Republicans actually
outvoted the Democrats, who nevertheless won because of the large vote
Roosevelt received on the American Labor Party line. There is credible
evidence to support the observation that many Italian Americans who previously voted Democratic went to Republican Willkie that year when only
42.2 % of city's Italians voted Democratic in 1940 as compared to 78.7 %
in 1936. Democratic Assemblyman Joseph Corso confirmed this defection
in my heavily Italian American Democratic neighborhood that voted for a
Republican German American that year as a vivid example of the damage
caused by Roosevelt's remarks.[110]

ITALIAN AMERICAN POLITICAL SPECTRUM

Although both major parties courted the Italian vote and big city Democrats generally were more successful, especially during Roosevelt's New Deal years in the 1930s and 1940s, there were significant exceptions. Thus one could find many shades of the political spectrum among Italian Americans, with a small but articulate and colorful group promoting a radical/socialist tradition usually outside of the mainstream Democratic and Republican parties. Numerically very small in number were a handful of committed Communists such as Brooklyn's Peter V. Cacchione, who was the first Communist elected to the City Council. As a dedicated Marxist, Cacchione was an anomaly among Brooklyn's Italian Americans who received limited backing from his fellow ethnics, compared to a high proportion of support from Jewish districts.[111] The available evidence indicates that very few New York Italian Americans were formally listed as Communists, thereby prompting one historian to conclude about "the failure of the left, even the liberal left" in East Harlem. Whereas in New York City as a whole, in the 1935 mayoralty contest "Socialist and Communist Party candidates received, respectively, 2.9 and 1.2 percent of the vote, but only 2.0 and 0.7 percent of the Italo-American vote."[112] More numerous were variations of socialists like union leader and co-founder of the American Labor Party, Luigi Antonini, whose outlook emphasized the centrality of the working class, but who opposed the Communists. The ALP would soon split with Antonini, leading his followers into the Liberal Party while others veered even further to the left. Political labels frequently were misleading as the career of fiery left-winger Vito Marcantonio manifests. At first an official Republican Party candidate, when he began his congressional career in 1934, he quickly belied his Republican Party label, becoming a factor in the leftist American Labor Party and the first of that organization to hold a seat in Congress. During this era, most New York City Italian Americans who achieved public office ran under the Democratic Party emblem, although a smaller but impressive number,

including LaGuardia and Marcantonio, were at least nominally Republicans. The rise of Fascism in Italy complicated political interaction of
Italian Americans. Some like Generoso Pope openly courted Mussolini's
favor for a time, while others like union leader Luigi Antonini, and left
wing elements such as the ardent radical Carlo Tresca denounced it. Divisions attributed to Fascist orientation became muted with the onset of the
Second World War as Mussolini's reckless foreign policy lost him support
among Italian Americans.

DETERIORATING INTERNATIONAL SITUATION

The international situation became even more ominous as Japan marched
into China in 1937, while in Germany, Hitler began a massive remilitariza-
tion program that led to annexation of Austria followed by marching into
the Sudetenland thus precipitating the demise of Czechoslovakia. When
the leaders of Great Britain and France assented to Hitler's aggression at
Munich in 1938, it was clear that liberal democracies were in great peril.
While these doleful events were transpiring overseas, the United States, preoccupied with an ongoing intractable economic crisis and in recognition of
the prevailing and vigorous anti-interventionist sentiment, remained hesitant
to overextend itself in assuming international obligations. Impartiality via
the enactment of several neutrality laws that was the official position of the
United States during the unsettled state of world affairs and that appeared to
comport with prevailing public opinion, proved to be no hindrance to curbing the appetite of aggressor nations. By 1939, the drums of war had quick-
ened as Hitler proceeded to gobble up Austria and Czechoslovakia while
Italy invaded Albania on April 9 of that year. Any pretense that all out war
could be prevented was shattered completely when Germany marched into
Poland on September 1, 1939. Complacency had succumbed to heightened
anxiety within Italian American circles as it became much more apparent
that war between the United States and Italy, as Germany's partner, might
well become a reality. When Germany's forces invaded Poland on Septem-

ber 1939, it became increasingly evident that the United States would have to alter drastically its policies.

For a few months following Germany's invasion of Poland, there was little military action prompting some critics to label it a "Phony War." The quietude came to an end, however, in the spring of 1940 as Russia, which had marched into Eastern Poland, quickly overwhelmed the small Eastern European nations of Lithuania, Latvia and Estonia, and then attacked Finland that put up surprising heroic resistance. At the same time, Germany took over a number of smaller nations: Denmark, Norway, Holland, Belgium, and Luxembourg, before it tackled France. Italy joined in the invasion of France, leading to Roosevelt's denunciation previously discussed. The fall of France was accompanied by the establishment of the collaborationist Vichy government made up of indigenous Frenchmen that administered southern France, while Germany occupied the northern portion. France's fall signaled many Americans that its own good fortune in avoiding war was now due almost entirely to the wide Atlantic Ocean and that the bulwarks of Great Britain and France that hitherto stood in Hitler's way had been significantly reduced. United States national security being at stake, the government took steps to patrol the western half of the ocean, thus relieving Great Britain of the full military burden. In June 1940, the United States passed the Selective Service Act, setting up compulsory one-year military training for young men between 21 and 35. On the screen in my weekly sojourn to the movies, I can still recall the blindfolded Secretary of War Henry Stimson pull out of a goldfish bowl the first draftee—the beginning of a scenario that soon became a reality on Himrod Street. A couple of young men on my block were drafted by the legislation and joked that it would be only for one year, but subsequently found themselves in the service for the duration of four to five years. Further bellicose actions by Japan and Germany in 1940 led the United States to place embargoes on the sale of certain scarce items, but singularly failed to affect the aggressor nations. Finally in March 1941, the United States approved the Lend-lease Act that empowered the President to lend or lease billions of dollars of war material to nations whose security were linked to the national security of this country.

PACIFISM

Formal pacifism was not a creed to be heard in our neighborhood. Aside from Italian American mothers like my own, who deplored war because of the death and destruction that would be the inevitable consequence of conflagration, the local atmosphere was bereft of the concept of non-violence. The only time it was discussed was in connection with the pacifist response of actor Lew Ayres who resisted entry into the regular army, but was able to resolve his conscientious objection by serving in a non-combatant role. Neither I nor my friends could quite comprehend refusal to fight in what obviously was a just cause. Although most of those who refused to fight were members of small Protestant sects such as Mennonites and Quakers that numbered few Italian Americans, there were exceptions. One was Simon Greco, a Chicago commercial artist whose motivation at how he arrived at the decision was a mixture of religion and personal preference. "First of all it had to do with my family. My parents were devout Christians. They're not very good Catholics in a real strict sense of the word, ... " he explained. He also referred to a personal incident of fighting as a young boy and receiving a lecture from the school principal about the difference between people and animals. "Then, I think, it was the whole idea of who I was, what I was going to do with my life."[113] With America's entry into war, pacifism faded away.

Chapter III
The War Begins
to Impact
Italian American
Neighborhoods

Pearl Harbor

On that fateful mildly cold Sunday December 7, 1941, while the Brooklyn Dodgers Football team played against the New York Giants squad before 55,000 people at the Polo Grounds, I was an active thirteen-year-old teenager who had just finished seeing a movie at a nearby theater with friends from the block. It was still afternoon with dimming daylight, when upon leaving the movie house, we heard people talking animatedly about the bombing of Pearl Harbor. The radio also called upon servicemen to don their uniforms and report to Brooklyn military bases either at the Brooklyn Navy Yard or Floyd Bennett Field. At first, we placed little significance on the incident, since in our limited understanding of geography our knowledge of important American harbors was confined to the more well-known ports, such as New York on the East Coast or San Francisco on the West Coast. In addition, at our house we were preparing to celebrate my sister's fourteenth birthday, and thus not inclined to be preoccupied with weightier matters. Our insouciance was soon dispelled. We learned that Pearl Harbor, although not part of the contiguous United States, was indeed a principal port in a major United States possession, that great harm had been done to the United States Naval forces, and that the nation was at war with Japan. Although it was approaching winter, I was impressed by the number of people out on the street talking about the event, and soon came to realize that a major shift in our way of life was imminent. Momentous events were to become commonplace and would be firmly reinforced by the indelible impressions that we saw repeatedly in somber Movie-tone newsreels. Who could forget the scenes of dense black smoke emitting from critically damaged or destroyed battleships lying prostrate in Pearl Harbor; President Roosevelt's stirring address to Congress about Japan's attack as "a day of infamy" and a solemn Congress passing a war declaration first with Japan, and in succeeding days, with Germany and Italy. Although not fully clear as to the implications, it was evident to my naive young mind that things would never be the same not only for the nation, but for people in my community. My world would change as it would transform life for all Italian Americans.

UBIQUITOUS UNIFORMS

Among the immediate symptoms of the transition from a peacetime environment to a war time climate was the ubiquitous military uniform. Up and down Himrod St. and the surrounding neighborhood streets, at Mass at St. Joseph's Church, in the subways and trolley cars, in the stores and movie houses, one could see men in Army, Navy, Marine, and Coast Guard dress replete with unit insignias, medals and other marks of distinction. One also could see uniforms were hanging on the racks in local dry cleaning establishments as well as in homes of friends and relatives. It was the same all over the country. A Washington observer noted the dramatic impact of uniforms "On December 6, you seldom, if ever, saw a uniform on the street. By the evening of December 7, there were uniforms all over the place."[114] Non-military businesses like American Telephone and Telegraph utilized the uniform metaphor in newspaper ads that illustrated company employees in familiar company garb as a way of bringing attention to their input in the war effort even though they were not wearing traditional military uniforms, "not all are in uniform—but all are in the Service." It seemed that to wear the uniform of one of the nation's armed services was tantamount to gaining acceptance as a patriotic American. Pithily describing his induction as well as that of his twin brother into the Army Air Force, Brooklyn's Nat Scammacca recounted the reaction of New Yorkers to the brothers in uniform. "All these well-dressed pedestrians saw us and looked our way. Yes, they stared at us because we had two silver wings on our olive-green officer jackets, and this meant we were valiant defenders of all that American good living and wealth ... We, the sons of Sicilian immigrants, were now considered the sons of America ... "[115]

WOMEN IN UNIFORMS

Although I recall few women in military clothing in my neighborhood, I was aware that a small, but nevertheless significant number of females were serving meritoriously in various military capacities as Women's Army Corps WACS (140,000), Navy's WAVES (100,000), Marine Corps Women's Reserve (MCWR) 23,000 and 13,000 with the Coast Guard's SPARS. Except for nurses, males in the armed services cast a disparaging eye on their role, while the general public regarded them with a degree of dubiousness and condescension. Women in uniforms had to endure "the spread of vicious rumors about WAC immorality in 1943 [that] dealt a serious blow to recruitment and demonstrated the extent to which women in uniform violated timeworn beliefs." That the press sometimes dubbed them "Petticoat Army," is a further illustration of the obstacles faced by women entering the service.[116]

One is left with a general impression that very few Italian American women receive extended treatment in studies of women's military participation during the war—possibly a reflection of their relatively small representation. Whether relevant statistics indicating white ethnic participation exist is unknown, it is revealing that the government regarded white ethnic resistance to enter the armed forces of sufficient importance as to launch specific drives aimed at encouraging them. One agenda that was translated into Italian, among other languages, emphasized WACS with characteristic foreign names enjoying life comfortably in "feminine barracks"—a plan evidently aimed at several groups, especially Italians.[117]

These obstacles notwithstanding, an untold number of Italian American women responded to the call for volunteers and thereby did their part to contribute to the war effort on the home front. One example was that of Jane Chianese who chose to volunteer in the Army Signal Corps as her personal way of doing her share to win the war. She was soon placed in the Intelligence Department and assigned to a high security code-breaking operation in Virginia where, "Our job was to decode messages as they were intercepted. They were Japanese messages and had been translated before they got to us ... We were warned never to tell what we did there, and if asked, to say we were just clerks." The indoctrination was so effective that fifty years later she confessed "I am not sure if we are allowed to talk about it even now."[118]

Others who joined the armed services intermittently received coverage in *Il Progresso Italo-Americano,* which highlighted their careers, thus bringing home the point of the outstanding Italian American female participation. One such instance included a picture of the Italian front where General Mark Clark pinned Bronze Stars on WAC technician Eleanor V. Spinola for her service with distinction in a campaign south of Rome. Another example is that of Dr. Giaconda Rita Saraniero of Brooklyn, who expressed her pride in being the first woman physician in the Third Naval District to be admitted as a Reserve Second Lieutenant into the Navy

Medical Corps. She would join three brothers who served in the navy. "It was the most thrilling moment in all my life. Now all the Saraniero children are all accounted for." [119]

There were, in addition, a number of Italian American women, like Adeline Vicario Hillman of South Ozone Park, Queens, who upon graduating from nursing school, enlisted in the Army Nurses Corp. She and other graduate nurses, many of whom graduated from Catholic colleges, were so deeply affected by the tragedy that befell servicemen—including a penetrating impression that registered deep in their consciences after seeing nurses lead a group of blind marines—that they felt it their duty to enlist. Notwithstanding a prevailing nagging misconception about the "easy virtue" of women in uniform, her immigrant father fully supported her as she donned a first lieutenant's uniform in the Army Nurses Corps. [120] For Catherine Vitelli who became a student nurse at New York Hospital in 1944, the U.S. Nurse Cadet offered the opportunity to fulfill a lifetime goal of studying nursing. It also provided an opportunity to aid the war effort significantly since every newly enrolled student would release a graduate nurse for military duty. Vitelli was deeply impressed with letters from enlisted nurses who wrote from the front lines as they ministered to the fighting forces. "If you could only read about what they say about how urgently nurses are needed you'd realize as we do, how important a part of this war we student nurses are." [121]

It is virtually impossible to provide statistics regarding the number of Italian American women whose support on behalf of the war effort came via service in the United Service Organization (USO), a quasi-government sanctioned agency that provided entertainment for the armed forces. That there was some involvement by members of the ethnic group is borne out in Sadie Penzato's autobiography in which she cites her own sister having such a role. "Less than a year after leaving the farm, Caroline joined the USO and was immediately sent overseas to entertain our troops." She traveled extensively, often close to the front lines and survived two airplane crashes.

We were very proud of her and, much to our surprise and delight, the people in the village of New Paltz were proud of her. They gave her a parade when she came home from overseas for a family visit. You wonder how Papa responded to her return? He welcomed his "hero" daughter with open arms and they embraced.[122]

MANUFACTURING UNIFORMS

Uniforms commanded respect from youngsters of my generation, most of whom were too young to enter the service in 1941, although that would change drastically in a couple of years. Of course, we absorbed government propaganda that extolled the privilege and honor that was extended to wearers of the attire of the nation's armed forces. We dreamed and verbalized of the time when we too would be able to share in that honored practice exploring the possibilities of diverse military services. While not equating it on a par with front line service, the government went out of its way to encourage clothing manufacturers and their employees that

Like many other neighborhood factories in major Eastern cities, this Brooklyn clothing company provided work for local Italian immigrant men and women. During the war, they produced massive amounts of uniforms and accessories that won the plaudits of high military officials.

PHOTO COURTESY FRANCESCA MAGLIOCHETTI

was not attended by the glamour of battlefield performance, nor that it would earn distinguished medals, nevertheless, the gesture of thanks by high military officers was appreciated. The ethnic press was fulsome in its report that no less than the commanding figure of General Eisenhower took the time personally to promote enthusiasm among garment industry workers. Government representatives exhorted tailors to create uniforms that not only provided sartorial satisfaction in the military apparel end product, but also that uniforms simultaneously be utilitarian yet grant protection from inclement weather—the "Eisenhower" jacket was one outcome. Few would dispute the observation that in New York Americans of Italian descent had become mainstay workers of the garment industry. "One of the most interesting aspects concerning the industry was that majority of workers are Italians or of Italian origin."[123] My home county of Brooklyn, in particular, was noted for the performance of its clothing factories in producing superior quality uniforms at an accelerated rate of production that was carried out in many factories owned and operated by Italian Americans—indeed on my corner, the Fontanetta family operated such an establishment. Because of the nature of the business, more than a few Italian immigrants found Brooklyn's garment industry an entry point into the entrepreneurship field. "For example, Albert Figuccio, Ernest Gallo, and Louis Isabella—all three of them natives of Italy who came to the United States about 1910—employed fifty to one hundred men each, in the manufacture of coats, suits, and dresses." Second generation Daniel de Vita was "general manager of the Naval Clothing Depot of Brooklyn, and designer of uniforms for the United States Navy."[124]

With the outbreak of the war, the Rovito Coat Company on Atlantic Ave., operated by the son of proprietor Stano DeSantis, an immigrant from Cosenza, that employed 330 workers, was cited for its leadership in the industry. For military clothing manufacturer Palermo-born Antonio Miceli and his wife, the knowledge that they were aiding the war effort was a bittersweet comfort since one of their sons was killed in action in the American Army. That overwhelming reality that they were aiding the war effort was what kept them going. The sorrowful mother explained, "All this is sufficient reason for my daily appearance at the factory." The role of Brooklyn Italian Americans in manufacturing uniforms was replicated in practically all the large cities that housed the garment industry. "In mid-January 1942, for instance, ACWA business agent Thomas Di Lauro, an Italian American himself, reported that '[clothing] shops are working in full capacity' for the production of uniforms for the armed forces."[125]

The omnipresence of the military uniform was further reinforced by the understanding that manufacturing was achieved by so many neighborhood Italian American mothers and their daughters who operated sewing machines or sewed linings or buttons on uniforms in the numerous small factories in which they employed. Previously occupied with manufacturing civilian clothing, such as men's sports jackets and overcoats, that were now no longer a priority, these plants now were acquiring desirable government orders for the manufacture of uniforms. I saw much of this first hand when I turned fourteen and went to work after school as a delivery boy in Manhattan that brought me into the bowels of mid-town lofts that housed countless clothing factories. One could also readily see many small factories similarly engaged in uniform production within the neighborhood. For example, various members of the Favara family owned clothing manufacturing factories in the vicinity. Mario Favara operated one only several blocks from where I lived on Wilson Ave. and Bleeker St. that normally produced coats and suits for a jobber in Manhattan, but during the war also produced uniforms. Although there was a sprinkling of male workers, especially as pressers, most of the employees were Sicilian-American women, the predominant background locally, many of them mothers with minor children, who lived within walking distance in the neighborhood, thus precluding the time and cost of travel and the comforting knowledge of proximity should demands of the home require—this included my mother who for a time walked several blocks to work in factory nearby. By the end of the war, as we children grew older, she went to work for a larger clothing factory in Manhattan that necessitated taking the subway. With the onset of war, workers in Favara's factory, who were members of the International Ladies Garment Workers Union (ILGWU), began to produce wartime clothing such as the famous "Ike" jackets, which his daughter Francesca proudly prizes decades later. The volume of work in this neighborhood clothing factory increased during the war to such a degree that even though he employed 50 workers, there was still a shortage.[126] In a flush of patriotic fervor after Pearl Harbor, Mario Favara changed his factory's name from Blue Ribbon Coat Co. to Victory Coat Co. Other Italian American factory owners sought to alter factory names, so as to blunt or completely obscure the Italian ethnic identity. The war-time name changing frenzy was a familiar scenario in the neighborhood where one could spot a faded German nomenclature "Hamburg Ave." signs that harkened back to the 1920s on the renamed" Wilson Ave." elevated lines a few block away. We saw it also vividly on December 8, 1941, at the nearby Rising Sun Diner—despite the absence of Japanese locally—but which hastily became Victory Restaurant.

Even among youngsters, the uniform was all-encompassing as child-sized military dress became the garb of choice. "Boys wore cast-off uniforms of all kinds ... Their favorite item of headwear was an aviator's cap." While khaki became the favorite garb, girls improvised by wearing sailor-like pea jackets. It was not unusual for mothers with sewing talent to make uniforms for their children. Susan Anzovino of Cleveland, who dreamed of becoming a Navy nurse, was thrilled with the uniform her mother made for her—a navy cape with gold satin lining and a gold star on each side of a stand-up collar.[127]

Among Italian American home front

Francesca Favara proudly wore the "Ike" jacket made for her in her father's factory where dozens of home front Italian American women produced military uniforms.

PHOTO COURTESY FRANCESCA MAGLIOCHETTI

contributions were the activities of specialized cloth manufacturing firms like the Scalamandre Silk Manufacturing Company of New York. Bringing with him a century-old family tradition of weaving and designing in 1924, immigrant engineer Franco Scalamandre was determinated to carry on the family practice. In 1929, he opened his factory in the Astoria, Queens, that would become the foremost producer of silk and silk-derivative cloth that employed dozens of people to keep more than fifty machines working constantly. The employees, mostly Italian immigrants who lived in the neighborhood, helped the firm gain world renown in its field, producing exquisite drapes and fine silk that graced finer homes, museums and the White House. Virtually from the outset of the war, the firm used its expertise to produce fine silk items that were critical to parachute manufacturing as well as other cloth that was essential to provide camouflage conditions on the ground. Scalamandre was also proud of his twenty-four employees who were serving in the armed forces, assuring them that their jobs would await them upon their return.[128]

All of these developments brought the war inescapably to us on home front. We saw other unmistakable signs all around us in the greater New York area: the darkening lights on famed Broadway, the dimming of the Statue of Liberty in New York Harbor, and the dispensing of floodlights along the shore lines of Brooklyn. For young Joseph Nastasi of Bensonhurst, Brooklyn, it was only a short bicycle ride to Fort Hamilton, a base originally built as a defense against the British in the War 1812, the fort continued to operate as an army post. From his bicycle vantage point, Nastasi saw segments of the fort's side open to allow for big cannons to protrude and after a time recede into the wall—obviously drills conducted periodically to be ready in the event of an enemy attack.[129] Newspaper headlines with accompanying dramatic photographs of the Normandie sinking in a harbor in New York City in February 1942 further brought the war to the home front. The fact that the huge French liner-transport was being converted for transport of thousands of American troops led immediately to fear that the disaster was the result of deliberate enemy disruption in the midst of our city. While subsequent investigation confirmed that the disaster was the result of accident, nevertheless, for a time, sabotage continued to be a source of speculation to us on the home front.[130]

DRAFT AND VOLUNTEERS

Since the dream of wearing a service uniform was inextricably intertwined with that of membership in the armed forces, my generation was acutely aware of the many young people who were in the service or about to enter it. There was little question about the popularity of the war; virtually all on the home front supported it, especially we young people. In this respect, this was undeniably a total war—one that involved not only those on the battlefront, but also we who did what we could on the home front. In my imagination, amply fed by movies that glorified their role, the Marines were at the pinnacle of the armed forces. It was not a diminishment of the Army or Navy or Coast Guard, but rather a belief that the United States Marines were usually given the toughest military tasks: the invasions, the extermination of particularly dangerous pockets of enemy forces, the heroic rescues of beleaguered comrades, etc. The personal accounts of relatives or neighborhood friends recently inducted into the Marines, who had come home on leave following basic training, confirmed the reputation that hard, rigid discipline was required and further enhanced the primacy of the Corps in our minds. For all that, most of those who entered the service in my block were in the Army, with a lesser amount in the Navy, and an even smaller number in the Marines.

It is not known whether there are extant statistics concerning the enlistment versus draft rate among Italian Americans. My impression was that locally, the draft call was the main catalyst for a military career, a notion corroborated in the autobiographical chronicle of Daniel Petruzzi and the biography of Philip V. Aquila, two recently-published accounts that underscore that being drafted probably reflected the experience of many, if not most. Petruzzi, who went on to a distinguished military career in Italy described his call up, "Then in June—only days after I reached twenty one and six months before Pearl Harbor—I was told to report to the draft board for a physical, among the first in the nation."[131] The Aquila story is similar: "All we know for sure is that the local draft board inducted four of the Aquilas' six eligible sons into the armed forces during World War II … Phil was twenty-one years old when he received his draft notice early in 1943."[132] Of course, there was a considerable number who, while waiting for the inevitability of the draft call, enlisted in order to determine the branch in which they would serve. In addition, it sometimes happened that young men, trying to spare their fearful mothers who worried about the harm that might come to sons entering the service, hid the fact they had volunteered by informing their mothers that they were drafted and therefore had no choice but to enter the Army. Such was the case with Sgt. Agostino J. Sorrentino of Brooklyn whose two uncles were fighting in Mussolini's Army, but nevertheless volunteered because "He was angry that Italy should let herself be used as a pawn by Germany and he wanted to avenge it. His family doesn't know he volunteered." In the course of the war, after the report that he had been captured, his mother, who spoke Italian exclusively, uttered the words of most Americans of Italian immigrant background. "We want America to win. We are over here now since 1904, we've never been back, this is where we get our bread and butter and we like it. We don't care about Italy any more."[133] It was a similar story with my brother-in-law Frank Sutera, whose Sicilian-born mother died in 2003 at age 105, never knowing he had volunteered for the Army, believing he had been drafted instead.[134] The enthusiastic response was echoed in Italian sections throughout the country. In his work on the Hill, the St. Louis, Missouri Little Italy, Gary R. Mormino describes the rush to enlist in the Marines. "More than one son conned immigrant parents to signing consent papers with the airtight logic of young Roland De Gregorio. 'Dad,' pleaded the young man to his Sicilian father, "the Marines are fighting in the Pacific and I won't fight against your brother and cousins in Italy."[135]   Some like next door neighbor Mike Rizzo entered the Army where he volunteered to train as a paratrooper—an assignment that also was highly regarded for the danger it involved. Although a few enlisted in the Navy, it was the khaki Army uniform that was predominant and that claimed inductees from virtually every family on the block where there lived those of eligible military age. This would encompass young men that otherwise did not convey images of rigor and vitality, and in fact, proffered a lethargic and sluggish countenance that one thought would have rendered them 4-F (unfit for military service). There were, in fact, a few in the latter category because of conditions like flat feet, circulatory, vision, heart, or auditory problems. For most families on the block, it was not merely one member of the family who served, but rather more than one since there usually were several children in each family. The Blue Stars in the center of satin white 7 x 10 inch banners, designating family members in the service, dotted the residential landscape of apartments in virtually every one of the 36 houses on the block. They stood as a ringing testimony to their contribution to the war effort. In time, some of the same windows displayed silver stars indicating a wounded serviceman, and most somber of all, the gold star that denoted a family member had paid the supreme sacrifice. Sometimes black and purple bunting would drape the house affected and passers-by showed respect by becoming a bit more silent. In addition to homes, organizations and institutions also displayed banners with multiple stars that indicated the number organization members of the service. This was the case in the Church St. Joseph where the service banner was situated to the right of the altar.

FAMILY PLURAL SERVICEMEN

The notion of multiple family members in the armed forces was a familiar phenomenon among friends on the block who had older brothers, such as the Sanfilippo, DiGiovanni, Giambalvo, and Aglialoro families. It was also vividly brought home in my aunt Fifi's (Philomena) family—the Gorgones—who lived a few blocks away. At least five of the eight sons of

Aunt Fifi, my father's sister, were in branches of the armed forces—two of them perished in war. To the country at large, the phenomenon of several members in the service was brought home vividly via "The Fighting Sullivans", a favorite wartime motion picture drama that recounted the tragedy of five Sullivan brothers—depicted as typical fun-loving American boys—serving as sailors on the same vessel that became a casualty of war. This severe misfortune was so overwhelming that the government rewrote its policy regarding the military assignments of plural family members (the central theme in the popular movie "Saving Private Ryan."); it likewise became the basis for much discussion on my block where in imitation we dubbed an Italian American household, the Castelli family with five young sons, "the Sullivans." I was further impressed with the admirable hard work ethic of the fathers of both families: the Sullivan father worked on the railroad, while the immigrant Castelli, worked as laborer during the day and after supper when weather permitted, pushed his cart while peddling lemon ices.

Given family fertility patterns of that era, it was inevitable that in numerous instances, several members of a given family served in the military simultaneously—a fact most abundantly evident among Italian Americans. For example, the six Quaranta brothers from New York, who were on active duty in Europe and the Pacific, were one of several area Italian American families that had six or more members in military uniforms. The De Angelo family of the Bronx's Little Italy claimed seven sons in military service—one of whom was born in Italy. Asked how she felt about this extraordinary display of patriotism, the widowed mother of the servicemen wistfully remembered the Italy of her childhood as a peaceful nation that excelled in art and science. "My appeal is modest to be united with others, also to become a great voice to help Italy," was her calm and dispassionate plea.[136] "I am the proudest father in the whole world" asserted immigrant Antonio Lorenzo of his seven sons in the service. An employee of the New York City Police Department, he expressed voiced gratification "of my sons especially because they are fighting for the people's liberty and against barbaric governments."[137] Pride intermixed with sadness marked the saga of seven sons of the Brooklyn's Adorno family that had emigrated from Bari in 1900. When one of the soldier sons who had been separated from the family met his younger serviceman brother for the first time in Italy, they planned a postwar reunion—only to have to postpone it again after learning that another brother, Anthony Adorno, had been killed in action in April 1945.[138] Similar tragedy impacted the extraordinary Conti family of Brooklyn that had achieved pre-war fame as aerial and tumbling artists that toured the country. Beneficiaries of excellent training since childhood because of their profession, two of them volunteered to submit to tests for the treatment of malaria, an action that earned them citation from the Secretary of the Navy. Four of the brothers joined the marines where they saw action in Guadalcanal and Iwo Jima, where one of them was killed on the battlefield.[139] The Maresca family that emigrated from Sorrento, Italy, and first came to Manhattan and to Jersey City, provided another striking instance of patriotism. Closely identified with their parish St. Paul of the Cross, where twelve sons were active in the Holy Name Society, three served in the First World War and one was killed in action. Subscribing to the slogan "For God and For Country", six Maresca brothers entered military service in the next World War.[140] The phenomenon of plural servicemen was also vividly demonstrated in micro "Little Italies" such as Glen Cove, Long Island, that saw hundreds of Italian Americans take the colors. The rate of participation can be gleaned from a local 1942 Honor Roll that, only a few months into the war, listed six members in the military services in each of the Nigro, Capobianco and Dileo families. Plural membership in the military was evident also in the eight brothers of the Faro family of Herrin, Illinois, and in the eight brothers and one sister of the Scerra family of Gardner, Massachusetts.[141] From New York City's West Side, Frank Noto proudly counted thirty-one members of the Noto clan in the armed services.[142]

As striking as these examples was the Red Bank, New Jersey D'Antonio family that probably set a record for plural servicemen within a family, when in March 1942, thirty-seven year-old Michael D'Antonio announced his entry into the armed services, thus joining ten brothers already serving. A twelfth brother would also soon be receiving his induction notice while it would be a few years before the thirteenth brother, then only fourteen, would receive his call. In addition, the three D'Antonio married sisters worked in war production plants. Since perhaps only one other family could lay claim to a dozen servicemen serving simultaneously, it rendered the D'Antonio achievement a rare and extraordinary phenomenon and prompted the Italian press to comment that "Italian immigrants brought over not only their intelligent work habits, and efficiency; but also exceeded their prolific expectations."[143]

A SECOND WAR

More than a few Italian American households caught up in the patriotic fervor that supplied men for the American military forces during World War I involved those who were of an age that could have precluded enlistment, but nevertheless were now ready to assume their patriotic duty in this war. One example from my neighborhood was Alex Pisciotta who had enlisted as a private in the First World War, remained in the active Army reserves, was instrumental in establishing a veterans post, and a member of the committee that helped raise funds for my parish St. Joseph's Church. Although he was married and a father of three children, and had become a lawyer and a magistrate appointee of Mayor LaGuardia,—all of which would have entitled him to deferment—a month after the attack on Pearl Harbor, he enthusiastically accepted a commission as a captain. That he regarded highly his military experience as part of the greatest generation was evident when I met and interviewed him a number of years later. Son of an eminent and titled archeologist, Italian aviator Captain Salvatore Curioni, who experienced his share of combat against Germany during the First World War, was still another example of those who served in two wars. An immigrant who became an American citizen in the 1920s, after

Pearl Harbor at age 47, he volunteered for the service.[144] The World War II memoir of Cornelius Kio Granai, based on his letters, relates the story of Barre, Vermont resident Kio Granai, who in 1917 at age 19, enlisted in the United States Merchant Marine, and then in 1943 at age 46, volunteered for his second war. One of eleven children whose forbears were from northern Italy, Granai became a lawyer. He enlisted because he "could not in good conscience continue to leave the fighting and dying ... to the youth of the community ... It is my duty to go if the Army will have me"[145] Ralph G. Mastalio (Big Ralph) of Glen Cove provides another remarkable instance of unbounded loyalty to serve in more than one war. Born in Salerno, Italy, Ralph enlisted in the American Army at the outbreak of the First World War, and this was followed by a career as a policeman. With the coming of World War II, although fifty-two years of age and therefore beyond the acceptable enlistment age, he was so determined to be in the army that he dyed his hair and managed to convince the draft board that he was still a young man. Assigned to duty in Asia, where he was the oldest man in the regiment, he was wounded in action, received the Purple Heart, the Bronze Star and several citations for bravery—he was clearly a source of inspiration to his younger comrades.[146] Perhaps the oldest Italian American to try to enlist was Peter Lado, who had served in the British Navy in World War I in the Italian Navy in the 1930s, and was prepared to join the American Army in the latest conflagration. Denied admission because of his age—he was 65—he appealed to President Roosevelt, who responded by suggesting he try the Coast Guard. Accepted into that branch, he was shipped out and saw combat twice, for which he was awarded a Marine Combat Bar.[147]

THE TWO-NESS DILEMMA

The attack on Pearl Harbor that brought the United States directly into the war against Italy and other Axis powers was a time of duress for Italian Americans. Products of an ethnocentric environment that effectively

meant a marginal status—American yes, but with a distinct Italian background, it became a "two-ness" dilemma for many who were faced with
the challenge of straddling two cultures. Traditional religion was the way
women in heavily Italian East Harlem and other ethnic enclaves dealt with
the problem.

> The women of Italian Harlem turned to the Madonna dur-
> ing the difficult years of the war, imploring her to watch
> over their men on the distant battlefields ... One woman
> gratefully observed after her son had returned from the
> Pacific, "I know that only through the aid of Our Blessed
> Mother was it possible [for him] to escape without a
> scratch." ... One woman expressed the tension felt by
> others in the community: "Many times in this long pe-
> riod of four years, I was without any news, and my heart
> suffered terribly, But I never gave up—instead I kept on
> praying.[148]

While the two-ness dilemma was particularly distressful to the older
generation, it also impacted young people. Even though too youthful to
enter the service, in my mind's eye I harbored no compunction about fighting against Germany or Japan, but to go to war against the land of our
mothers and fathers caused me to pause. Initially, this may have been the
prevailing view among second generation Italian Americans; however, it
quickly receded into the background as they energetically responded to the
call of the colors.[149]

SWELLING PATRIOTIC FERVOR

Utilizing his particular talent, songwriter R. Solly Pellegrino mailed
out to military camps 15,000 copies of his war-inspired composition of a
waltz titled "American Ever Free," essentially his personal contribution to
the war effort. In elucidating his motivation, he undoubtedly echoed the
sentiments of the overwhelming number of Italian Americans on the home
front. "In this hour of great need, we Americans of Italian origin shall do

all we can to show our love and patriotism for this great country."[150] From the Orchard, Glen Cove's Little Italy, Alfred "Freddy" Carbuto, who was a local musician before the war, joined the Marines soon after Pearl Harbor and saw extensive combat in the Pacific theater, including the bloody battle of Guadalcanal, wrote a song borne of fighting in the trenches. Carrying his guitar with him, he went from one battle to another alongside his column of weary leathernecks, who would stop for breathers until the sergeant yelled out "Get your gear on boys, we're moving out again." The repetitive catchphrase served as his inspiration and as the title of his battlefield song that became very popular in the jungles of the Pacific and back on the home front where it was also featured on commercial radio stations in New York. Years after the war, it continued to be included in Marine Corps reunions.[151]

There was really no serious question about Italian immigrant loyalty in the United States—a fidelity that can be discerned in the unsophisticated yet heartfelt sentiments of a Westbury, New York barber who kept a diary and whose simple account of his entry for December 7, 1941, Pearl Harbor Day, stands as eloquent testimony to immigrant patriotism.

> December 7, 1941
> 172 Post Avenue
> Westbury Barber,
>
> I am Italian Born -
>
> Thank you. Uncle Sam, for giving me a home and letting me become an American. I am proud to be one of you and I shall help in every possible way to keep American on top of the world.
>
> American Citizen A. Cesare.[152]

This sentiment, it might be added, was genuinely representative of the home front, one in marked contrast to the uninformed crass hypocrisy demonstrated in Jerry Della Femina's recollections of growing up in the Gravesend, Brooklyn Italian enclave. "When World War II came to our village, there was a real problem for my family—they weren't sure which side to root for."[153]

Patriotism could be demonstrated in other home front acts that were performed outside of military service, even by mere youngsters. Caught up in the prevailing patriotic euphoria and without informing his parents, diminutive and frail fourteen-year-old Brooklynite Louis D'Ambrosio unsuccessfully tried to enlist in the Army, Navy, and Marines. Equally unsuccessful in an attempt to donate blood because of his own frailty, he finally was given an assignment by the Junior Red Cross—namely overseeing his junior high school contribution to the war effort. He soon received public recognition for his efforts in organizing the collection and sale of newspapers, knitting, collecting tin foil, clothing, and rags for sale, with all the proceeds for the Red Cross.[154]

THE SUPREME SACRIFICE

There were indeed many ways to demonstrate loyalty: donating blood, buying war bonds, developing victory gardens, working in defense plants, joining the armed services, among others, but the sacrifice of one's life would surely be the greatest of all proofs of devotion to the nation. Italian Americans made their contribution in this regard from the outset of the war. Perhaps the first was Oreste Datorre who had volunteered for the service in 1940, and died at Pearl Harbor after the December 7, 1941 Japanese attack. Given my recollection of neighborhood, Italian American mothers who genuinely dreaded the thought that their sons might have to fight and possibly lose their lives, the reaction of Oreste's immigrant mother is incredible as it is remarkable. "America means more to me now. Yes, for I have given a son to America and whenever I look at the Star Spangled banner, I can visualize my son among the stars and stripes." The Italian language newspaper marveled at her expression of patriotism and opined "What greater love can an immigrant show for his or her new land than giving a son to the nation."[155] Notwithstanding the brave words of this mother, the reality was that the loss of a son was devastating and deeply felt on the home front. This can be gleaned from the recollection of Frank Cavaioli who wrote of the heartbreaking reaction of his neighbor, Tessie Curcio, "screaming as I lay awake one Sunday morning in June 1944, when she received word that her son Todd had been killed in action by the Japanese during the invasion of Saipan."[156]

FULL EMPLOYMENT

The mobilization of the nation's labor force was one of the most astonishing developments we witnessed on the home front as it seemed to reverse almost overnight the dreary picture of extreme unemployment that characterized the prior years. Of course, the reality was that transformation, while not instantaneous, however, by 1943, it was a discernibly brighter picture because now "the problem was how to find workers for all the jobs that needed to be done."[157] The lesson I learned in my social studies class was that the law of supply and demand finally favored the workers. Another assessment succinctly captured the impact of the war. "The war did not merely banish the decade-long scourge of unemployment. It also provided jobs for the 3.25 million new job-seekers who reached employable age during the conflict, as well as to another 7.3 million workers, half of these women who would not normally have sought work in even in a full-employment economy."[158] Historian Kennedy's summary of the impact of the war on employment trends toward full employment is an apt description of what happened in my Brooklyn neighborhood, over the course of several months. It was a stark reversal of fortunes for older men who had struggled for years to earn enough for their families at low-paying jobs or who were dependent on the WPA for work but could now afford a few luxuries.

For many Italian Americans on the home front, working in war production plants not only provided welcome improvement in income, but also helped to salve anxious consciences: they were hereby conspicuously contributing to the war effort by helping to build the equipment to defeat America's enemies. It was with pride, for example, that Neapolitan-born Gennaro De Angelis, the father of a Hartford, Connecticut family stated that not only did he work in a war plant, but so too did nine of his children who worked around the clock in three eight hour shifts.[159]

The employment climate brightened perceptibly for young men on my block whose pre-war aspirations would have been amply satisfied if they were fortunate enough to land jobs at $16.00 a week, but it now seemed the demand for workers was so great they could go beyond their wildest dreams. The fabled Brooklyn Navy Yard satisfied a voracious appetite for workers by employing at its height 71,000 workers who sought easy commute at its three shifts. Brooklyn's Todd Shipyard Corporation, and the Sperry Gyroscope Co., among others, hired thousands while defense companies and instrument manufacturers in nearby Queens, along with Long Island airplane construction plants all clamored for help. In its Times Square employment office, the Wright Aeronautical Corporation of New Jersey advertised in an Italian language newspaper under the slogan "Get in the Fight—Work at Wright" for "Husky Men" to work in its foundry for salaries of $44.20 for 48 hour week.[160] Companies like the Bulova Watch Co. now shifted from watch making to manufacturing of precision instruments called for workers at attractive salaries. Italian Americans were substantial beneficiaries of these gains and could well agree with sentiments that were expressed in other parts of the country. For example, a Virginia worker was overjoyed at the prospects. "I went from forty cents an hour to a dollar an hour ... At the end of the war I was making two seventy-five an hour ... I couldn't believe my good fortune."[161] Moreover, it was not only men who engaged in war work. In a unique example of contributing to the war effort, many Italian American women participated in WOW, an acronym for Women Ordnance Workers, by the War Manpower Commission and established at Marcy, New York to train women aircraft workers thus replacing men called into service.[162] One instance whereby Italian American women capably assumed jobs previously in man's domain was that of Rosa Penna and Ann Mandore, who took on the jobs previously held by their husbands, now in the army and had previously worked for the Long Island Rail Road.[163]

Not only was the basic pay much higher than the recent past, but jobs now also provided the opportunity to work overtime. A concept rarely heard during the Depression years, overtime work and pay at time and a half now became part of daily lexicon as virtually every employed person worked far beyond the typical 40-hour week. The major complaint that I heard from the neighborhood men engaged in essential defense plant work that granted them a deferred status from the draft, was that they were so busy putting in additional hours that they did not have time to spend and enjoy their newfound wealth. Severe shortage of workers found employers prepared to ignore federal child labor laws that had been enacted only a few years earlier to prohibit employment in factories of those under sixteen years; and under eighteen, where there were dangerous machines. Although I was too young to be employed legally in factory work, as soon as I turned fourteen, while still under age, I nevertheless obtained an after-school job in a Manhattan bookbindery factory where I served in various menial capacities, including delivery of diverse items to companies in mid-town lofts. Since the bookbindery was not engaged directly in war work, it was typical of many such small establishments that scrounged around for workers that normally would be by-passed. They included the sixty-year-old proprietor; and his son, who according to rumor was 4-F; the owner's mute brother-in-law, an apparently homeless local street person who projected an offensive odor and who mercifully came to work sporadically; another older worker, and myself aged fourteen—not one of us was soldier material. On several occasions, proprietors of the companies to which I delivered my firm's products, notwithstanding their friendship with my employer, nevertheless offered me jobs with their companies. I recall several occasions even while riding elevators total strangers would offer me a job, surely a reflection of the desperateness of employers for workers. We were at first surprised, and then came to marvel at the skill and ability of women performing industrial tasks that previously were the provinces of males. It filled them with a sense of accomplishment and pride that they were more than doing their bit for the war effort. A popular poster appeal that highlighted their role featured a woman at work wearing a polka dot bandana, with her sleeve rolled up and flexing a muscle under the caption "We Can Do It!"

The impressive improvement in wage earning was reflected in another aspect of economic life on the home front—income taxes. Prior to the war, the working people in my neighborhood, because their incomes were low, were not normally concerned with paying income taxes. However, early in the campaign, in part to finance the war and in part to curb potential high inflation, the government passed a withholding income tax law that was felt instantly as monies were deducted from every weekly salary. Most of us regarded it as an unwelcome but necessary wartime intrusion; indeed one of my teachers, in what turned out to be a totally erroneous projection, prognosticated that the tax was strictly a wartime measure that would disappear with the conclusion of the war. In my naiveté, as a young student who took seriously my teacher's clarification, I tried to explain the same to many skeptical older people whose attitude was that once the government became accustomed to taking tax monies, it would never reverse its course.

"GOING AWAY PARTIES"

Only thirteen years of age at the onset of the war, I was the youngest in my gang and too callow to enter the military service, I thus confined myself to partake vicariously of the experience via my imagination. It was more than daydreaming, however, as I witnessed the induction of so many around me into various military branches. The first to go were the older brothers of my friends and my older cousins. Then as the war lengthened the older members of my immediate group three to four years my senior began to be inducted. It struck me that I was becoming a fixture at so many "going away" parties that I could serve as a guide for the occurrences.

These affairs, which usually were hosted in the home of the future induct-ee, provided food, drink and a supportive atmosphere to accompany the good cheers. On several occasions, I accompanied fellows on my block to the induction center on Chambers St. in downtown Manhattan or to Penn Station where innumerable servicemen awaited trains to take them to vari-ous parts of the country. One could not fail to find signs of the war liberally sprinkled throughout the mammoth terminal in the form of posters urging Americans to "Save Scrap", and "Buy War Bonds".

SIGNS OF WARTIME CHANGE

Inevitably, the war wrought emphatic change in all manner of life on the home front. It was apparent within weeks in the January 1942 cer-emony that marked for me the termination of grade school and preparation for high school. A prominent part of the ritual consisted of martial music such as "Anchors Away" and "From the Halls of Montezuma"—ready reminders that we were in the midst of a war. The change was apparent in my vocational high school, Brooklyn High School of Automotive Trades where, in recognition that buying war bonds was beyond our financial abilities, we were encouraged to buy 25-cent war stamps. The war mental-ity immersion was further advanced when in 1943, the principal of my high school announced to seniors that they could graduate six months ear-ly—on condition of being drafted.[164] As a member of my high school glee club, I learned to sing, in addition to traditional American folk music like "Ol Man River," a great deal

Acclaimed the nation's greatest singer / entertainer in later years, for the Italian American community, Frank Sinatra was an important positive icon during the war. His award-winning rendition of "The House I Live In" served to promote tolerance and brotherhood in the late war years.

of military music such as "The Battle Hymn of the Republic," "Anchors Away," "Coming in On a Wing and a Prayer," This is the Army Mr. Jones," and "Over There". By the end of the war, our school chorus learned to sing an archetypal paean to the promotion of brotherhood: "The House I Live In," that captured the sense of striving for a higher objective. We heard the song on the radio, watched and were enthralled by a young Frank Sinatra who sang it in a movie short by the same name for which he received an award.

MUSIC

In the realm of popular music, there were of course loneliness love songs such as "Don't Get Around Much Any More," "You'll Never Know," "Saturday Night is the Loneliest Night of the Week," and "I'll Walk Alone," that evoked memories of those who went off to war. The war theme suffused much of the world of popular music that we young people heard constantly on the home radio, at the ice cream parlor jukebox, and at the dances we frequented. We were all acquainted with "I'll Never Smile Again," "I Had the Craziest Dream," and "I'll be Seeing You," "Don't Sit Under the Apple Tree," "My Buddy," and "Coming in on a Wing and a Prayer." The ballad "They're Either Too Young Or Too Old," that lamented the absence of young men on the home front was a song that effectively caught the mood of our neighborhood as did "P.S. I Love You," that reminded young sweethearts to write often to their loved one.

CONEY ISLAND

To go the beach at world famous resort Coney Island in the summertime was another diversion that I enjoyed in the midst of the war years. It required a one-hour subway ride on two separate lines to reach the famed beach as well as enduring the discomfort of returning home sunburnt and itchy from sand in the crouch of my bathing suit in hot, stagnant, non-air-conditioned subway cars at the end of a long day in the sun. But it was an inexpensive outlet that occupied practically every Saturday and Sunday from June to September. The 20-cent expenditure for the 5-cent subway ride and another nickel each for a Nathan's hotdog and soda to supplement homemade Italian sandwiches appeared an eminently good deal. On gloriously hot sunny summer days, it seemed new record crowds jammed every available space on the beach where on Bay 14, in addition to surfing, we could cavort in an unrestrained manner. Yet even here, there were reminders that a war was going on in the form of debris that floated ashore from the sea and occasional oil slicks that were attributed to vessels engaged in war off shore. Whether all the rubbish that floated onto Coney Island's beach was in fact due to military activity may indeed have been the work of fervid imagination. However, there was evidence of military action off the West Coast. Likewise the saving of oil-begrimed survivors struggling to reach the beaches in Florida, the rescuing of survivors from a torpedoed ship off Provincetown, Massachusetts, and the probable sinking of an enemy submarine off Montauk Point, Long Island rendered plausible our Coney Island sightings.[165] The occasional newspaper reports that described the rubbish we saw as the consequence of naval military action and the presence of people in military uniforms, including military police in and around Coney Island's amusement facilities, further reinforced our impressions about the proximity of the conflagration and the notion of a war atmosphere.

MOVIES

Going to the movies that became such a major feature of social life for young people of my generation, frequently meant to see films that revolved around the war. That Hollywood was tuned in to the immediacy of war was borne out by a study which indicated that thirty-eight out of eighty-six pictures in production between July and October 1942 were war pictures. The motion picture industry was exhorted to make "war content" films that focused on various themes: why we fight, the nature of the enemy, the camaraderie of our allies, the home front, and the fighting forces.[166] Although obviously propagandistic, we nevertheless willingly absorbed the centrality of the message that the United States and its Allies, especially Great Britain were the "good guys" while the Japanese and the Nazi Germans were the "bad guys." The biggest stars in the film industry frequently appeared in such movies. Among them was Humphrey Bogart who played the lead in the 1942 spy thriller "Across the Pacific," as well as in "Action in the Atlantic," a 1943 adventure film wherein he adroitly avoided menacing German U-boats. He likewise was the lead in the 1942 classic "Casablanca," wherein he fought against the Nazis in Algeria. In the 1945 film "Blood on the Sun" a tough and popular James Cagney was the hero newspaperman stationed in Tokyo who uncovered Japan's treacherous plot to bomb Pearl Harbor. In 1942, Cagney won an Academy Award for his portrayal of George M. Cohan in "Yankee Doodle Dandee," a film that harkened back to pre-World War II, yet was set against a backdrop of loyalty appropriate in the present conflict. It propelled a paroxysm of patriotism in me and my friends by promoting enthusiasm to the notion of patriotism. Cagney likewise played a resourceful government agent that exposed a devious German plot to infiltrate the American intelligence service in "13 Rue Madeleine" in 1946. In 1942, rugged John Wayne heroically led his troops against the vicious Japanese in "Back to Bataan." Undiscerning between the diverse Asiatic people, we were unaware that many of the actors who played treacherous Japanese were in fact Chinese—accounted for in part by the shortage of Japanese American performers in circulation.[167] Nor was it solely the major movies that focused on the war as many of the campy B-grade productions also concentrated on the conflict via melodramas film. Thus one could be amused by adventures of "Charlie Chan" hunting down spies and Sherlock Holmes, who amazingly was transported from Victorian to modern times turning his remarkable powers of deduction to defeat the Allies' enemies. Also in that genre were documentaries, short films, and movie tone news that were the frequent fare to which the moviegoing public was exposed. We especially admired the film stars who interrupted their professional careers and went into the active service such as Clark Gable and James Stewart, while also aware and unsure of what to make of conscious objectors such as the celebrated actor Lew Ayres.

The home front was also the central subject of several films. One was the award-winning film "Mrs. Miniver" that commemorated the pluck and spirit of a typical British family as it carried on in the midst of war. The 1944 Hollywood movie "Since You Went Away", starring Claudette Colbert, Joseph Cotton, and Jennifer Jones, celebrated an American family's resourcefulness and determination under wartime circumstances as typical. This movie was basically a saccharine story of a formerly pampered housewife, whose husband had gone off to war, now adjusting to the responsibility of running a household that included two teenage daughters. Viewers were asked to empathize with the archetypal American home front heroine's spirit of sacrifice as she forfeited her genteel circumstances by taking in a boarder to supplement the family income and obtaining a job as a welder, but implausibly still retained her domestic help who cooked and cleaned the house. Although a well-acted tearjerker, it was not overly convincing to Himrod St. inhabitants who never in their wildest dreams had paid domestic help. The film reference to Joseph Cotton's fighting in Italy elicited the inevitable stereotype as he remarked, "There was a dame in the middle of Salerno in Italy with a big plate of spaghetti." Although restrained by comparison to depictions of Germans and Japanese, it nevertheless reflected an attitude of triviality regarding Italians.

PASTIMES

My friends and I learned the rudimentary techniques of sports on the stoops, the sidewalks, and the street. The major participatory block sport was stickball, a game that was comprised of bases as in baseball, shaped however, not in the form of a diamond but in a rectangular configuration that could be accommodated on the street. That is, home base was a sewer plate in the center of the street, second base was another sewer away (perhaps 100 feet), with first and third bases mid-way between the sewers and chalked along curbs. Whenever space on the block was available, which was frequent during the Depression years since most block residents did not own cars, or when drivers were away or would acquiesce not to park where it might interfere with the game, and whenever there were enough players, we had exciting games. The batter would attempt to hit a rubber ball with a stick (a discarded broom handle) and run the bases as in baseball. Handball was game that we played that utilized four or two players along clear expanses of wall usually at an end of the block or in the nearby schoolyard. A single stoop of two or three steps in front of house was all that was necessary to play stoop ball. In this game, a player hurled a rubber ball against the steps hoping the ball would fly out 15 or 20 feet or more beyond the player on defense. Some of the older fellows played baseball in local parks on more formal teams that played in organized leagues. Much of this activity, however, was on an ad hoc basis rather than in organized teams or leagues. On occasion, players from one block would challenge those from another. There were some capable athletes, nonetheless, who did engage in formal, organized teams that played baseball in larger ball fields in the area and competed with teams from other city neighborhoods. Although there were talented players in the neighborhood, I do not recall any that attained major league status.

We also followed professional sports, particularly baseball, although we did not frequently attend such games. I was about fourteen-years-old when I went to my first major league baseball game at Ebbets field to see the Brooklyn Dodgers play gratis via the Brooklyn Dodger Knothole Club, an opportunity provided by the Dodger organization to allow a number of youth to enter the ballpark free. For some (perverse) reason I chose to be a New York Giant instead of Brooklyn Dodger fan, a decision that found me enduring my share of derision from Brooklyn fans over the course of the years.

Roller-skating was another sports activity that I enjoyed in various skating rinks that were located a short train ride away. Ballroom dancing was a popular pastime during the war. Undoubtedly, due to increased familiarity with music as result of radio popularity, ballroom dancing became even more acceptable in the middle of war across country. Although my first venture to attend a dance in a facility in the nearby neighborhood occurred when I was 14, it was not auspicious—deeming it an activity for which I was too young, my mother came to the dancehall to bring me home causing me embarrassment and resulting in a quick and premature exit from the hall. By the time I became 16, I was able to attend dancehalls more frequently, including the famous Manhattan dance meccas, the Roseland, and the Arcadia, along with less well-known but convenient neighborhood dance facilities located in high school gyms, church halls, and social clubs.

In that period, local social clubs were organizations that were housed in rented vacant stores that dotted the neighborhood. While these clubs sometimes sponsored athletic activities, they also became the hangouts for local gangs, that is, groups of young men who enjoyed a close relationship and went out together or sponsored dances. Too young to join such a club then, (although I did as an older teenager), I witnessed the inner workings of a typical "clubbu" as the Sicilians called them, as a shoe shine boy on those Saturday afternoons in one of the social clubs that usually held dances, especially on Saturday nights.[168] My friends and I looked up to the older young men who were either late teenagers or in their early twenties and prided themselves on appearing well-groomed by sporting the latest fashion in young men's suits for these dances, on providing the latest music in the club record collection holdings, and in bringing pretty girls to the affairs. In time all my friends developed considerable expertise with the lindy hop, the rumba, and most of all, the foxtrot, which was the most popular dance at the time.[169] Not only were servicemen frequently present on these occasions, but also dance functions were held especially in their honor.

ALIEN REGISTRATION—
MY MOTHER WAS ONE OF THEM

Clearly one of the most onerous actions to impact my neighborhood, and particularly my family, was that which required non-citizen aliens of nations at war with United States to register as enemy aliens. Because of a variety of circumstances, 600,000 Italian Americans who had lived in this country peaceably for years formed the largest group of enemy aliens in the country and accordingly in the suspect category—one that subjected them to an assortment of humiliating and exasperating restrictions including requirements that they register and be fingerprinted. In addition, they could not own cameras or short wave radio receivers, not travel beyond a 50-mile radius, and were ineligible to be hired for war work.

This rankled then and decades later because my mother was one of them—an enemy alien. She had arrived from Sicily with my father in 1927, and like many of her co-nationals, had not obtained citizenship because of preoccupation with raising a young family and dealing with the ravages of the Depression and unemployment. In addition, she experienced the adversity and privation of being a single parent following my father's death after a lengthy illness in 1938.[170]. The topic of Italian American alien status has begun to receive more attention of late. In

2004, popular mystery writer Lisa Scottoline published *Killer Smile* that reverts to that policy as the backdrop for her mystery. She acknowledged that she received the idea for the plot from the real life ex-

Italian immigrant Maria LaGumina, author's mother, was required to register as "enemy alien" and subjected to various restrictions that were extended to American born children as well. She attended evening classes and received citizenship during the war.

perience of her paternal grandparents in Philadelphia who were required to register as enemy aliens. [171]

In our home, we did in fact have a short-wave radio that brought in overseas stations such as those emanating from Italy that I marveled at. What a wonderful instrument was the radio; that through it, sitting in one's own living room, one could hear live broadcasts from different countries in foreign languages, such as those I listened to occasionally. Learning of the restrictions placed on foreigners from enemy nations, we became concerned because my mother was technically an enemy alien and to avoid any problem with the law, I personally carried the receiver to a radio repair shop a couple of blocks away to have the short-wave reception band disconnected. Two months after Pearl Harbor, on February 22, 1942, my mother registered, and from then on, carried her alien registration book that showed the print of her right index finger, a black and white photograph, and other pertinent data that presumably was to be presented, if asked by government authorities. Although I do not ever recall such an instance, it was, nevertheless, such a source of embarrassment and diminishment for her to be regarded an enemy alien, that she endeavored to correct the matter by attending night classes in English which she completed successfully at Bushwick High School. We children thought it amusing that our mother attended basic elementary classes; however, the instruction finally allowed her to become a naturalized citizen on January 24, 1944.

Statistics confirmed that naturalization was a vital subject on the home front at the time nationally and locally. Whereas an average of 148,291 aliens were naturalized in the 1934–1939 period, the figures for 1940–1945 show an average of 295,872 aliens became citizens—442,000 in the peak year of 1944, the year in which my mother received her papers.[172]

WEST COAST

The situation for Italian Americans on the West Coast was even more drastic after military authorities deemed their presence near the coast a danger to national security. Although not a subject that received much attention at the time, and even little known decades later, wartime policies severely impinged on California Americans of Italian descent. Recent scholarly research by Lawrence DiStasi, Rose Scherini, and Stephen Fox shows that in the period that following Pearl Harbor, 10,000 Italians were forcibly relocated from their homes, sometimes just a few blocks away and in other instances miles inland from a "prohibited zone." They were also required to carry photo identifications at all times or risk immediate internment. In a few cases, Italians were excluded from California for the war's duration.[173] Not satisfied with the degree and extent of such restrictions, some American leaders would have enacted even more drastic steps. Congressman Clarence Lea of California, for example, called for exclusion of all aliens from California, Oregon, and Washington. Within a short time, 1,500 Italian aliens were arrested for violating curfew laws. What in retrospect seems incredibly unbelievable and contrary to all evidence, authorities believed that the Italian Americans were part of a huge Fifth Column movement and ordered Federal Bureau of Investigation (FBI) agents to confiscate short wave radios, guns, flashlights, and binoculars, in the belief that this would frustrate sabotage. To say that this completely disrupted the work and home life of Italian neighborhoods is an understatement—their lives would never be the same. In addition, commencing the night of December 7, 1941, government agents rounded up 231 "dangerous" Italian aliens and interned them in detention camps. The FBI apparently deemed dangerous any individuals who were members of the Italian War Veterans, editors and writers for Italian-language newspapers, and announcers on Italian-language radio, and instructors in Italian-language schools sponsored by the Italian consulate.[174] The severity of the arrest order may be gleaned from a letter of Filippo Molinari,

> I was the first one arrested in San Jose the night of the attack on Pearl Harbor. At 11:00 p.m., three policemen came to the front door and two at the back. They told me that by the order of President Roosevelt, I must go with them.

They did not even give me time to go to my room and put on my shoes. I was wearing slippers. They took me to prison ... and finally to Missoula, Montana, on the train, over the snow, still with the slippers on my feet, the temperature at seventeen below and no coat or heavy clothes!"[175]

TRAUMA AND TRAGEDY

For some the "enemy alien" designation constituted such a severe penalty and a hardship, especially for a few labeled "dangerous", that they committed suicide. On a cold February night in 1942,

> Martini Battistessa, aged 65, unable to complete his naturalization before his adopted country classified him an enemy alien and expelled him from his home of twenty years, went to a bar and offered a friend $50 to shoot him in the head.
>
> The friend laughed and Battistessa left. A short later he threw himself in front of the southbound passenger train as it passed through Richmond, California ...
>
> When authorities told Giovanni Mecheli that he could not live in his Vallejo home after February 24, the 57-year-old fisherman cut his throat with a butcher knife.
>
> Before 65-year-old Stefano Terranova leaped to his death from a building, having refused to leave his home as ordered by the Justice Department, he left a note that read in part "I believe myself to be good, but find myself deceived, I don't know why ... [176]

There is additional irony in that from some of the "enemy aliens" homes came forth servicemen who performed patriotically in various branches of American military units.

In some of the most egregious instances, "enemy aliens" could no longer earn a living in their accustomed trade. For enemy alien John Bronzini of Oakland, California, the label meant he could no longer operate his small fruit and vegetable shop that was in the prohibited zone, while his wife, also enemy alien, suffered a mental breakdown at the interruption to their way of life.[177] For the thousands of Italian Americans engaged in California's fishing trade, the war constituted a huge interruption—witness the plight of Joe DiMaggio's father, Giuseppe, who was forbidden to carry on his life-long fisherman trade. Nor could the father even visit his son's restaurant on Fisherman's Wharf, now in a prohibited zone. Italians were subject to a curfew from 8 p.m. to 6 a.m., and not allowed to travel further than five miles from home. The nature of the fishing industry meant so much for those engaged in it since it functioned as a family enterprise—older sons frequently followed their fathers to the sea, and wives were occupied with making intricate nets and processing the fish that were caught. Italian immigrants brought over their knowledge of the industry that was characteristic of Mediterranean fishing, including lateen rigged schooners with long hulls that were narrow and deep. They developed complex sets of nets that ranged from large meshes to smaller one for different types of fishing.[178] Since most of California's coastal fishermen were Italian, the government order had the virtual effect of shutting down the entire fishing industry, at a time when fish was in critically short supply. There was indeed something incongruous in this dilemma as illustrated

 by a singular demonstration of support in behalf of American military needs following the Pearl Harbor attack—that of the Monterey, California Italian American fishermen who voluntarily and without compensation, gave up intricate fishing nets to Army.

Baseball great Joe DiMaggio was the undisputed source of pride among Italian Americans. Ironically, because his parents did not have citizenship, they were listed as "enemy aliens".

Previously, up to 600,000 square feet of net—enough to
equip thousands of soldiers with head and body camouflage—to the Army by the same fishermen, many of them
Italian aliens and naturalized Italian-Americans ... The
nets, while worn out according to fishing standards, are
of a much finer weave than those issued by the Army and
represent a huge saving to the government ... [179]

PINZA

The roundup of enemy aliens did not spare even the most heralded Italian Americans, including the most famous basso of Metropolitan Opera
House Ezio Pinza. Born in Rome, Italy, in 1892, and blessed with a beautiful natural voice, he began to sing for the Met in 1926 where he achieved
conspicuous success. Pinza married an American woman and was on the
verge of becoming an American citizen when the United States entered the
war. Unfortunately for him, the naturalization process was not completed,
thus causing him to be officially designated an "enemy alien," a classification that subjected him to a repugnant experience. Subsequently, his wife
Doris described his shocking arrest on March 2, 1942.

Ezio was alone in an upstairs room of our home in Mama-
roneck, NY doing paperwork at a table when he suddenly
became aware that two strange men were approaching him.
They had entered through the unlocked back door without
either knocking or ringing the doorbell. They then walked
through the lower floor and up the stairway. One of them
said, "Are you Ezio Pinza?" Ezio replied, "Yes, what can
I do for you?" The men showed their FBI identifications,
and one said, "In the name of the President of the United
States we place you under arrest!"

Ezio immediately stood up. He was shocked and puzzled.
He asked if they would mind waiting until his wife came
back from the village. They handed Ezio a warrant and
said, "There's plenty of time. We intend to search your

house anyway. "When I returned to find the strange car—
and men—I was shocked to hear Ezio say to me, "They
have come to arrest me." ... We never suspected this could
happen in the United States.

Ezio told the judges why he had decided to become an
American citizen and how he had attempted to help the
American war effort by performing, without remuneration,
for the U.S. Treasury Department at rallies to sell Defense
Bonds and for the American Red Cross in their drives to
collect funds and blood. He tried to help them understand
that he cared only about his family and his musical career.
He later told me that he was so nervous and confused by
the ordeal that he had put on the worst show of his life.[180]

For a time, it seemed that the subversive charges would have sent him
to a detention camp, except for the energetic intervention of prominent
supporters including New York City Mayor LaGuardia. Stripped of tie,
belt, and shoelaces, he was held in detention for several weeks. The incident left him seriously depressed for a time, however, he gradually not
only resumed his operatic career, but in addition, became a matinee idol
for his 1949 role in the musical "South Pacific."

RATIONING

With America's entry into war rationing became an intrusive but inevitable aspect of civilian life on the home front. Under the leadership
of Leon Henderson, head of the Office of Price Administration, in early
March 1942, the government printed 190,000,000 ration books that became the constant accompaniment for Americans when purchasing a
plethora of articles. It was ironic for people who had to do with little for
so many years because of the Depression to now experience deprivation
of selected items in spite of improved economic circumstances. This paradox, as one historian expressed it, "was especially irritating and frustrating
in that some of the rationed goods were at the heart of the good life as

most Americans defined it."[181] It became easy to criticize the government for supposed "foul-ups", and indeed more than a few Americans did not comply, resorting instead to partake in a black market economy; however, rationing was a fact of life on the home front in my neighborhood.

Owing to limited inventory of rubber and because the regular sources of rubber resources in Asia were no longer available due to the war, rubber was one of first items to be rationed. Faced with a freeze on new tire sales, car drivers resorted to recapping old tires or simply severely limiting driving habits. The challenge to car drivers intensified when by the spring of 1942 gas was added to the list of rationed items. A sticker and coupon system four categories: "A" for pleasure driving vehicles, "B" for vehicles to drive to work, "C" for those driven at work, "E" for emergency vehicles. Unless motorists possessed car stickers entitling them to additional gas because they were essential to the war effort as, for instance, those who worked in war production plants, drivers were allowed three gallons a week for pleasure driving. Some in my neighborhood resorted to the use of naphtha, a flammable, oily liquid product made by distilling petroleum as a gas substitute. This chemical was available at a few gas stations in the area and was not rationed; however, it could cause engine damage. While rationing of these items seriously impinged upon car drivers, it did not seriously impact many of us who lived in the city since we were accustomed to taking public transportation via subway, elevated trains and electric trolley cars. Food rationing, on the other hand, affected all of us much more deeply as we became accustomed to figuring out whether our government-issued War Ration Books contained the requisite stamps to purchase an assortment of foods such as meat, sugar, coffee, and canned meats, and fish, among other items. The ration books contained points to purchase scarce articles on a monthly basis. When a family ran out of points, it could not purchase such items for the remainder of the month. Under these circumstances it became prudent to cultivate the good will of local butcher who exercised informal discretion over the sale of his limited meat supply. The conversion of our heat-furnishing stove from wood and coal to kerosene found us negotiating the proper amount of ration stamps needed to purchase the fuel with Mr. Frank, the iceman who now supplied kerosene. We needed stamps to purchase no more than two pairs of shoes annually—not really hardship for me since I did not buy shoes that frequently. My sister and especially my brother who went through a few pairs of shoes annually, however, were grateful when they could use my unused ration stamps for that purpose.

SHORTAGES

Americans became accustomed to living with a variety of shortages, that were apparent in the neighborhood even while they were not officially rationed. Thus with a Pontiac rolling off the assembly line in early February as the last car manufactured for private use, one saw no new cars on the road. Car owners on Himrod St. learned to carefully conserve their vehicles and make do with rebuilt parts for repairs. Severe shortages in raw material altered certain practices that endured in the postwar period. Tailors dealt with the wool shortage, for example, by eliminating vests from men's suits, narrowing lapels and promoting "victory pants" without cuffs, while women lost the option for pleated skirts and had to settle for two piece bathing suits.[182] Although not officially rationed, certain items like cigarettes were always in limited supply as was milk leading my family to experiment with canned milk, a trial that was short-lived owing to our dislike of the bland product.

COLLECTING SCRAP AND VICTORY GARDENS

Along with other young people, I joined in aiding the war effort by collecting scarce items: lard that was turned into the local butcher shops, and silver that was obtained from discarded cigarette wrappers that tested our ability to roll them into spheres as large as baseballs. Americans were exhorted to develop victory gardens as a means of producing vegetables that were becoming scarce in the markets. Because the back yards on Himrod St. were small, since they had to accommodate six families, in some instances neighbors combined their gardening efforts. However, it seemed that where there were resident landlords, it was they who were most likely to plant the victory plots. Given a heritage of successful intensive farming traditions, it was not surprising that Italian Americans achieved remarkable success in transforming small 8 x 10 plots in Brooklyn to produce an assortment of vegetables. Indeed, it was observed that Italian Americans had a head start in this endeavor since for years they had cultivated seemingly insignificant small sections of soil for the purpose of growing flowers and fresh vegetables for their tables. Exhorted to produce these scarce foods because the military had priority on normal farm vegetable production, Italian American victory gardeners responded enthusiastically not only to help the national effort, but also because of their desire to enjoy fresh vegetables. [183]

CHAPTER IV
DEMONSTRATING LOYALTY AMIDST AN ATMOSPHERE OF SUSPICION

SUSPICION

A vexing consequence of Italy's declaration of war against the United States after Pearl Harbor was that it ushered in a more severe testing time and increased suspicion regarding Italian American loyalty. For many Americans already inclined to look askance at those of Italian descent even before Pearl Harbor, the outbreak of war on December 7, 1941 intensified uneasiness as a veritable loyalty scare gripped the nation. "Stigmatized by other Americans as fifth-columnists and potential traitors, Italian Americans were frankly divided as to how they should respond to the prospect of war between their ancestral land and the land they had adopted."[184] Among historians, there exists difference of opinion as to how damaging the anti-Italian experience was, although they are virtually unanimous in concluding that in comparison with Japanese Americans, it was relatively mild. The start of war fundamentally upset the pre-war pattern of Italian

American life—one that had not been easy at best. "Not yet fully accepted by American society ... Like other recent immigrant groups, the Italian-Americans, largely unskilled and unlettered, ordinarily commanded only the worst kinds of jobs, and even those had been hard to find during the Depression."[185] The institutions that they previously created to promote self-esteem, church, fraternal societies, social and political clubs, would now have to make considerable adjustment.

The prevalence of ethnic intolerance, especially against people associated with America's enemies, was a customary phenomenon on the home front in virtually all of the nation's Little Italies. The woeful atmosphere is confirmed in a recent study of the Philadelphia Italian American experience where "ethnic intolerance became again a major concern for Italian Americans." Fueled by nationally influential journals like *Fortune* that fulminated against possible subversive activities perpetrated by fascist "fifth column" operatives—largely poor immigrants conditioned to believe that democracy was becoming decadent—it negatively impacted Italian Americans employment opportunities, not only in defense work, but in non-defense employment as well.[186] An atmosphere suffused with distrust, and restrictions encouraged "a smoldering suspicion on the part of American-born citizens against all citizens with foreign-born names, particularly those of German, Italian, or Slavic origin."[187] Simply put, many Americans felt they had good reason to suspect Italian Americans of subversive intent."[188] Although the focus of attention on the West Coast was on the removal of Japanese Americans, inflexible American officials like General John DeWitt, in charge of the Western Military Defense Command, had authorization to evacuate all enemy aliens from designated regions by blanket inclusion of Italians and Germans. Granted that there was some amelioration of the policy in June 1942, many onerous restrictions remained.[189] Even aside from extreme solutions, Italian Americans, along with other groups were confronted with the virulence of ongoing prejudice—a phenomena that has exposed a central contradiction—that is, in spite of enthusiasm for the war, "there existed deep, racial, ethnic, and cultural animosities that occasionally exploded into violence." Among the buried vignettes of life that revealed the fractures that rend the home front, William Tuttle cites the experience of Italian American Rick Cesare, who recalled with distaste what his second-generation mother experienced when called before a federal official to attest to her loyalty. "I remember feeling like they thought we were on the side of the Italians, and it scared me." Rick described growing up in a Jewish neighborhood and his feeling of relief to be taken for a Jew while in school. On one occasion, he acknowledged that he was Italian, rather than Jewish, "and all the kids booed! This was in 1944, I was seven ... They called me Mussolini and chased me home." As unpleasant as these experiences were, Tuttle nevertheless maintained that on balance Italian Americans endured less suspicion than German Americans and certainly far less than Japanese Americans.[190]

That hostility toward things Italian could have a profound damaging effect is borne out by the autobiographical account of writer Helen Barolini. Subsequently destined to become a distinguished author, whose works are steeped in Italian language and culture clearly demonstrate a fondness for her Italian roots, her childhood evinced little to indicate such a path. Her upbringing was deliberately devoid of familiarity with the Italian language—a result of her father's deep repulsion of his Italian heritage during the pressure-laden days of the Second World War. "I knew nothing of Italian. It was not a popular subject at home. We had just come out of World War II in which Italy had been our enemy, and my father was at once scornful and touchy about Italy's role in the conflict. It never occurred to him to speak his father's language to my brothers or to me, so we grew up never speaking to our only two living grandparents."[191]

Like my neighborhood contemporaries, I was convinced that anxiety about Italian Americans was totally unwarranted, and in retrospect, one wonders how such a prevailing excessive atmosphere of alarm could so grasp the mindset of American society. It was nonetheless an unpleasant reality. The loyalty of even so respected an Italian American leader like Mayor LaGuardia was called into question as he was asked why he did not return the medals Italy had bestowed on him for his combat duty in that country during the Great War.[192] Under the pressure and stress thus engendered, the ethnic group discovered the existence of considerable hostility and wariness that bearers of Italian names were forced to endure during this distrustful period. It was, in short, a time of unbidden and distressing tribulation. Generally overlooked by a public understandably preoccupied with conducting a grueling war, those Italian Americans who were characterized as recent newcomers by the broken English they spoke or by other transparent ethnic patterns, were frequently regarded with mistrust, if not as outright threats to American life. The circumspection about Americans of Italian descent often extended to American born as well. In his fittingly titled book, *What's Your Name?* Louis Adamic, the discerning Yugoslav American writer, captures the menacing atmosphere as he recounts the blatant pressure applied to a young Italian American to change his name if he wished to obtain a position as a teacher. A twenty-year-old graduate of a college in Pennsylvania where he studied pedagogy, John Pedrotti described the generally positive reaction from a prep school headmaster to his application for a teaching position.

> With helpful recommendation from the college I managed to secure an interview with the headmaster who was very nice and seemed pleased with my qualifications. From his talk I gathered the job was mine; we discussed salary, what was expected of me, etc. Next week he would write me a letter confirming the substance of our conversation, and then he would expect to see me next September. I waited for his letter, but none came for ten days, three weeks, almost a month. Finally I wrote to him. No reply. Then I heard from the College Alumni secretary who said he had a long conversation with the headmaster concerning me. (The headmaster is an alumnus too). It seems there was the "little problem" of my last name. Could I change Pedrotti to Peters, or something similar? If I did that, the appointment was mine. "I am sure you will agree," read the letter, "that although they have distinguished them-

selves in many other fields, the Italians have not done so
well in education ... Mr. H—(the headmaster), feels the
parents of the boys in his school would take exception to
an Italian name on the faculty ... Your qualifications far
outrank those of the other applicants, and Mr. H—hopes
you will make the necessary change (a simple legal matter) and accept the position."

I was hurt. So were my father and my mother and my
two sisters, both schoolteachers, and good ones. I wrote
the headmaster, ... and explained that I did not want the
job under that condition. I pointed out that Angelo Patri,
Leonard Covello and Pestalozzi were people with Italian
names distinguished in the field of education in this country. If his school objected to my Italian name because of
the war and Italy's position in it, I wished him to know
my sympathies were completely with England and Russia
and the occupied countries.[193]

Pedrotti was aware that Italian immigrants and their children frequently
were required to Anglicize their names to gain positions. Although he was
definitely upset about not getting the appointment, he nevertheless confessed, "I would have been very miserable if I had discarded Pedrotti."
The letter-writer then went on to say that he was working in a coal-mine
along with his father while also speculating about a career in the Army
with an Italian name. Adamic's analysis of American society in June 1942
gave some reason to pause. Although the Army maintained no official policy concerning "foreign names", he suggested there could be a problem.
"Thousands of top sergeants find the daily roll call one of their toughest
jobs, for in some outfits half the personnel have names are difficult to
pronounce. Their owners are kidded and tossed undignified nicknames. Of
course, they take it with a grin, but it affects them ... Our names are more
important than ever before."[194]

While to later generations it may seem an exaggeration to maintain that
names could be the bases for discriminatory practices, it was indeed the

case in the wartime environment. Reflecting on those times, writer Sandra M. Gilbert, who grew up in New York City, recounts as "most disturbing" her childhood years that coincided with America's entry into war and the consequent identification of Italian names with Mussolini.

> Noticing the Italianness of my name, with its vulnerably open vowel ending (so different from the clipped decency of an Anglo-Saxon consonant), other kids did kid me, implying that Mussolini had something to do with me. And it didn't help that everything about the culture in which I was growing up made me want to be a "real" American—what we'd now call a WASP—instead of a weirdly "foreign" outsider.[195].

Those of us with Italian names realized that with few exceptions, these nomenclatures could serve as concrete impediments especially in obtaining choice jobs. Notwithstanding the wartime need for workers to efficiently utilize manpower resources, there were still too many instances in which an Italian surname was a barrier to employment in defense or in war-related employment. A competent study of discrimination in the defense industry in the early 1940s states "Discrimination against ethnics focused on the aliens, but radiated out to individuals who, while they might be citizens, were identified as belonging to 'undesirable' ethnic groups.[196]

DISCRIMINATION

While it would be a gross hyperbole to assert that all Italian Americans suffered from discrimination at the time, there were, nevertheless, numerous instances that caused deep concern within the ethnic community. One example was that of Italian American John Occhino, who in response to a 1941 employment agency newspaper, applied for a position as a guard only to be refused because "the employer specified placement of a person of Anglo Saxon, Scotch, Irish, or English ancestry."[197] Even more revealing was the court decision that Occhino did not have a case, maintaining the employer's right to hire whomever he pleased. In another instance, a fifteen-year-old boy wrote to Mrs. Roosevelt that his father, a World War I American Army veteran, who had been wounded and decorated, had been denied employment repeatedly for failure to produce a birth certificate. "Prospective employers, he noted, were unmoved by his discharge papers or by a presidential citation he had earned." That anti-Italian intolerance pervaded ethnic enclaves is discernible in the testimonies of residents of Providence, Rhode Island. One of them complained about rejection of job applicants because of their Italian ancestry. "Last week I applied for work at Brown & Sharpe and saw men being interviewed. They were Americans, too, but I noticed that the moment a man appeared to be an Italo-American, he was told there was no work."[198]   A mid-1941 survey in Boston's North End found that Italian Americans overwhelmingly felt that they faced greater difficulty obtaining employment than those of other backgrounds—a perception substantiated by a federal official called in to look into the issue. In 1941, anti-Italian discrimination in employment may have been even more egregious in the West where major defense contractors customarily rejected workers of Italian, German, and Russian background.[199]

To deal with the problem of anti-Italian discrimination, the Italian-language newspaper *Il Progresso Italo-Americano* established a division to elicit examples of prejudice and enlisted the cooperation of professional social workers. Among samples of bias uncovered by this effort were instances in which contractors denied employment to experienced Italian-born bricklayers on the grounds that such well-paying jobs were only for native born Americans.[200] The issue of discrimination in employment was a major one at the outset of the war, one which encompassed far more Americans than those of Italian ancestry—indeed, African Americans were the largest group to suffer from such practices. Although Congress was not prepared to do much about the situation, a presidential executive order established a Committee for Fair Employment Practices (FEPC) as an agency of the War Labor Board to counter discrimination on racial as well as national origin grounds in war work. Notwithstanding the order, aliens and naturalized citizens of Italian heritage often were denied jobs due to employer unwillingness to comply or to avoid the encumbrance involved in obtaining government approval. Italian American New York Congressman Vito Marcantonio was one of the strongest and most consistent voices advocating not only adhering to FEPC policies, but also strengthening it.[201]

Italian language radio under siege Foreign language broadcasting went into sharp decline during the war years dropping from 205 programs in 1942 to 126 in 1948.[202] These were clearly unpropitious times for Italian language radio broadcasts in the New York Metropolitan area and beyond as pressure mounted to terminate them. A case in point was "The Voice of Local 89" sponsored by the Dressmakers Local 89 of the International Ladies Garment Worker's Union whose 40,000 members composed entirely of Italian Americans. Competently led by Luigi Antonini, it was the largest local union in the United States. Beginning in 1934, the labor-oriented program evinced a firmly anti-Fascist stance, including condemnation of Mussolini's invasion of Ethiopia. Its emphasis on the virtues of democracy and Americanization while urging naturalization, found the number of its listeners grow from WEVD, its original station and base in New York, to a point where it was heard in local stations in New England, New Jersey, Delaware and eastern Pennsylvania. Speakers from mainstream political parties, prominent local politicians, and leaders from the ethnic community frequently could be heard on the broadcasts. The outbreak of World War II virtually placed this program, along with other foreign language radio programs, outside of the pale of acceptability with the ominous decision by a number of local stations to eliminate the Italian language format, notwithstanding an apparent substantial following.

In response, leaders within the ethnic community marshaled their forces in an attempt to counter this unfortunate development. In December 1943, Antonini testified before the United States Senate Interstate Commerce Committee, informing the committee that stations that had been broadcasting the program for many years were, without warning, summarily terminating it. "But at this very moment, when our work became more indispensable than ever, we were hit by a blow in thunderbolt fashion as if out of a clear sky." He informed the committee that efforts to have the management of WELI in New Haven, Connecticut, and WPEN in Philadelphia suspend its termination order had failed.

> Now we appeal to you to draft such legislation as will prevent the undoing of years of non-commercial education work to be discarded for out and out commercial projects ... To suppress Italian language programs, regardless of the valuable character and property of their contents, would mean depriving Americanism of a powerful weapon, would mean denying us a most effective instrument for bringing this message to a vital section of our population. I feel that such a denial will give this population of Italian origin in our country, a sense of frustration. They will feel a keen disappointment at being deprived of this means of their becoming more rapidly an integral part of the life of our country. [203]

Proponents of Italian language radio were heartened by the studies of Irvin L. Child, whose research, under the auspices of the Institute of Human Relations of Yale University, was originally published in August 1942, under the title *Italian or American? The Second Generation in Conflict.* Child's scrutiny demonstrated that among New Haven's population of 160,000, some 42,000 were first and second generation Italian Americans for whom the Italian-language radio medium constituted a major source of information, entertainment, and socialization.

> Additional forces making for change in group affiliation lie in the institutionalized media of mass communication and of entertainment. The most varied and most accessible sources of information ... in the community are the American newspapers, magazines, radio programs, and moving pictures. They undoubtedly exert a profound influence on the second generation, and in at least two fairly distinct ways. In the first place, there may be effects that are relatively independent of the goals of the individual.

He is acquainted with facts about American people and American ways that he might not learn in his experience with his own friends and acquaintances. To the extent that he feels himself into the events and the characters that he reads about, sees on the screen, or hears over the radio, he is likely to pick up attitudes and modes of action in a rather automatic manner. But among the facts that the second-generation Italian becomes cognizant of through these media are the variety of rewards to be obtained in American life, and it is by this route that he is perhaps most significantly influenced.

... They provide him a picture of the humblest American as living a respectable, secure, and enjoyable family life in which the mention of spaghetti, bocce, or a mother country would be more that a little incongruous. The total effect is a continuous, subtle suggestion that just to be a plain American would bring such ample gratification that it is a goal eminently worth striving for.[204]

In other words, Child' study adumbrated that the radio, along with other media, constituted an indispensable medium that served to familiarize Italian-speaking residents with acceptable and congruous American customs that effectively articulated and promoted Americanism. Child's observations about the role of Italian language radio found affirmation in my neighborhood where so many first and second generation people obtained a considerable portion of their understanding of contemporary issues via listening to Italian language programs.

WORLD WAR I VETERANS

World War I veterans Italian Americans dealt with the issue of loyalty head on, demonstrating their irrefutable devotion to America dating long before the outset of the war. Articles in the Italian language press praised the role of Italian American soldiers "as among the finest of the Great Army which is now being formed for a more secure defense of the vital interests of the nation."[205] After the attack on Pearl Harbor, Italian American veterans groups whose wartime service in behalf of the Allies during the First World War should have warranted favorable consideration, were among the first to proclaim their fealty. In one example, the Florio Post of the Italian American War Veterans of Waterbury, Connecticut, reminded Americans that just as in the Great War, they were once again ready to support the nation's cause against its enemies by working assiduously in behalf of Civil Defense and the Red Cross. Assembled at a dinner / dance, these same veterans recalled the heroism of Americans in the Bataan death march by shouting "Viva l'America. Viva MacArthur!" In another expression of loyalty, veterans at the Colonel Francis Vigo Post held a position of honor at the head of the American Legion march in New York City on "I Am An American Day," and proudly proclaimed their fidelity to the United States. A figure virtually impossible to corroborate, it was estimated that 300,000 Americans of Italian descent served in the American armed forces during the First World War. It was further claimed that 50,000 of them were members of the Italian American World War Veterans organization, which used its next annual meeting following Pearl Harbor to reiterate robustly its devotion to the United States against enemy forces. The organization recalled that although during the earlier war, Italy was an allied nation, it was now the destiny of thousands of Italian American soldiers to defeat the enemy regime and bring to Italy a better peace.[206]

ITALIAN AMERICAN ORGANIZATIONS

Within twenty-four hours of the Japanese attack, Italian American organizations responded positively. The United Italian American League, a metropolitan New York confederation of ethnic organizations that claimed to speak for 50,000, sent President Roosevelt a telegram informing him of their support in the effort to defeat Japan. Likewise the strongly anti-Fascist Mazzini Society, that as previously observed was made up of approximately 1,000 prominenti (prominent) in over forty branches, also pledged loyalty to the president. Despite the society's commitment to combat Fascist propaganda in the United States and promote cultural and educational activities to unmask Fascism, and notwithstanding the prominence of individual leaders in these organizations, it is doubtful that it registered deep impact on rank and file Italian Americans, whose opinions were more likely to be shaped by associations such as labor unions.[207]

New York Italian American unionists and their socialist allies were in the forefront of efforts to rally fellow ethnics unstintingly in favor of the American cause. One of these was Sicilian-born Vanni B. Montana, who in the course of his life had been a Communist, an informer about Italian Communist activities, a Socialist and union newspaper editor for various left-wing and union newspapers.[208] In his autobiography, Montana described the swift action of union leaders who met on December 8 at the Manhattan offices of Local 89 to deliberate on the cascading calamitous events following the attack on Pearl Harbor.[209] Especially infuriated over Italy's declaration of war against the United States, they realized that labor union leadership rather than the Mazzini Society would be more effective in rallying Italian Americans. Accordingly, they organized the Italian American Labor Council, swallowed their pride while eschewing their opinion of Antonini as imperious, and chose him as its president. In deferring to the influential Antonini of Local 89, the Italian-speaking unit and one of the largest locals within the ILGWU, in which he also served as first vice president, the other leaders clearly acquiesced to pragmatism. The council then convened a massive rally of its members on December 20 on behalf of an Allied victory. Antonini, who also was a founder of the American Labor Party (ALP), and later helped found New York's Liberal Party that was resolutely anti-Communist, utilized his stentorian oratory both at large mass meetings and on the radio to animate Italian Americans. He was one of the first spokesmen from organized labor to use this medium to spread the union's message, and soon became the most listened to figure among Italian Americans on the East Coast.[210] Although only a young teenager, I recall my mother listening to Antonini's radio broadcasts in which he vociferously thundered condemnation of Fascism and rallied Italian Americans to support the government in that period of great crisis. Even though I only partially understood what he was saying, my impression was that he was an extraordinary leader who used oratorical flourishes one heard only from accomplished speakers of the old esteemed Italian school. Antonini was, of course, not the only Italian American unionist to fulminate against Fascism as he was joined by leaders like Eduardo Molisani, Joseph Catalanotti, John Gelo, George Baldanzi (of the textile industry), and Augusto Bellanca, among others. Fileno DeNovellis, business agent for the overwhelmingly Italian American shoemakers of local 69 of United Leather Workers Union, was another outstanding example of an Italian-born labor leader who enthusiastically supported the war effort. A constant critic of Mussolini and Fascism, De-Novellis led his shoemakers to cooperate fully in purchase of war bonds and donations to the Red Cross. "Without exaggeration, therefore, it is affirmed that local 69, under his direction, and his more unassuming associates, have given the maximum contribution to a United States victory." [211]

ITALIAN AMERICAN POLITICAL LEADERS

Virtually all the prominent Italian American leaders in public life raised their voices to proclaim the devotion of the group to American ideals of liberty and democracy. Three of the four Italian American members of Congress at the outset of the war spoke out in their defense, including Louis Capozzoli who reminded listeners of the devotion and sacrifice rendered by Italian Americans in his congressional district, citing instances in which friends and neighbors rallied behind mothers of local servicemen and other instances of solid support for bond drives locally.[212] Baltimore's Congressman Thomas D'Alessandro, Jr. proved to be a reliable and steadfast defender of the ethnic group, and frequently broadcast messages in Italian to citizens of Italy urging them to defy Mussolini.

The fiery East Harlem Congressman Vito Marcantonio's concern for the welfare of Italian Americans was never manifested more than during the war. Criticized for his earlier stance against American participation in the war until the invasion of Russia, he now became a strong proponent of the Allied cause. More so than any congressman, Marcantonio emerged the ethnic group's most consistent and conspicuous defender. Eschewing the defensive, he objected to the denigration of Italian American patriotism by diligently researching and highlighting instances of Italian American heroism. He cited the heartening response of the ethnic group to war bond drives, and recounted episodes of outstanding participation in defense and war plant activities. Aware that many Italian aliens were denied work in such industries, he denounced it as unworthy discrimination that prevented full mobilization of American power, and fought unstintingly for the right to employment in such plants. Nor did he stop with speeches in Congress as he utilized the public media to instruct the public of Italy's enduring role in the history of democracy. Finally, he protested to President Roosevelt himself repeatedly until a degree of justice was rendered.[213]

On many occasions, New York City Mayor LaGuardia, used his rather influential political pulpit to counter rising hysteria by reminding Americans of the unquestioned loyalty of Italian Americans, and recalling to his audience that to discriminate against them with "enemy aliens" labels was to play Hitler's game of divide and conquer. He assailed specifically those instances wherein local organizations seemed to be too eager to harass aliens—a reference to a policy of encouraging civilians who were linked to local defense councils to transmit evidence of hostile activity to the nearest FBI office. The consequence was "a number of instances where city and local organizations have taken the law into their own hands ... Such activity can only lead to hysteria."[214]

NON-ITALIAN POLITICIANS

Speaking in defense of the ethnic group also were a substantial number of non-Italian politicians from national state, and local government, particularly those whose districts included large segments of the group. For example, even before Pearl Harbor, Congressman Thomas A. Flaherty, of Massachusetts, whose district represented a constituency composed of a considerable number of Italian Americans declared, "I have close association with hundreds of Italo-Americans and can bear testimony to their high place in the ranks of loyalty as real Americans." He was joined by Massachusetts Congressman John McCormack ,who also condemned "unwarranted attacks from any source upon all Americans or all racial groups particularly attacks made on those fine Americans of Italian descent ... "[215] In April 1942, New York Senator James M. Mead, took note of the many resolutions adopted by Italian American organizations, representing tens of thousands of members that demonstrated unhesitating loyalty. Similar testimonies of loyalty were also voiced by local government officials, as for example, New York City Councilman William Carroll, and Council President Newbold Morris, who hailed the contribution of Italian Americans for their dedication as reflected in their young men joining the military service and their purchase of war bonds.[216] The cumulative effect of these voices was to help balance those voices of alarm and would gradually cause the national government to revise its "alien enemy" classification.

ALIEN REGISTRATION AND DETENTION

Many years after the war, I became acquainted with writer Jerre Mangione, who had worked for a time in the Federal Writer' Project, and then as special assistant to the United States commissioner of immigration and naturalization. I recall his sensitivity to the alien registration and detention problem and his hope that the history of this episode be recorded. As ominous as was the pre-Pearl Harbor 1940 atmosphere, the condition became even more depressing. The hovering of war clouds saw the government pass the Alien Registration Act (Smith Act) that required the registration and fingerprinting of aliens—provisions that forecast an even more baleful and portentous time for Italian aliens. In its original form, the legislation was fraught with frightening impositions. However, since implementation of the alien registration order was the task of Attorney General Francis Biddle, it proved to be a fortuitous development according to Mangione because Biddle resisted the more severe aspects of the originally proposed manner of registration. "Originally, the aliens were to have been registered and fingerprinted at police stations, but Francis Biddle and Earl Harrison, in their determination to minimize the unfriendly implications of mandatory fingerprinting, insisted that the registration take place in the nation's post offices instead."[217]

One of the very few Italian Americans working on the Immigration and Naturalization staff, Mangione left a picture of the inner workings of the department as well as telling profiles of government officials charged with executing government edicts. Along with social service agencies and the ethnic press, his job was to allay fears about the registration campaign and implement it by writing news releases and pamphlets that explained to aliens what was required of them. The results were mixed; in February 1942, aliens by the hundreds of thousands, apprehensive despite their compelling innocence, trudged to post offices with photographs of themselves, ready to provide information about employment, organizational affiliations and other personal data. Notwithstanding Mangione's efforts to explain the necessity of registration, it left many with deep distrust.

> The nervousness and indignation it engendered was reflected in some of the messages I received from my Rochester relatives. My uncle Stefano wanted to know if an "alien enemy would mean deportation to Italy. They could not understand why the American government would consider them dangerous since by now they been here so long they could not imagine having any other homeland. One angry relative wrote: "Don't those imbeciles in Washington understand that to have American-born children is to become an American for the rest of your life? ... My uncle Stefano put it neatly in a letter to me: "We Italians have become Americans in spite of the Americans. It should

not be held against us that we speak this country's language badly or not at all. The most important language is
the language of the heart."[218]

To be an "enemy alien" was to be regarded an outsider, one subject to
potentially emotionally scarring experiences that could lead to bitterness.
Matters were made even more disturbing due to the fact that so many
members of the American armed forces came from the homes of "enemy
aliens." It was calculated that only two months after the Pearl Harbor attack, ten percent of these homes provided family members for the armed
services—a number bound to increase as the war unfolded.

INTERNMENT

Studies estimate that hundreds of Americans of Italian heritage were
interned during the war, in addition to many thousands in California who
were forced to relocate, and were subject to curfew laws.[219] Some were Italian nationals, such as seamen whose ships were in American ports when
war broke out; others were Italian diplomats or members of the foreign
service, while still others were so-called hardened Fascists who remained
loyal to Mussolini even after the declaration of war. As we have seen,
the decision to classify 600,000 Italian residents of the United States as
"enemy aliens" was deeply disturbing, and no sooner had the government
edict been issued, a determined effort to reverse the policy was underway.
Leaders both within and without the ethnic community lent their voices to
a call to reverse the policy.

CARUSI

Within Italian American circles, diminutive and dynamic Ugo Carusi,
who despite entering federal government service during an earlier Republican administration, was retained by the Democrats, held the office
of Assistant Attorney General within the Department of Justice—the

highest post in government held by any Italian American. He was called upon to play a prominent role, frequently serving as spokesman for the government regarding the alien registration policy. For three consecutive days, Carusi was interviewed on a New York City Italian language radio program titled "Lo Zio Sam Parla" (Uncle Sam Speaks), where in an effort to define the legal aspects as well as to urge compliance, he fielded numerous questions concerning the policy from anxious Italian Americans on the home front. He emphasized that it was the patriotic duty of presumably literate Italian American citizens to assist the government's registration program by clarifying the need for the program to parents and others who were non-citizens and over fourteen years of age. They would thus be performing a valuable patriotic service, asserted Carusi, who worked assiduously to ease the minds of fretful Italian Americans by explaining that in a democracy we have the right to expect our government employ a proper rationale for the policy. "The only reason is that we are at war. When a nation declares war, people who live in that nation and are citizens of another nation—because of the fact that they have not become naturalized—are called "Enemy Aliens." Carusi reiterated the opinion of Attorney General Biddle that although the majority of Italian aliens in the United States were loyal, there were some who were not. Therefore it was an issue of national security. "In other words, because we are at war, we cannot take risks."[220] This was part of Attorney General's campaign to effect compliance with the registration effort, and an attempt to deflect the denigration associated with the "enemy alien" term. Biddle implored lawyers within the ethnic community to assure people that "enemy alien" was not a term of dishonor when they truly loved their country and the ideals for which it fought.

Many questions were of a pragmatic nature. Accordingly, Carusi informed his audience that it was necessary for aliens to submit travel plans to Department of Justice officials in order to travel beyond the prescribed zones. In answer to the question of what should such aliens do if they were in possession of restricted items such as short wave radio receivers, maps and cameras, Carusi ingenuously advised owner to bring such items immediately to local police stations as the law prescribed, where law enforcement personnel would ascertain their danger, and give people a receipt for items involved which could be retrieved at the war's end. Carusi also informed aliens that they could indeed apply for naturalization during the war.[221]

JOINING THE ARMED SERVICES

With the outbreak of war, the unique political rhetoric that enfolded became an effort to demonstrate that "At last, it was clear that Italian-Americans were more American than Italian."[222] More than mere eloquence or pomposity, the profession of loyalty was borne out by concrete actions, in the form of enlistment into the armed services by ethnic group members, at a rate proportionately higher than their percentage of the total population. So swift was their induction that in less than a month of war, Major B. T. Anuskewicz, an official of the Selective Service Boards in New York exclaimed "The American soldiers of Italian extraction are capable and ready to take their places alongside their brothers-in-arms for the defense of America."[223] In New York, the Selective Service System, popularly known as the draft, required all men, even aliens, of eligible draft age to register by February 16, 1942. Since many of the aliens were unable to read or write English, the Selective Service System provided interpreters from Italian American volunteers within the community. Over two hundred interpreters working through the Italian Division of the Foreign Language Bureau of the Selective Service were available for practically all city draft boards. By March 1942, the government announced that regardless of whether or not Italian subjects had applied for citizenship papers, they were subject to induction into the armed forces. This was, in effect, a vindication of the effort of "loyal Americans" desirous of joining the armed forces, but had been denied because of their non-citizen category, and yet had been assiduously petitioning government officials to enable them to enlist.[224] In addition to serving as interpreters, Italian Americans played a prominent role in facilitating the task of registering and drafting men for America's military forces. One example from my neighborhood was Sicilian-born lawyer Victor Anfuso, who served as the chairman of the Advisory Board for Local Conscription. Proud of his work of achieving the local board's quota for the armed forces, he was even prouder to note that at least fifty percent of the young men conscripted from his board were of Italian descent, and who thereby fulfilled their solemn duty and obligation.[225] Local residents rewarded him when he ran for public office. Enjoying great popularity in the neighborhood, I can distinctly recall the picture of his solid mustachioed face and receding hairline featured on posters placed in practically every small store front for blocks around when he ran for Congress—he eventually become the first Sicilian-born member of Congress.

CATHOLIC MILITARY CHAPLAINS

Among the unmistakable signs of the war's impact on the home front was the enlistment, not only of the rank and file young men in the neighborhood, but also of Italian Americans from various professions, doctors, lawyers, and even clergymen. With respect to the latter for those of my background, it was the enlistment of priests of our ethnic group that was extraordinary because in our mind's eye, that could be associated with the positive image of chaplains frequently portrayed in movies which depicted military chaplains as enduring the hardships and deprivation of the ordinary GI while extending themselves to bring not only religious assistance, but also

Monsignor Ottavio Silvestri, an immigrant priest who became founding pastor of St. Joseph Patron of the Universal Church of Brooklyn and a leader within the Italian American community.

PHOTO COURTESY LOUIS PIERINI

psychological and medical help to suffering soldiers. It has been estimated that thousands of clergymen served as military chaplains in the war and that eighty-three of them were killed, performing their unselfish duties.

The ethnic press identified several Italian American priests from the New York area as military chaplains including Fr. Arturo Denelfo, Fr. John Battaliata, Fr. George Rosso. In September 1943, they were joined by Fr. Anthony DeLaura, an assistant pastor in my own parish of St. Joseph's Church. Born and raised in Brooklyn of Italian immigrant parents, he was educated at Cathedral High School, St. Francis College, and St. John's University in Brooklyn, and upon ordination to the priesthood in 1933 was assigned as assistant pastor for the Brooklyn churches of St. Lucy and St. Rita—de facto Italian parishes before coming to St. Joseph. At St. Joseph, he served as moderator of the Holy Name Society, the St. Vincent DePaul Society and also organized sports and other activities for young people. In September 1942, he enlisted in the Army, received a commission, and was assigned to the 85th Infantry Division.[226] That his deed was especially pleasing to Catholic circles was evident in the testimonial farewell dinner tendered him by the pastor, Monsignor Silvestri, the four other assistant pastors of St. Joseph, all of Italian descent, other leading Italian American prelates and his own family.

Many years after the war, I had the pleasure of discussing that period with Fr. DeLaura who regarded that time as a formative experience. He saw his chaplaincy vocation as one of bringing solace not only to Catholics, but to men in general who needed assurance and guidance—many of them non-Catholics. The experience also prepared him to see his post-war role as a priest not only for Italians, but beyond. In 1946, with the end of the war, the Irish-American pastor of St. Brigid in Westbury, New York, importuned Fr. DeLaura to accept assignment as assistant pastor there, specifically to accommodate parishioners of Italian descent. Fr. DeLaura resisted the narrow ethnic-based assignment. "I have to repeat I just came back from the war. I was in the regiment as a chaplain. I took care of Italians, Jews, Poles, everybody. I'll take care of all the people and the Italians too."[227]

UNEQUIVOCAL LOYALTY

There was no question where the sense of loyalty lay for the nation's Little Italies—no matter what their regard for the old country, now that the United States was at war, there was undivided and resounding support for the American cause. Baltimore's Italian ethnic community was a case in point. Thus although ambivalent over Fascism in the 1930s, the hesitancy "lasted only until World War II broke out in 1941 ... From that day Little Italy rallied to the American cause—vigorously and unequivocally." By August 1945, the enclave assembled to dedicate a service flag title "For God and Country, In honor of Our Boys." "They cheered as a large flag—containing a blue star for each of Little Italy's 85 fighting men—was stretched across Eastern Avenue between the roof tops of two houses. Each family had contributed toward the purchase of the flag."[228] It was the same in every Little Italy—a total commitment illustrated in St. Anthony's Church in the Italian American enclave in Watertown, New York. The church census showed that at the outbreak of war the parish counted 3,500 parishioners of Italian extraction. "To a man, that population pledged total commitment to the United States ... The Italians feel its America first," said Monsignor Claudio Sechi, who had previously endorsed Italy's venture into Ethiopia.[229] Singular contributions to the war effort was the sober legacy of Brooklyn Italian American neighborhoods such as East New York where Our Lady of Loretto Catholic parish recorded 60 of its young men—virtually all of Italian heritage, including a set of twins, were killed in action. It is doubtful that many parishes in the New York area sustained such a concentration of casualties.

NEW YORK RESPONDS
TO PEARL HARBOR ATTACK

The direct response of common men and women of Italian extraction was manifest in numerous ways. It could be seen in the unprecedented number of humble Italian Americans spontaneously flocking to de facto Italian churches in ethnic neighborhoods, where people went there to pray and light candles for the country and for American servicemen. It could be observed in the action of New York Italian American restaurant owners, who within a week of the outbreak of war, offered free meals to all servicemen. The attitude of positive support was also well exemplified in the willingness and readiness of ordinary Italian Americans to serve as air raid wardens, volunteer firemen, and civilian defense workers. For instance, Italian American residents who accounted for over a third of Harrison, New York's population were cited for the ethnic group's heavy representation among its volunteer air raid wardens.[230] Endorsement of American war goals was apparent in less visible but important morale-boosting activities, such as local organizations sending packages and town newspapers to servicemen.

For many of us my age on Himrod Street who lived through that period, air raid drills were regarded with a mixture of seriousness, bemusement, and annoyance because they intruded into our daily home routines including hanging out on the street with friends. As young teenagers, we looked upon the portly middle age air raid warden who lived next door with some amusement as he went up and down the block making certain no light emanated from our windows. During air raids, I used to peek out from a corner of a curtain in a darkened room to see him and other wardens walking by. A novelty and somewhat exciting at the outset, in time I became a bit jaded with the drills, nevertheless we came to accept them as part of the reality of a nation at war. In reminiscing about that time, Florence Gatto offered a terse description of blackouts that recaptured the essence of the experience to younger Brooklynites.

> I have vague memories of sirens screeching, all lights out, shades drawn and everyone remaining indoors when I was a youngster in Brooklyn. It was a "blackout" in the early 40s during the World War II. These were practice drills in case of enemy air invasion ...

During the Civil Defense Drill a warden dressed in khaki with a white helmet and an arm band patrolled the block, blew his whistle and through a megaphone ordered, "All lights out." The warden was usually someone who did not qualify for the draft and was 4F perhaps because he had flat feet or was a bit older.

I was very young then but I have a flashback of being huddled into our kitchen and my grandmother attempting to console us by making Pizza.[231]

MELTING POT

In striving for acceptance during a hostile period, Italian Americans, even while focusing on their ethnicity, stressed the "melting pot" theme. After an excursion throughout Italian enclaves in the northeast, a reporter observed that although preoccupied with the war, both the Italian-born generation and their children were solidly behind the American cause. He noted that the First World War promoted the melting pot concept—the powerful assimilative force that superceded loyalties to their ancestries among the various peoples in favor of a new American personhood.[232] The present war he deemed a consolidation of the notion that was celebrated on "I Am An American Day." Originating during the First World War and post-war period, when various American groups sought to measure patriotism by highlighting nationalist activities, while simultaneously denigrating immigrant cultures, that special day in May had become an occasion to promote loyalty. By the 1940s, it assumed renewed interest among us Italian Americans, who saw it as an opportunity to proclaim our patriotism. Unaware of the suppressive aspects of Americanization, I followed with pride the declarations of public spirit that were treated with uncommon fulsomeness by a nationalist press that we eagerly absorbed in those heady super-nationalist days that characterized the home front. Accordingly, the New York *Journal American* used the May 1942 "I Am An

American Day" festivities, which featured operatic tenor Giovanni Martinelli singing patriotic songs, to commemorate the positive role Americans
of Italian descent played in the development of American democracy.
"The roots of Italian migration go back to early Colonial days, to the very
foundation of the republic. The Italians have ever shown a growing love
of freedom in this great country which they helped carve out of the wilder-
ness. They backed their belief with their lives. They have died for it. It is
what America means to them."[233]

WORKING FOR VICTORY

Home front Italian American support for the war effort was even more
visible in the multitude of exceptional examples that found them employed
in various capacities to produce items essential to the war endeavor. Virtually every Italian neighborhood housed junkyards, like the one on the
next block from my home, that we ordinarily regarded as of minor importance, shopping there infrequently for a used appliance part, but now
in the midst of war, it assumed greater significance for its miscellaneous
holdings of scarce materials. The results were in some cases noteworthy as
in the instance of Ralph Attonito of Waterbury, Connecticut who received
a certificate of merit for the amount of iron that he recovered from the
scrap holdings in his yard. There were numerous instances in which multiple family members were employed in vital war production, such as the
Formichella family of New York, whose eight family members did their
part working for national defense plants. There were singular instances of
exceptional cooperation on the part of senior citizens like Mrs. Carmela
Zarillo of Orange, New Jersey, who converted her kitchen into a virtual
laboratory where she repaired asbestos gloves used by Westinghouse
workers. Rose Marie Juliano of City Island, New York claimed the rare
distinction of launching a minesweeper for the Robert Jacobs Shipyard,
thereby continuing a tradition begun fifty years earlier by her Sicilian-born
father Charles. During World War I, Charles helped construct ships for the

American Navy, a task he continued during the present conflict, joined now by three other family members. So dedicated to his work was Charles that he did not take time off to be present when Rose Marie swung the bottle of champagne that launched the naval vessel in April 1942.[234]

INVENTIONS AND CREATIVITY

Among the extraordinary displays by Italian Americans extending themselves for an American victory were the actions of ingenious individuals who invented machines or modified extant techniques to improve production. In June 1942, twenty-four-year-old Margaret (Peggy) Ferrone made a singular contribution at the Picatinny Arsenal of Dover, New Jersey where she had been employed for only several months. A brilliant and pretty high school math student, Ferrone who found production work tedious, conceived of an idea to emend the operations and consequently, invented a new machine that accelerated and rendered more accurate the production of fuses that were required to detonate bombs delivered by naval aircraft. She followed up by developing another apparatus that made it possible to operate the machine without the need to occupy both hands. Remarkably, she had no prior experience with machinery, except that which was in the kitchen for cooking purposes. Her simple and forthright motivation reflected the overwhelming attitude of the ethnic group engaged in war work. "Our young men on the front lines need the greatest amount of munitions as soon as possible. We must do all that we can to hasten production to win the war."[235] Later that same year, the War Labor Board conferred its distinguished certificate of honor to Frank LiVoci for his invention of a speed-up procedure to produce spark plugs and increase efficiency of operation that would significantly benefit other industries. Born in Calabria in 1927, LiVoci came to New York where he went to high school and college, before being employed by the Aero Spark Plug Company. So impressed was the government with this development that the Office of War Information prevailed upon

LiVoci to broadcast a "brother to brother" appeal on Italian radio, urging Italian workers to abandon their alliance with the Nazis and Japanese. Secret at the time, one of the most noteworthy scientific contributions was that of Dr. Cledo Brunetti, who won the 1941 award as the Outstanding Young Engineer in the nation, and who during the war worked for the National Bureau of Standards. Described as an engineer, scientist, and physician, his development of a radio proximity mortar fuse, was called by some as "No. 2 Secret Weapon" (after the Atomic Bomb), because it significantly improved bomb delivery first used with devastating effect against the Germans in the Ardennes offensive in December 1944. It was also deemed essential in developing the atom bomb.[236]

As the war progressed, additional creative Italian Americans on the home front continued to make contributions that the ethnic press proudly proclaimed demonstrated that in entrusting them with wartime responsibilities members of the group were validating their role. In recognition of some of the extraordinary contributions attributable to the ethnic group, the War Production Board cited Dominic Pirozzo of Newark, New Jersey for developing a small device to inspect grommets thus speeding up a normally time-consuming process and consequently, saving thousands of hours of labor. Likewise, the agency cited machine operator Samuel Giudetti, for figuring out a faster way of truing up brass elbows procedures used on sparkplug conduits that also saved precious time, while it commended William Yasoni for designing a cam-shaft turning tool that also sped production significantly. Undoubtedly, Brooklyn's Dominic A. Albanese was perhaps the most prolific of the young inventors within the ethnic group. Born in Reggio Calabria, where he studied at an Italian technical school, Dominic and his parents immigrated to the United States in 1935. Four years later, at age 19, Dominic joined the Army where he soon impressed his superiors with his mechanical knowledge, was promoted to a sergeant's rank, and placed in charge of supervising hundreds of men. Credited with 18 inventions that significantly aided

American military aviation, including perfecting visual angles for bullets, a Smoke Tank Adaptor, and a radar adaptation, he earned The Legion of Merit and the sobriquet "G. I. Edison."[237]

UNFEIGNED PATRIOTISM

There were innumerable instances of unfeigned patriotism traceable among Italian Americans, from the most illustrious figures to the more humble. Recognizing that the war emergency required changes in long-held practices, the world-acclaimed symphony conductor Arturo Toscanini broke a self-imposed rule that he had adhered to for many years of broadcasting. For the first time, he now allowed a live audience—1,000 sailors, soldiers, marines, airplane pilots and their wives to listen to his NBC Symphony Orchestra radio broadcast on behalf of the Defense Bond and Stamp Drive. Pasquale D'Agostino, President of the New York State Food Merchants Association, and a member of the Food Committee of the War Production Board of the OPA exhorted Italian language readers to do their part in bringing about victory. Specifically, he urged them to accept the need for meat rationing and forgo their normal preferences for choice meats because that food was a priority item for the American fighting forces, and for the nation's allies. He likewise asked them not to purchase meat from the "black market"—the illegal practice of purchasing rationed items by paying vendors above the approved market rates. Such practices were particularly dif-

Considered the greatest conductor in the world, the renowned maestro Arturo Toscanini, also encouraged the home front with his unflinching anti-Fascist stance.

ficult on people in poor neighborhoods.[238] As the war unfolded, the "Restaurant Division" of the Italian American Commission of the National War Fund, announced its particular contribution. The division set aside one day in which most of the Italian-owned nightclubs and restaurants in New York metropolitan area announced a contribution of ten percent of their proceeds for the National War Fund. Officers of the division, including proprietors of some of the most elegant establishments in the city, went on Italian language radio to announce pledges and to encourage others to join in the drive.[239] Determined to do his bit for the war effort, New York master barber John Albano defied his labor union by offering uniformed servicemen a rebate on their haircuts and shaves. His gesture was appreciated by neighborhood women who slugged union pickets that marched in front of his shop in opposition to the lower prices.[240]

WAR BOND DRIVES

In addition to taxes, the United States government sought to finance the war by relying on citizen loans to the government via the sale of war bonds. To stimulate this funding, the government undertook periodic War Loan Drives that not only raised necessary funds, but also saw the drives as a means of measuring public support for the war effort. For ethnic groups like Italian Americans on the home front, these also provided an opportunity to demonstrate patriotism. Bond drives therefore were important not only for financing the war, but also because they served "as constant reminders for those on the home front that there was, in fact, a war being fought an ocean away."[241] They were reminders that home front sacrifice was connected with front line action. Thus they were promoted as an indication that in purchasing bonds, they not only were helping the war effort, but also were making a wise financial investment; leaders within the Italian American community were very active in the fund-raising endeavor. With New York Lieutenant Governor Charles Poletti as honorary chairman, leaders in the ethnic community organized the Defense Savings Committee for Americans of Italian

Origin in May 1942. The real working chairman of the committee, Paolino Gerli proved effective in promoting the sale of war bonds not only among adult groups of Italian Americans, but also among high school age youngsters. The effort of these youngsters in various schools throughout the city and beyond was given much coverage as an act of patriotism. Among the students who were lauded for their effort was Salvatore Pacella, a senior at Commercial High School in New Haven, Connecticut, who made it his patriotic goal to get people in the school in offices nearby and distant to buy war bonds and stamps. In January 1942, he achieved a local record of selling $4,556 of the government issues.[242]

Generoso Pope was another leading activist in this regard, utilizing his newspaper not only to regularly report on the amount of bonds Italian Americans in various locales purchased, but also became a chief advocate of bond buying by providing cut-out coupons that newspaper readers could readily use.

> It is a coupon which can be easily filled out by anyone who wants to buy Bonds and Stamps, on the installment plan or otherwise, in order to give a spontaneous contribution to the financing of the was which American is fighting for the salvation of our democratic institutions, of our independence, of our homes, and which, at the same time, will provide a saving which will bear a definite and secure interest, savings which can be of invaluable help in our old age and for the future of our families ... Those who have already made previous purchases are asked to indicate this in the lower part of the coupon, which, sent to this newspaper, will permit us to publish the names of the loyal and conscientious citizens who are thus enrolling themselves in this great army of the subscribers to the colossal economic effort that the war is imposing on America and whose investments constitute public testimony of high patriotism of the Americans of Italian extraction.[243]

In promoting the Third War loan, Secretary of the Treasury Robert Morgenthau sought record-breaking sums to finance the war and enlisted

Italian American leaders in the effort, naming Pope Chairman of the Italian American Committee for the Third War Loan. The publisher then responded by forming a committee of prominent Italian Americans, including Judges Albert Vitale, Samuel Di Falco, and Anthony DiGiovanni. He also exhorted employees within his business enterprises to respond to major war bond drives via extensive coverage in *Il Progesso Italo Americano*, replete with examples of signed employee pledge cards together with accompanying photographs and lists of amounts of their subscriptions. One notable aspect of the drive was that five thousand Americans of foreign birth were enlisted to encourage people to cooperate. In addition, famous personalities within the ethnic group also joined in advancing the drives. For example, in July 1942, comedian Jimmy Durante was featured in the cause, while in subsequent months, stars of the Italian stage like Gilda Mignonette and Farfariello urged their fellow Italian Americans to help by participating in war bond purchases. Frequently, the newspaper contained photographs showing Italian Americans in the city's Little Italies purchasing bonds and kissing the American flag.[244]

TERMINATING THE "ENEMY ALIEN" POLICY

From the outset, the government "enemy alien" policy rankled. To Italian Americans, the procedure that 600,000 aliens who had not yet obtained United States citizenship, be required to register under the defamatory classification was at best, a bother and at worst, a heartless and unjust policy. To be regarded along with large numbers of German and Japanese subjects who were in similar positions, or who despite their naturalization, nevertheless were somewhat suspect, was devastating to morale. Any intimation that they were associated with internal foes or that their actions bordered on betrayal was offensive. Thus, they called for an end to the policy. Accordingly, the movement to change the policy was swift and unrelenting, as leaders from within and outside the Italian ethnic community, with an effusive display of testimonies and statistics, demonstrated that the encumbrances of the policy were at variance with the unassailable loyalty of the ethnic group. They entreated the government to terminate the rule, citing Italian Americans patriotism and participation in the First World War, and the outpouring of inductees from the ethnic community in the present conflict as justification. They reminded Americans of the astonishing response to join the colors on the part of tens of thousands astoundingly from the very homes of those labeled 'enemies' —by February 1942, the American Committee for the Protection of the Foreign Born reported that 60,000 had been inducted. By September 1942, it was estimated that 75,000 inductees into the service came from such homes. Given this realization, it was argued that the affected people should be called "Friendly Aliens."[245] This latter point was utilized as the basis for beginning to change a callous policy whose travel restrictions prevented Italian subjects living in America from freely visiting their own sons who were serving in the armed forces. Frank Grillo, secretary-treasurer of the United Rubber Workers of America, echoed the sentiments of many when he said, "I do not believe there is a more important objective than to consolidate the nation in a united front for combat ... Let us unite, therefore, with our foreign born brothers and sisters in this great American enterprise, to complete and bring ultimate victory." In September 1942, the Grand Lodge of the Order of the Sons of Italy in Massachusetts, with the cooperation of New York's Mayor LaGuardia, proposed that the government pass legislation that would extend naturalization to non-citizen parents of American servicemen. Even traditional feasts, like the celebrated San Gennaro Feast in September 1942, became occasions for so-called "enemy aliens" to demonstrate their patriotism. Notwithstanding the offensive label, "in their hearts and in their actions they proudly exhibited the greatest patriotism among Americans." Furthermore, the profits gleaned from the feast were allocated toward a community drive for the purchase of war bonds.[246]

The political antennae of the political parties also came into play as the Democratic Party realized that its standing within the ethnic group had eroded as evidenced by the fall-off of the vote for Roosevelt in the last presidential election. A student of the subject explained that although the decision to change the policy was made by the spring of 1942, a decision to make the official announcement was purposely delayed until Columbus Day October 12, for maximum political impact. "According to Roosevelt's election-campaign strategists, the postponement would let the President's decision have a broader echo in Italian-American communities nationwide and have a deeper impact on the vote, which was scheduled for early November."[247] From mutual aid societies, labor unions, leading professional figures, and religious leaders, there was such a constant appeal to change the policy that it was merely a matter of time before it was terminated. As the fall of that year approached, proponents of a policy change became more encouraged, an attitude reflected in a Generoso Pope editorial. "And we hope that Attorney General Francis Biddle, who has accepted an invitation to be among us on October 12, on the occasion of the solemn Columbus Day ceremony at Carnegie Hall, will bring us a precise, generous and welcome word in confirmation of the policy against discrimination which he has many times, in clear and effective terms, authoritatively and publicly sustained."[248] From states heavily populated by residents of Italian ancestry like Rhode Island, the influential voice of Democratic United States Senator Theodore Green was raised in their support. Green noted that those labeled as enemies were discriminated in employment, deprived of right to fish offshore, and subject to other restriction on the West Coast. "Here in Washington, our nation's capital, they are prohibited from working as barbers, as hotel and restaurant employees—all because Italians occupy an inferior position than the Germans in the war against the United States. Green suggested that instead of the derogatory term of enemy they should be regarded as "Loyal Aliens."[249]

Although Jerre Mangione described the end of the "enemy alien" stigma, which Attorney General Biddle announced on Columbus Day 1942 as a surprise, in reality, it was not, in view of the political considerations just discussed. For a few weeks before October 12, prominent leaders like Pope more than intimated a fundamental change was in the offing, as illustrated in the following comment. "The American government has, therefore, entrusted Francis Biddle with the noble task of giving our people a world of kindness, of encouragement and justice as a result of so many evidences of loyalty given by them to America at war, of the large contribution—in soldiers, work, and money—given by them for the defense of the united States and for its unfailing victory."[250] Even Mangione conceded as much when he wrote, "This momentous action, based partly on the statistic that of the 10,000 aliens interned by the Department of Justice less than 250 of them were Italians, had wide repercussions."[251] This was, in fact, an understatement when one realizes that it dramatically accelerated naturalization steps and also encouraged the Italian underground movement with important consequences for Americans.

> The change of policy was widely embraced by Little Italy residents as a belated but welcome confirmation of their commitment to the American cause. Attorney General Biddle announced not only the end of the "enemy alien" designation, but also that 200,000 Italians living in the land and over 50 years old, would automatically become citizens without having to pass the Literacy Test. On behalf of the Office of War Information, Ugo Carusi explained the Attorney General's order was of great meaning to Italian aliens. Speaking on Italian radio, he tried to convey the seriousness of the new policy and his exhortation to spread the word within Italian American communities. "What I have to say is very important to every Italian alien, and I shall speak slowly so that none of you may miss my meaning. If you are a citizen, listen carefully and pass on my information to those friends and relatives who are not American citizens.[252]

The reaction among affected aliens was spontaneous and enthusiastic, and clearly reflected in the unadorned and befitting words of seventy-five-year-old immigrant Rosa Giarusso.

> It is such happy news. What can I say. What can I really
> say just with words. For 48 years this has been my home.
> I have raised my family here and the American soil has
> been the only one that I have walked upon. Here I have
> earned my bread and here is where my husband made his
> living. And it is here that my son works and raised his
> family too.

Salvatore La Miceli, who lived as an alien in the same Little Italy for
thirty one years and whose two sons were in the armed forces while a third
was shortly to enter, was equally approving of Biddle's announcement.

> I have always wanted to have citizenship papers. But I
> had to work and could not go to school at nights and it
> was difficult for me to apply for my papers. But America
> has been my home and the home of my children and I
> have obeyed all the laws. We Italians are not enemies of
> the United States. And I am happy that America recog-
> nizes that now. We love America.[253]

From the large Little Italy of East Harlem came similar expressions of
joy. "This is another proof that America is the greatest country in the world,
and that President Roosevelt knows and loves the Italian people," opined
café owner Temistocle Lanzara. Biddle's order had immediate impact in
California where the midnight curfew was terminated. The new policy
also had ramifications in Mexico, where over 4,500 Italian aliens lived and
who were now no longer regarded as enemies. In a broader expression of
gratitude, the Italian American Labor Council honored Attorney General
Francis Biddle with its Four Freedoms award at a ceremony in Carnegie
Hall.[254] Happily, the new government policy would mark a turning point
for the ethnic group on the home front.

CHAPTER V
ITALIAN AMERICAN RESPONSE: 1941–1943

THE FIRST TWO YEARS OF WAR

Fervently and avidly, Americans on the home front followed the slow tortuous unfolding of the war throughout the first very anxious months following the attack on Pearl Harbor. While allowance was made for the necessity of censorship and for the predictable propaganda, inevitable concomitants of bellicosity, the newspapers could not entirely mask the seriousness of Allied desperation during the first half of 1942. The *New York Daily News* and the *Daily Mirror* were the most popular tabloids in my neighborhood, as they were in many a city Italian American neighborhood. The anticipation that awaited the *Daily News*, in Greenwich Village in the evenings could have described my neighborhood. "People began milling around their favorite candy store up to an hour before the truck was scheduled to pass, enough time to socialize and exchange gossip."[255] These tabloids provided its readers with bold, sensational, if exaggerated headlines while the more staid *New York Times* and *New York Herald Tribune* informed their readers with subdued but nevertheless alarming front line information. In the Pacific and the Far East, Japan followed its devastating attack on Pearl Harbor by simultaneously launching assaults on the Philippines, Guam, Midway Island, Hong Kong and the Malay Peninsula. January and February 1942 found Japanese invaders forcing the surrender of American and Filipino defenders of the Bataan peninsula with its Corregidor fortress in the Philippines, along with accompanying accounts of cruel torture perpetrated by the conquerors. Within the first six months of conflict, Japan completed the first phase of the Pacific war, with the conquest of British forces in Malaysia and the East Indies. Japanese advancement continued until May 7–8, 1942, when American naval forces halted them in the noteworthy Battle of the Coral Sea, and the even more important American victory at the Battle of Midway. Having arrested the deadly aggressive thrust, the long, arduous task of retaking lost territories and bringing the war to the Japanese mainland remained.

On the home front, we learned that the prosecution of the war during the first several months in the Mediterranean and European front was also unpromising. By 1942, Germany, the principal Axis nation, faced serious opposition on the continent primarily from the Union of Soviet Socialist Republics. France had surrendered and entered into an accommodation arrangement with Germany, while Great Britain, with bulldog tenacity, steadfastly persisted in defending itself from punishing air attacks while simultaneously establishing itself as the assembly point for American aid, a constant source of reinforcement. There was understandable concern over the frightening cost to the Allies exacted by Germany's U-boat campaign that required major efforts by United States workers to build new merchant ships in record time to meet the emergency. In conversations with older war workers in the neighborhood, in newspaper reminders, in movie houses, railroad stations, etc., we became aware that it could be dangerous to talk loosely about defense matters. "Loose lips sink ships." The dimming of the "Great White Way," the Broadway marquees, the subdued car headlights, the air raid drills that compelled all the homes on the block to emit no light onto the street, also brought home the point. In short, because of the omnipresent array of exhortations not to disclose information that could be used for sabotage, we were quite conscious of the menace the nation was facing. The bold, but ultimately unsuccessful German venture at espionage was brought close to home in May 1942 when a group of saboteurs was captured on Long Island. I recall avidly following the events in the newspapers that ultimately led to their trials, convictions, and in most cases, executions. The lesson that these were dangerous times was not hard to miss.

Great Britain was also to be the locale for the buildup of an Anglo-American force that would eventually cross the English Channel to bring the fight into Germany itself. That, however, was in the future; meanwhile in the spring of 1942, Russia, seemingly on the point of collapse, needed enormous assistance. While an invasion on the western front was premature, an Allied landing to reverse sensational German advances was settled upon and became a reality before the year was out. It became clear to us on the home front that we faced a long and grueling road.

LETTER WRITING ON THE HOME FRONT

We followed war news in a variety of ways: in jarring newspaper headlines and accompanying reporters' accounts, enhanced by numerous front line action photos, in stirring radio reports wherein leading newsmen intoned in dramatic timbre somber military developments, and in the black and white movie house newsreels features. We also tried to follow events via the United States mail as letter writing became an absorbing, patriotic, almost sacred homage. Government propaganda that promoted correspondence to servicemen and women as critical to maintaining esprit de corps found ready acceptance. In this light, it is not surprising to find Hollywood movie productions that revolved around military service frequently featured the "mail call"—that period of the day in military camps, near the heat of battle, when sergeants delivered mail from home. Scenes of joy as soldiers received letters from home or utter dejection in the faces of those who waited anxiously, but in vain for communication from loved ones made memorable impressions and served to augment our resolve not to disappoint our relatives and friends.

The importance of receiving letters from home in bolstering morale was more than propaganda. Leading political figures, civic leaders, teachers, and newspapers regularly reminded readers of their obligation in this regard. Students in my sister's public school class were encouraged to write to servicemen—brothers or cousins whose names and addresses were supplied by students and placed on bulletin boards. Indeed, the value of writing letters to servicemen was brought home to my sister when Tullio and Gemma DeMichele, who lived on the third floor above us, came to ask her to write to their son Augie who was away in the Navy Seabees. Since they could not write in English, they depended on my sister who happily fulfilled the chore. Another example of how this played out on a community level took place in the Orchard House, a settlement house in the heart of Glen Cove, Long Island's Little Italy. Once a week, a nun from St. Rocco Parochial School marshaled together young teenage girls after school to write letters to local servicemen. Taking their assignment seriously, the girls wrote to men in the service and kept them abreast of events in their neighborhood. One of the most extraordinary letter writing achievements was that of Queens resident Teresa Daniello, who convinced of the comforting value that letters from home represented to lonely young men, not only wrote regularly to her five sons in the service, but also to many of their comrades as well. Regarding her promise to write as a sacred responsibility, for three years she wrote an average of twenty-five letters per week, aided by her husband who enclosed them in envelopes, placed stamps on them, and posted them, Altogether, it is estimated she wrote 3,200 letters—probably a record of this kind of patriotic activity.[256]

Persuaded that letter writing was valuable and comforting to young soldiers thrust into strange and frequently hostile environments, I took the responsibility seriously and wrote more letters then than I ever had written before to several older friends who had been drafted, to acquaintances, and to a few cousins serving in the military. Interestingly, the correspondence was to people that I normally did not write to either before or after the war. Letters I received from servicemen confirmed their appreciation for hearing some news from back home. Most of the correspondence was of a trivial nature as I related current neighborhood events such as the names of the newest neighborhood inductees, local dances events, current movie favorites, or about popular bands that we had seen in the city. Nor was the subject matter that much more substantial in the missives my correspondents sent to me as they informed me of the trails and travails of basic training, or the seemingly inane assignments given them. Occasionally, my friends wrote about mores in different parts of the United States. Most interesting to me were those that revolved around front line combat. I remember one sent by Joe Basile, an acquaintance who had entered the army and who was caught up in the "Battle of the Bulge"—Germany's last ditch but ultimately futile effort to stop the American and British forces in December 1944. Joe's letter described the harshness and difficulty of combat in extremely cold weather—corroborating accounts of the cruel battle that I read about in the newspapers back home. Almost all letters that dealt with combat activities showed assiduous signs of concern for security as censorship agents blocked out references to specific locales and theaters of war.

Perhaps the most poignant aspect of letter writing was that involving mothers or fathers whose command of the English language, especially in written form, was non-existent and thus unable to communicate effectively with non-Italian speaking children. There were many such people in virtually every Italian enclave as indicated in the instance just related. In her charming article on her mother's letter-writing, Octavia Capuzzi Locke provides a vivid illustration of how an immigrant woman dressmaker, "became the neighborhood letter writer" first to her own son.

Every night she would sit at the big square table in the kitchen and write a letter to my brother who had been drafted the preceding summer and had not been heard from since "Pearl Harbor Day."

Mamma wrote the same letter every night. Her only concern was that perhaps Johnny couldn't understand what she wrote. Because while we were bilingual and Mamma could read both languages, her writing was Italian. "Maybe if I keep writing the same thing, one day he'll understand every word." Mamma would say "Anyway he'll read my name. He'll know it's from me."

Her faith was rewarded because in a couple of months she did receive word from Johnny away in the South Pacific. In due course, neighborhood Italian Americans learned about the persistent custom clothes maker letter writer and sought her help, especially those who were unable to write either in English or Italian.

Then one morning something happened that marked the beginning of a flood of letter writing which was to last long after the duration of the war. A little woman with gun metal hair knocked on the Mamma's door. She was wearing a black smock, and she carried a shopping bag over her arm. He voice trembled when she asked,

"Is it true that you write letters?"
"I write my sons."
"Do you read too?"
The woman whispered in awe, "Si si."

The woman opened her shopping bag and pulled out a stack of sealed air mail letters. She was terrified of them. "Read ... read them to me, please.

Mamma opened one letter and read it to the woman. It was written in English. It was from the woman's son, a boy with red hair, fighting in Europe. But the woman didn't understand, and she wrung her hands and wept. Mamma translated the letter into Italian.

> One by one, she translated all the others. The little wom-
> an's eyes sparkled. "Now I must answer," she said. But
> she couldn't write.

> "Does your boy understand Italian?'
> "That's all we speak at home."
> "Can he read Italian?"
> "I think he can, if its simple." ...

So Mamma told the woman that she would write a letter.

> One day, the little woman came to Mamma, and from
> the look in her eyes, Mamma knew what had happened.
> Mamma couldn't do anything except stare into the little
> woman's eyes, and see the hope had gone out from them.
> They sat together for some time, with their knees touch-
> ing and their hearts locked as one. Then Momma said,

> "Maybe we'd better go to church. There are some things
> too big for people to understand."[257]

For Joseph Bentivegna who grew up in a small town in Pennsylvania, it
was much the same as he became the informal letter writer for many of his
Italian American neighbors. He reveled in the role as one of the few townspeople who not only understood Italian, but also could write in English. He
became a local favorite because of the joy he could bring in reading letters
written in English to the basically Italian-speaking neighbors, informing
the parents what their children were doing, that they were in good health,
etc. Unfortunately, there were those few dreaded occasions when he would
have to tell a neighbor of a son who had been wounded and most dismaying
of all, when he brought messages of a loved one's death.[258]

IN RECOGNITION OF MILITARY SERVICE

Over the years, various estimates of the number of Italian Americans
who served in the armed services during the war have been offered; how-

ever, definitive authoritative figures are hard to come by. One recent research on the topic maintains that each army division contained at least 500 soldiers of Italian descent leading to a total of 750,000.[259] Difficult to substantiate, nevertheless from the outset of the war *Il Progresso Italo-Americano,* engaged in an effort to put the best possible face on ethnic group participation employing a tendency to inflate the numbers by undoubtedly grasping on what were obviously favorable estimates. Accordingly it proffered the testimony of army officials such as Major Benjamin Anuskewicz, administrator of New York's Selective Service Boards, who was profuse in his declamation of their loyalty. Anuskewicz referred to records of the Regular Army, which showed Italian American enlistment rates to be the largest of any ethnic group—that model became the basis for his impression that the percentage of Italian Americans in Army camps was far greater than their proportion of the population.[260] This was the view held by many who were under the impression that prior to the Selective Service Act, in the Second Corps Area, Italian American enlistment rates led all others.

The Italian language newspaper provided periodic statistics that purported to show that they counted for some 12% of the members in the armed forces as for example, an August 1943 reference to a projection that altogether 10 million Americans would be in uniform before the war ended. Since, in fact, there were over 14 million servicemen and women before the war ended, if one accepted the 12% proportion as a guide, then the number of Italian Americans would be well in excess of 1 million. Utilizing similar

Italian Americans on the home front cheered the awarding of the Congressional Medal of Honor to I. William Bianchi, the first of his nationality to achieve this coveted tribute.

rationale in November of the same year, allusion was made to the approximation rendered by an Army officer overseeing Army enlistments in New York City early in the war, who commended Italian American enlistees as comprising 40% of the total. Expressing his gratitude, Col. Arthur McDermott further opined, "God bless these good old fashioned Italian mothers who came to America, for they are giving us two, three, four, five and even more of their sons. Yes, and they make darn good soldiers, too. We can trustfully say they are among the best disciplined, courteous soldiers in the Army."[261] With the conclusion of the war, another *Il Progresso Italo-Americano* item further revealed the underlying theory in arriving at the rate of Italian American participation.

> We do not know the exact number of Italo-Americans called into the armies. But it is certain that it is not less than 750,000 men, approximately 15 percent of the Italo-American population of the United States, that is assumed by the last census of five million people. It is a very high percentage, higher than other ethnic groups in America. We have, instead, an exact index of the local Italo-Americans losses, offered by local New York newspapers that encompass a considerable part of the Metropolitan area, including outside New York; seven New Jersey counties and two counties in Connecticut. From one study, the tally of deaths and wounded in the area indicates they constitute 12 percent of the total population. The losses to the Italian American population according to the estimate of the above-mentioned lists attains to 24 percent of the total in some cases, while the medium losses is always above 20 percent. The percentage from every side is highest in relation to the number of Italo-Americans.[262]

In addition, the Italian language media maintained that not only were children of Italian extraction serving in extraordinarily high numbers, but they were also sustaining casualty rates in greater percentages to their portion of the population. Less than a year into the war, Italian American enclaves were erecting honor rolls in their neighborhoods and their churches to acclaim the ethnic contribution to the war effort. The Italian Catholic of the Church of the Nativity in Manhattan parish proudly referred to over 600 parish members in uniform, including two fatalities as a demonstration of uncommon patriotism.[263] Readers of New York's newspapers also quickly learned that the ethnic community was producing more than its share of heroes, such as Bronx Seaman William A. DeRosa who died while helping to save the lives of his comrades on a ill-fated ship, or that four Italian American soldiers were caught up in the problematical but heroic defense of Bataan, and that Sergeant Salvatore Battaglia, who had sacrificed his life for his fellow troops was labeled "hero of Little Italy" by the *New York Daily News*. "Thus, all is over, Sammy Battaglia. The lower East Side, for whom you are the 'the flying hero', knows its every hope and pride. Your mother knows it. Your father, your brother Louis and your two sisters know it well. They are sad, Sammy, Oh Lord! How proud they are today." Italian Americans read about Captain Sam Mauriello, "A man at twelve, a parachute jumper at seventeen, today a World War II hero, with the Distinguished Flying Cross for shooting down five Nazi airplanes". They also learned of the fantastic adventure of Brooklyn's Cpl. Peter Brescia who had been captured by the Germans in Tunisia and then incredibly, together with another soldier and two discarded rifles, turned the tables on their captors leading to the arrest of 100 enemy troops.[264]

As the war progressed, increasingly, Italian Americans on the home front honored ethnic servicemen cited by the press for their battlefield intrepidness. Thus, a *New York Sun* reporter, covering the war in North Africa, related the stirring account of Sgt. Frank Caprino, Corp. Anthony Ricciardi, Pvt. T. Cincotta, and Capt. Ciccolella of Brooklyn, whom he encountered at the Battle of Kasserine Pass in which they captured 88 German soldiers, and became the first to enter the town of Gafsi.[265] Coming in person to greet Sgt. Joseph Forti at New York's Pennsylvania Station, the mayor of New Brunswick, New Jersey held a special ceremony as the city's Number 1 hero, Waist gunner Forti, one of the most decorated members of the Air Force, was cited for his unstinting service in several theaters of war that earned him numerous wartime decorations. In March 1943, the large Italian enclave in Frank Sinatra's home town of Hoboken, came out en masse to pay tribute to the large contingent of Italian American servicemen and their parents for their contribution to the war effort. It prompted Hoboken Mayor Bernard McFeely to resort to stereo type as he emphasized the city's pride in its people from "Sunny Italy, land of Heroes, poets, and artists." Still another example was that of the Italian American community of Detroit, Michigan that conducted a drive to finance a Victory Mercy Ship in honor of Sailor Joseph Polizzi, the first of Italian descent in Detroit to lose his life in the war. Fittingly, the ship dedication took place at the foot of the city's Columbus Monument with city dignitaries joining the Polizzi family.[266]

One of the most astonishing stories of an unsung hero unearthed by the Italian language press was that of Pvt. Richard Romano whose father had served in the First World where he lost his life as did two of his brothers in the Second World War. Richard had enlisted in the British armed forces in 1939, was credited with shooting down eleven enemy planes, and was shot down himself a number of times, lost an eye and was grounded. He managed to join the British Commandos where because of other wounds, he was discharged. Classified 4-F upon his return to the United States, he once again managed to join the Army—a background that prompted excessive praise. "Such is the spirit of our American soldiers—such contributions to the Army by our young men of Italian origin."[267] Whether the American public at large was conscious of these names, it was certain that the Roosevelt Administration was well aware as Attorney General Biddle used his Columbus Day speech to laud Battaglia and recent Congressional Medal of Honor winner William Bianchi for their heroism in combat.

DEALING WITH LINGERING DENIGRATION

Although Italian American wartime participation did much to win general acceptance, there were always pockets of prejudice with which the ethnic group had to deal. One example involved the vicious remarks of Mississippi's Senator Theodore Bilbo in response to Josephine Piccolo, an Italian American woman from Brooklyn who had the temerity to criticize him for his opposition to a fair employment practices bill. Bilbo had the sheer gall to address her as "My Dear Dago," ushering an immediate Italian American response. Another letter writer, Teresa Daniello, reminded Bilbo that her sons and thousands of other Italian American soldiers, while proud of their ethnic heritage, fought valiantly for the American cause. Fiery Congressman Vito Marcantonio assailed Bilbo's tactics as exactly the type used by Nazis and Fascists, demanding an apology, and pointing out that the Brooklyn woman had three brothers in the services, one of whom died. The arch segregationist senator not only refused to apologize, but further criticized Marcantonio.[268]

Although not a Marcantonio supporter, *Il Progresso Italo-Americano* joined in the denunciation of Bilbo by suggesting he read the reports of the many Italian American heroes fighting in defense of the United States, like Lt. J.K. Barbieri who performed heroically in Okinawa. "Even Lt. Barbieri is a "dago" as are "dagos" super-ace Captain Gentile and Sergeant D'Alessandro, decorated with the highest honor for his bravery in action, as is "dago" Sergeant Basilone, who returned honored in glory in the lower Pacific, who voluntarily returned to the line of fire, and lost his life for the honor of the stars and stripes."[269]

CAPRA

The contribution of certain individual Italian Americans was noteworthy, if ironic. A case in point was famed Hollywood director Frank Capra who was born in 1897 in Bisaquino, Sicily, and came with his family to Ellis Island in 1903, and eventually settled in Los Angeles. Following his service in the American Army during the First World War that earned instant citizenship, Frank worked in a variety of jobs and attended college before he entered the newly emerging movie industry working in the background as prop assistant, film cutter, and gag writer for silent films. His opportunity came in 1933, when he directed a comedy that he followed with "It Happened One Night," winner of academy awards in five categories including best director. The list of succeeding films he directed that won critical acclaim include "Mr. Deed Goes to Town, (1936); "Lost Horizon" (1937); You Can't Take it With You" (1938); "Mr. Smith Goes to Washington" (1939); "Meet John Doe"(1941); "Arsenic and Old Lace" (1944); and "It's a Wonderful Life" (1946). The latter film that celebrates the essential goodness of the individual, the family, and the community served to reinforce fundamental values; it has become a classic that is shown regularly at Christmas time into the 21st century. Capra won Oscars for best director three times for commercial films and was also nominated three other times for the same award.

During the Second World War, despite the government's designation of his Italian-born non-citizen sister Ann as an "enemy alien", Frank Capra once again demonstrated his patriotism. Even before Pearl Harbor, the Department of Justice called upon him and other Italian Americans, such as Fiorello LaGuardia, sculptor Attilio Piccirilli, bandleader Guy Lombardo, singer Frank Sinatra, and airplane designer Giuseppe Bellanca, to demonstrate their allegiance in a Justice Department-sponsored "I'm an American" radio program. Capra once again enlisted in the Army where he became a major and produced a number of wartime propaganda movies that also won awards.

> Capra's "Why We Fight" films "were intended to be shown to servicemen in order to educate and clarify for them the reasons for United States involvement in the Second World War. The choice of Capra, an Italian immigrant and naturalized U. S. citizen, to oversee the series is an interesting one. The Army could easily have delegated the project to another Hollywood filmmaker like John Huston or John Ford (both of whom had enlisted) or even a documentarian like Pare Lorentz, but instead they chose Capra. One can only assume that Capra's prior credits

like *Mr. Smith Goes to Washington* (1939), a film that led one critic to label Capra "a sentimental reverent patriot at heart," played a key role in his selection. However, it seems likely that Capra's well-known and well-publicized ethnic background would also have made him the person to undertake the project. Here was Capra, an Italian by birth, telling Americans why his new homeland of the United States was the right country to back in a confrontation with his former homeland. Certainly that added some credibility to the film's rhetorical stance, even if viewers were not shown credits on prints of the films.[270]

There is every indication that Capra, aware of the stereotypes Hollywood used to depict Italians, sought to soften and subtly change the images. In contradistinction to Germans and Japanese who were depicted as wholeheartedly behind Hitler and Hirohito, Italians were regarded as being exploited by the dictator. Capra endeavored to discourage audiences from connecting Mussolini and his fascist supporters with rank and file Italians and Italian Americans who were treated more benignly—"In Italy, then the problem is Mussolini while in Germany and Japan the problem is national identity."[271] Accordingly, "Why We Fight" films eschewed references to Italians as "wops" or "dagoes", or insinuations that they were lazy, sex-preoccupied, or always overeating. Capra's films "not only determines the reasons for U.S. involvement in World War II, but also establishes greater respect for the Italian community in the United States."[272]

To aver that Italian Americans welcomed the content of Capra's message is an understatement. Although Capra was not an overriding household name within Italian American homes at the time, we all desired a more positive image for the ethnic group. So starved were we for affirmative portrayals of Italian names on the screen that we extended that empathy to those, who regardless of their nationality, played them effectively. One such instance that my friends and I deeply appreciated was in Hollywood's production of the war movie "Sahara" that featured movie favorite Humphrey Bogart, but we also found notable for the role of talented Irish American actor, J. Carroll

Naish. Filmed in 1943, the movie described the adventures of a tank commander (Bogart), who cut off from his unit following the Allied defeat at the Battle of Tobruk, meandered through Libya in search of water and picked up various individuals along the way, one of whom was Giuseppe (Naish), a repentant and humane Italian soldier. Stabbed in the back by a hard-line Nazi prisoner, Giuseppe alerts Bogart before he dies. The sympathetic portrayal of a compassionate but doomed Italian war prisoner, desperately trying to survive in a losing cause in North Africa, won Naish a nomination for an Academy Award for best supporting actor—it also won our compassion for one of the more appealing portrayals of Italians on the screen.

A BELL FOR ADANO

Another memorable film that I remember seeing and that I thought portrayed Italians and Italian Americans caught up in the war rather sympathetically was John Hersey's Pulitzer Prize (1945 Fiction) winner, *A Bell for Adano*. Starring John Hodiak and Gene Tierney, this is a somewhat bittersweet novel about Major Victor Joppolo, an Italian American from the Bronx, who was placed in charge of Adano, Sicily, and wins over jaded townspeople when he replaced the 700-year-old town bell that the Fascists melted down for bullets. The major also imparts lessons about democracy.[273] To become aware that the film's theme was derived from an authentic Italian American source rendered the movie even more acceptable. In spite of the usual parody about Italians, and notwithstanding the fictitious names of Adano and Joppolo, the story was indeed roughly based on the real life drama of Col. Frank E. Toscani. Born in the Bronx to Italian immigrant parents, he had worked for the local sanitation department until he entered the Army when World War II began, and became major in the 3rd Infantry Division headed by General George S. Patton. Since Major Toscani possessed knowledge of the Italian language and customs, Patton promptly named him American Military Governor of Licata, Sicily, and as such, at only thirty-two years of age, Toscani became the youngest official of such a grade in the army of occupation. In a short period of time, To-scani proved himself to be an appealing conciliator as well as responsive to humane needs.

In the course of his duties, Toscani was approached by a delegation of the townspeople, who he suspected they would ask for food because everyone was hungry. Their request surprised him—they wanted a bell—the Italian army had melted down their bell, and so there was no way to signal the births, deaths, marriages, and the beginning of liturgical celebrations. A week later, Toscani mentioned the need to some naval officers; a bell was found on one of the destroyers and given to the villagers who acted as if a miracle was taking place. A clear indication of how Toscani endeared himself to the townspeople could be gleaned in an account of his farewell dinner that saw Licata's grateful mayor with unabashed tears flowing wishing him well.[274] As a war correspondent then in Licata, Hersey witnessed the unusual event and modeled his Major Joppolo after him. Ironically, Toscani was soon transferred to Palermo and did not then see the bell installed. Years later, in 1962, he was invited back to Licata where for three continuous days, townspeople rang the bell each hour in his honor. Later in an interview, he said "Sometimes I think I can still hear it."

PROMOTING CITIZENSHIP

Attorney General Biddle's enunciation of the termination of the "enemy alien" label on Columbus Day 1942 was gratefully received in the Italian community. With the way now open for tens of thousands to obtain citizenship papers, the ethnic group responded enthusiastically as 250,000 obtained citizenship in 1942 and 318,000 in 1943—the latter constituting the greatest number since the peak prior year of 1907. Italian Americans on the home front were active in this patriotic promotion. Women in Greenwich Village, for example, formed neighborhood clubs to promote citizenship, schools sponsored citizenship classes, while news accounts exulted in the record numbers of Italian Americans who became Americans officially and swore allegiance to their adopted country. In Italian enclaves throughout the country, the response was enthusiastic, occasionally tinged with ironic tragic twists as in the case of the proud Italian father of five servicemen who looked forward to obtaining his citizenship papers, only to fall dead on the morning of their issuance.[275] Thousands within the ethnic group could now do their part by joining the Civilian Defense Corps, continuing their efforts in defense plants, and joining the armed services. Notwithstanding the elusiveness of corroboration, the number of Italian Americans attributed to the armed services is indeed remarkable. *Il Progress Italo Americano* consistently reported extraordinary numbers within months of Pearl Harbor: 400,000 in June 1942, of whom 60,000 were sons of non-citizens; 500,000 in September 1942, of whom 70,000 were from "enemy alien" parents. Even Attorney General Biddle, in his 1942 Columbus Day speech declaring an end to the "enemy alien" classification, referred to 500,000 Italian American servicemen, 75,000 of whom came from homes of non-citizens.[276]

SICILIAN AMERICAN HOME FRONT SPAWNS INTELLIGENCE OPERATIONS

A little-known but important endeavor that was virtually exclusive to the ethnic group, one which underscored the Italian-American patriotic essence, was that of utilizing their linguistic, cultural, and familial connections to promote American victory. From various "Little Italies", many an Italian American served in military activity that required extensive knowledge of the Italian language, and thus served as translators, or wrote propaganda material in the ancient language. Gathering of vital military intelligence was another significant activity unique to the ethnic group, one that expressed itself in an unexpected way in Middletown, Connecticut in a peculiar form of espionage. Although I was not conscious of it at the time—indeed because of the secret nature of the enterprise Americans, in general, were unaware of it until many years later—fortuitously, I became cognizant of the operation in the generation following the war as a result of teaching courses on the Italian American experience at Wesleyan University, Middletown, Connecticut, where Frank Tarallo, one of my more affable older students, enlightened me on the subject. Just under six feet, with ample-sized arms and legs, powerful neck, face and head, the mustachioed dark olive-skinned World War II veteran, even in middle age, revealed a football player physique. He was, in fact, a star football player for Middletown High School, and recruited with a scholarship by the University of Alabama for its football squad, where he played until an injury cut short a career in the sport—he continued his education and graduated. Tarallo was thoroughly Sicilian American, one conversant with the Sicilian language and customs, and one who had a host of relatives in Melilli. The more I became acquainted with his story, the more I realized it was a significant chapter in the untold story of Italian Americans on the home front. The fact that this was an essentially Sicilian American operation that helped the war effort exceedingly struck a responsive chord with me because of my own Sicilian background.

Located in central Connecticut, Middletown in the late nineteenth century began to attract so many Italian immigrants that by 1941, they became the largest single element in the community. The overwhelming majority were descendants from Melilli, Sicily, a town founded by Greeks in eastern Sicily.[277] Moreover, although most Middletown families retained strong

bonds with family members in the old country, there was no hesitation

Frank Tarallo, (second from right) and Max Corvo (lower right), Sicilian Americans from Middletown, Connecticut joined in OSS operation with actor Douglas Fairbanks Jr. (lower third from right).

when the United States entered war. Sicilian Americans not only volunteered in the regular armed forces, but also served as the inspiration for launching a striking intelligence operation that would facilitate invasion and liberation of the island of Sicily and the entire Italian nation. Biagio (Max) Corvo, a short, energetic, loquacious, and confident Middletowner, was the catalyst for the plan.[278]

In his autobiographical account, Corvo relates how he foresaw that a successful Allied invasion force required development of subversive warfare—an effort to which he committed his energies unstintingly.[279] Sicilian-born Max was the son of Cesare Corvo, militant anti-Fascist editor and publisher of the Middletown *Bolletino* (Bulletin), whom he assisted in publishing the Italian-language paper, thereby acquiring extensive knowledge of political issues as well as the acquaintance of many anti-Fascist activists. He joined the Army in 1942, and remarkably concocted an ingenious plan to engage Sicilian American,s who were familiar with the Sicilian language, colloquiums, and characteristics, and whose relatives lived in Sicily, to gather intelligence. This information would then be transmitted to the military as it planned the invasion of Sicily and the Italian mainland. A relatively simple plan, it was simultaneously bold and promising. As an indication of his resourcefulness, Corvo, although then only an army private, was able to gain a hearing from high administrators in the O.S.S. military intelligence apparatus then being spawned by Gen. William (Wild Bill) Donovan.[280]

Previously reliant on British intelligence services, on July 11, 1942, President Franklin D. Roosevelt entrusted Donovan with the important task of developing an American intelligence unit capable of conducting shadow warfare by accumulating a flow of knowledge that could support regular military operations.[281] Since Italy was one of the places where this service would be used, it was imperative to search for and utilize Italian-speaking personnel like Anthony Scariano, future member of the Illinois State legislature who enlisted for the Italian operation. "I was a young Italian American looking for adventure. Wild Bill Donovan of the OSS was looking for adventurous types. He wanted people who could speak Italian."[282]

By spring 1943, the Allies had developed "Husky"—a plan for the invasion of Sicily—aware "that they had no Italian or "Sicilian"-speaking personnel available."[283]. The problem was even more pronounced because incredibly, the Allies were noticeably deficient in establishing "close connections with significant Italian resistance organizations by the summer of 1943."[284] Infighting and competition between the regular Army and the O.S.S. undoubtedly contributed to the failure to utilize rapidly O.S.S. intelligence as did envy and anti-Italian American feelings. "Finding no other motivation, they attributed it to the fact that most of the recruits were of Italian origin and were not shy about being heard."[285]

Uncertainty seemed to characterize the situation. On the one hand, the Army, apparently becoming aware of the desirability of having specially trained personnel conversant with Italian culture, began an eight-month intensive program at Yale University to prepare personnel for assignment in Sicily and Italy, following the invasion. Sicilian-descended Brooklynite Barney Levantino was one of several Italian Americans selected for the program that concentrated on study of Italian languages, geography, economy, and customs in anticipation for duty to establish rapport with the Italian populace after American forces took over the country. Yet on the other hand, the very length of the program would seem to have negated its potential since it was abruptly terminated before the allotted time. The explanation given to Levantino was that the since the Italian people were so receptive to American forces, the special program was no longer needed. His training in Italian culture was not wasted, however, because he was then assigned to work with Italian prisoners of war in Pine Camp.[286]

The Sicily Campaign resolved to achieve Allied control of the central Mediterranean. Accordingly, Italian-American O.S.S. special operations, including men who had fled Sicily years before and now returned singing popular songs of the 1920s, began to arrive in the theater in force soon after the initial landings.[287] It was in connection with this critical purpose that Middletown's Sicilian Americans showed their remarkable resolve—namely to facilitate and render victorious "Husky"—the largest amphibious invasion in history up to that point—indeed, some aspects were larger than the better-known Normandy invasion of 1944. Fortunately, minimal but useful steps to correct the O.S.S. deficiency in Italian-speaking personnel had begun with the creation of the Italian Section of Special Intelligence (SI) whose administrator Earl Brennan, a diplomat with extensive experience in Italy, had learned about Corvo's plans for the invasion of Sicily, replete with a personally financed, homemade, and uncannily accurate topographical map highlighting the island's harbors, rivers, mountains, etc. Clearly, Brennan regarded Corvo as indispensable to the task. "As you may recall Max Corvo was my 'one man brain trust' from the beginning of the Italian Section, and later he made his enviable mark in the field ... "[288]

One example that confirmed Brennan's faith in Corvo was the knowledge that Corvo recruited men familiar with Sicilian language and customs— many of them were descendants from Melilli living in Middletown.[289] The recruits were, for the most part, professional and college-educated individuals such as Emilio Q. Daddario, Wesleyan University graduate, former Middletown mayor, future member of Congress, and candidate for governor of Connecticut. In addition, the included Middletowners Marine Captain Sebastian Passinisi, Catholic University graduate and Tarallo who later became my student. Tarallo entered the Army and soon was promoted to the rank of captain. In January 1943, Tarallo received an urgent message from his friend Corvo, who aware of his knowledge of Italian and the Sicilian dialect, requested that he join the Special Intelligence (S.I.) Italian Section, O.S.S. then being developed. Friends of many years, Corvo and Tarallo nurtured a deep filial attachment to Sicily. As Tarallo put it,

> We were always talking about Melilli, Sicily. It was natural because our parents were Sicilians and from Melilli.
> I had never been there but was well acclimated because

> whenever I stopped at the *Bolletino* office, there were
> maps of Sicily on the wall and all sorts of literature.[290]

These experiences augured well for the projected plans of the Italian Section that were designed to have properly trained men who could penetrate enemy-held territory, blend in and mix with the native population, sometimes even contact relatives and friends, and thus obtain vital military information. The SI unit was really a cross of regular military professionals like Tarallo and others who were less military—that is, "they were really military in name only", and not expected to enter into combat, but rather garner intelligence.[291] Once the SI unit was assembled, it reported to Allied Headquarters in Algiers, North Africa, where it coordinated activities with G-2, Army Intelligence in General George Patton's command. In a typical operation, Patton's headquarters would request combat intelligence from SI; Corvo, in turn, would assign Tarallo and his infiltration men to learn about German troop concentrations, heavily fortified positions, and other peculiar obstacles that invading Allied forces might encounter in enemy-occupied Sicily. Tarallo "would study the situation, then at night under cover of darkness, go in a jeep to the front lines and the team knew what the consequences would be if we were caught."[292]

The importance of such intelligence gathering became evident during the invasion of Sicily as Italian military forces "had virtually ceased to exist. Although thousands of Italians were happily sitting in Allied POW cages, while other thousands had simply doffed their uniforms and melted into the civilian population," there were nevertheless, 60,000 German troops in Sicily who presented a formidable obstacle that caused the Allied campaign to bog down.[293] Any information that Corvo, Tarallo, and SI could obtain was extremely important. Accordingly, Tarallo and his SI men filtered into enemy-occupied southern Sicily in the coastal region of Gela and Licata. There they met with Sicilians who welcomed them because they spoke in their dialect and demonstrated familiarity with the local customs and culture, and were thereby able to glean information as to road-blockages, demolitions, mine-fields, ammunition dumps, concentration of German forces, etc. They also succeeded in recruiting some Sicilians to serve as local agents supplying additional valuable military information.

As to the question of whether or not Italian American individuals with criminal background assisted Allied operations in Sicily, opinions vary with some writers maintaining that notwithstanding his notoriety, Lucky Luciano did indeed have a hand in paving the way for American intelligence efforts. Other historians acknowledge it is a murky area. "The question of the American Mafia's contribution to the liberation of Sicily is clouded with ambiguity and contradiction."[294] Corvo and Tarallo were adamant in their denial that these elements, especially that Lucky Luciano, had any role whatsoever with the OSS. Understandably, SI personnel had some misgivings in carrying out their missions in Sicily—the land of their parents and ancestors—mindful that they might be fighting against their own relatives.

> It was a traumatic experience in a way because we knew that villages were being bombed and there was a war going on. I knew that I had cousins that I had never seen but that they were about my age. Whenever we had prisoners I was always looking for names to see if any were my relations. If they were and did have some [military] experience, then we would recruit them."[295]

These emotional feelings were mitigated, however, in the knowledge that they were liberating Sicily.

As the Allied conquest of Sicily proceeded to a successful conclusion, it occasionally afforded opportunities for extended families to reunite or to meet in person those whom they knew only by hearsay. One of these remarkably benevolent moments occurred when Corvo granted Tarallo and Fiorillo a three-day pass to visit their relatives in Melilli. Borrowing an Army jeep loaded with gifts of food and sporting two-week old beards, they proceeded to drive to the town in eastern Sicily. Upon reaching the plaza at Melilli, they were struck by an extraordinary spectacle in the person of an old man sitting on a chair holding a book in his lap. Tarallo recalled, "I was going to ask him for directions when all of a sudden he jumped up and said "figlio mio, figlio mio". It was my grandfather holding my high school picture in his lap. That was traumatic."[296] Although the grandfather and the Army officer from Middletown had never before met, and in spite of an absence of communication between them prior to this, the grandfather was certain Frank was coming—they immediately recognized each other. Among other Middletowners who likewise met close relatives were Max Corvo and Pvt. Louis Fiorilla, the latter was reunited with his uncle Fr. Fiorilla, the parish priest of Melilli. Ever on the lookout for possible agents, Tarallo scrutinized his relatives, but since they were for the most part country folk, he could find no one who possessed the requisite training for espionage.

RACIAL AND ETHNIC PROBLEMS; JUVENILE DELINQUENCY

While events of great moment were taking place on the battlefront, on the home front, young people of my generation were affected by a number of other issues, including racial problems and juvenile delinquency. Abnormality in wartime effectively exacerbated racial conflict with worrisome racial and ethnic consequences for society in general, and with particular impact on home front Italian Americans. For African Americans, the Second World War provided the backdrop to further promote equality. Dealing with entrenched views about racial segregation that were vivid in the South's Jim Crow laws, African Americans also regarded de facto segregation in the North as unsatisfactory. Threatening a massive march on Washington, they extrapolated from Roosevelt, the Fair Employment Practices Committee (FEPC) that prohibited discrimination on account of race, creed, color, or national origin of workers in defense industries or in government employ. Although FEPC did successfully resolve a number of cases, it nevertheless had limited impact.

Housing was one of a number of other trials between the races. "The migration of blacks and whites into urban centers of war productions strained housing and transportation facilities. Blacks found their housing choices limited, and therefore concentrated in ghetto areas that became strained to the breaking point."[297] The result in certain northern cities was race riots—the most serious in Detroit in June 1943, which cost the lives of twenty-five blacks and nine whites. We read about the incidents, saw gory photographs of the accompanying ugliness in the tabloids back home in Brooklyn, and also spoke to those who witnessed riots in Harlem in August that same year, which resulted in the death of six African Americans and hundreds of injuries. Vivid memories of the ugly riots between African Americans and Italian Americans in Harlem in 1935 caused Mayor LaGuardia to assign a third of city's police force in the area; he also obtained Governor Dewey's support to place several thousand state guardsmen on alert.[298]

The riots reflected long simmering resentment over social, economic, and particularly housing issues that had ripple effect even in my high school where there was a sizeable minority of African American students, alongside a considerable number of Italian Americans. With emotions mounting because of the notoriety of race riots roiling the country, one day, word went throughout the institution that after school, a fight between blacks and whites was to ensue. Carried forward by the emotion of the crowd in front of the high school, I found myself in the front line of whites taunting the blacks—it was hardly my finest hour since I really had no problems with any of them. Fortunately, alert teachers and administrators moved in and dispersed us before any serious violence occurred.

Although there was not then a huge Hispanic element in my Brooklyn neighborhood, we were aware of and somewhat conflicted about California riots we read about and the movie newsreels that featured United States sailors and Mexican Americans. These disturbances were known as "Zoot Suit" riots because of the distinctive dress of Mexican youth that featured long jackets and pants that were very wide at the knees, but extremely narrow at the ankle. On the one hand, as wearers of zoot suits ourselves, we could not logically register criticism because of their attire beyond that of disparaging their clothing as exaggerated. On the other hand, we denounced their clashes with sailors as harmful to the war effort.

JUVENILE DELINQUENCY

It was perceived that juvenile delinquency increased during the war-time environment that found many young people on their own because of parents' work or military obligations or because young people were increasingly employed in a labor-starved economy. Moral preceptors decried the practice of married women with children working in defense plants because it resulted in absence from the home where young children were unsupervised and neglected. In some ethnic neighborhoods, social workers associated with local settlement houses developed programs to bolster traditional family relationships. For my family, such concern was ironic because after my father's death my mother became the breadwinner and had no choice, but to go out to work. We were not left alone, however, since my mother paid a small amount of money to a neighbor to watch over us.

Most members of the older generation believed that the problems of youth were getting out of hand; however, the alarmist perception, is debatable.[299] According to one study, one in five schoolboys aged fourteen and fifteen, and two in five aged sixteen and seventeen were gainfully employed. Understandably, this disruption of normal adolescent development had societal implications, and although officials like Mayor LaGuardia initially attempted to downplay the extent of the problem within the city, the reality was otherwise. My high school, along with most city schools, conducted systematic programs warning us of the perils of juvenile delinquency by urging us to stay in school and avoid truancy. In addition, some neighborhood youngsters took advantage of programs offered by the community center run by our parish.

While juvenile delinquency impacted the nation in general, it had particular bearing on Italian Americans prompting a New York City Parole Board official to offer a disturbing yet discerning analysis in which he lamented the lack of religious training as playing an extremely important role. He observed, in addition, that for the ethnic group the crisis could be traced to young people who came from good homes, with hardworking parents, but were nevertheless, embarrassed about them. "Unfortunately, however, some of these young people are ashamed of their parents. The reason for this seems to be because the youngsters have had an American education and their parents have been brought up 'the old fashioned way.' But that way has been proven to be a good, honest way."[300] To my everlasting regret, I too temporarily suffered embarrassment over my mother's broken English whenever she spoke to non-Italians. Fortunately, this was a short-lived period and really did not reflect fundamental feelings that I, along with others whose parents also had limited English facility, shared. Although sometimes the objects of teasing in an atmosphere that celebrated Americanism, and thus subject to scrutiny that might well have caused us to rebel or escape, that did not happen. Even though I do not recall a community center near where I lived, in other Italian neighborhoods like the Bronx, such institutions were established to assist Italian American teenagers in combating juvenile delinquency. For example, the Belmont Community Center developed programs that sponsored a baseball team and boxing matches, which included professional boxers from the community such as Tami Mauriello. It also provided the facilities, including a library, juke box, radio, and a room for meetings.[301] The social environment on Himrod Street was, for the most part, considerate even if narrow. We knew and liked the fact that we were children of Italian immigrants.

Chapter VI
In Search of Heroes

The Liberation of Italy

By early 1943, Italy's liberation had become a preoccupation in the Italian American home front where for some time, the prospective invasion of Sicily was emerging a lively topic of speculation and rumors of such an eventuality accelerated. For months, leaders in the ethnic community had been active in promoting a drumbeat of calls for an invasion, confidently offering assurances that Italians would willingly welcome the move. "More and more the invasion weathervanes are pointing to Italy. The air is thick with rumors," was the way *Il Progresso Italo-Americano,* described it.[302] This view was reinforced by English language newspaper reports that analyzed and described patterns of air raid attacks as a sure signpost of the future course of war and "suggested strongly that Sicily may soon become the next objective of the 1943 Allied land forces."[303]

Messages From Home Front to Italy

From the beginning of the war, home front Italian Americans played important roles in communicating messages to Italy via short wave radio program schedules that were broadcasted to the Italian populace three times a day. In an effort to sway Italian public opinion, Italian American speakers on the home front, resorting to their ancient language, informed listeners in Italy about the contributions of their blood relatives to the achievement of an Allied victory—especially the patriotism that found so many of the young people of Italian ancestry in the armed forces. Clearly distinguishing between the Italian Fascist dictatorship and the Italian people burdened by Mussolini, the broadcasts sought to encourage listeners to hope and work for liberation. Many an Italian American leader spoke to Italians in this manner, including Mayor LaGuardia, for example, who used his influential voice to appeal to members of the Italian Navy not to resist the Allies and was believed to have made considerable impact.[304]

One of the more effective messages was that of Baltimore's Congressman Thomas. D'Alessandro, Jr., who in September 1942 broadcasted a stirring radio speech to the Italian people, reminding them that because they opposed Germany during the First World War, his hope was they would soon do the same against Nazi Germany.

> Today, twenty-six years later, you have lost your liberty, and justice has fled from your land. Yours is well-named the largest German-occupied nation in Europe, for your government, while nominally called the partner of the Nazis, has in fact sold your food, your clothes, your homes, and your lives to Adolph Hitler ... Today the millions of Americans whose vein flow with the same blood as yours, call upon you to join them and to join the United Nations and to turn from the false gods who are destroying you.[305]

To Italian Americans on the home front, such communications were not only highly desirable, but also important in bringing about an end to the Italian Fascist regime.

Ugo Carusi's broadcasts proved to be among the most influential messages sent by home front Italian Americans to Italy. In addition to his regular Friday broadcast in which he presented the American viewpoint and encouraged partisan activities, he also made noteworthy appeals on special anniversaries and other occasions. Writing near the end of the war, columnist Drew Pearson affirmed that these psychological pleadings rendered an exceptional service.

> U.S. officials have just received proof that Carusi's short-wave talks in 1942, 1943, and 1944 were extremely successful. They encouraged the Italian patriots to fight the Nazis and assisted in inducing the surrender of Italian forces to the Allies.
>
> One Italian army colonel, now a prisoner of war in a camp near St. Louis, has revealed that he surrendered, with his entire force, as a direct result of Carusi's radio appeal to the Italians in Tunisia to lay down their arms to the Allies. "Not a shot was fired," the colonel reported ... Another Italian officer in the same camp revealed that he had been learning English by translating Carusi's shortwave broadcast scripts.[306]

ITALY INVADED

With Allied forces compelling Axis armies to retreat, and with the success of "Torch," the amphibious operation that by the end of 1942 landed American and British troops in North Africa, it was increasingly apparent that the fortunes of war were going against Italy and its partners. With May 13, 1943 marking the formal end of the North African campaign, the attention of military planners now focused on Italy, particularly Sicily. The result was the "Husky" operation—the invasion of Sicily by air and sea on July 10, 1943, that as previously described, was significantly facilitated by Italian American intelligence operations and constituted the next nail pounded into Mussolini's war machine coffin. Largely a clandestine operation, there were contemporary reports that revealed such sufficient knowledge about the forthcoming operation that astoundingly, within days of the invasion of Sicily, columnist Pearson wrote a succinct and informed report that confirmed the critical role of Italian Americans.

> Greatest tribute in the invasion of Sicily should go to cer-
> tain unheralded heroes who paved the way in advance.
> They were Italo-Americans who spoke Italian, knew
> Sicily and did most of the dangerous work of any war,
> behind-the-lines sabotage of the enemy. It is no military
> secret that these operations are and must be carried on by
> the American Army in every theater of the war. But in
> Sicily they were especially effective because the Army en-
> listed the patriotism and bravery of Italo-American boys.
> Many of them of them had never been in Sicily. Some
> had friends or relatives there. Some of them spoke Italian
> with such an American accent that they had to brush up
> their language before undertaking such a dangerous mis-
> sion. The manner in which they were sent to Sicily well
> in advance of the Allied landing must remain a secret.
> But once there it was the job of these unsung heroes to
> blow arsenals, bridges over which the enemy might bring
> troops, and lay plans for civilian revolt. This undoubtedly
> was one reason why certain key civilian leaders acted so
> promptly in helping the Allied invasion.[307]

That Italian Americans in New York's home front responded to the
news of the invasion of Italy positively was evident in the outpouring
of American flags and broad smiles in the ethnic communities as well
as cheers of exultation, such as "wonderful," and "tickled to death."[308]
Notwithstanding the bravery and crucial role of Americans of Italian ancestry back on the home front, the Italian ethnic group, especially those
of us of Sicilian roots, continued to endure defamation and insult from
well-known publications. A column in the widely read weekly *The New
Yorker*, demonstrated its own innate haughtiness when it facetiously
opined that it was serving its readership with truthful knowledge in writing about the intrinsic failings that constituted the fabric of Sicilian and
Sardinian society—shortcomings that caused even other Italians to shun
them. It trotted out the old vicious canard about Sicily as a land in which

murder and untruth reign, where religion is debased and from which no one "has ever made a place for himself in history."[309] The positive and valuable accomplishments that constituted Sicily's history were entirely overlooked, as was the admirable military role played by its citizenry to defeat the Germans. It was comforting to us on the home front that at least some sources acknowledged the importance of Italians to the Allied cause once Mussolini's government was destroyed. "It is a significant commentary on dictatorship that, whereas the cowardice of Mussolini's men has been the butt of jokes from Guadalcanal to El Alamein and Bizerte, thousands of our own immigrant Italians, fighting for America, have been in the front rank of the battle for freedom in both the Pacific and Atlantic theaters."[310]

While Italian military resistance in Sicily rapidly melted away, resistance on the part of German forces on the island remained formidable, but in the end unavailing as the conquest of the island was completed in a matter of weeks, thereby assuring greater safety to Allied shipping in the Mediterranean, and also providing a nearby springboard for the invasion of the Italian mainland. Albeit a degree of controversy abounded about the strategy of extensive and exhaustive Allied involvement in Italy, the consensus view "is inclined to agree with those who say that if a primary aim of the invasion of Sicily and Italy was to divert German troops from action elsewhere, that purpose was accomplished."[311] These developments encouraged Italian Americans on the home front to press for steps designed to alleviate suffering in liberated areas, and simultaneously pressured the government for ready acceptance of Italians who took up arms to now fight alongside with American and British forces against the Germans. Generally speaking, Americans were much more willing to accept the latter while the British demonstrated a hard line position.

VINDICATION PURSUIT

From the Italian American viewpoint, the course of the war had been progressing satisfactorily toward the end of 1943. The portentous threat that the Axis powers previously represented had diminished as the Allies successfully blunted their outward aggressive moves and were now bringing the war closer to the enemy home territories. Americans were doing their part, churning out weapons of war in the nation's factories and plants, conserving scarce defense items, and buying bonds that resulted in financing such a prodigious amount of production of war material that, in effect, it rendered this country the indisputable arsenal of democracy. Of particular significance in 1943 was the fact of Mussolini's ouster that presaged the expectation that Italy would soon be out the war and perhaps join the Allies in their crusade. Strangely, Italian American reaction to the momentous events varied—with the Chicago ethnic community responding enthusiastically to Mussolini's downfall while New York's historic Little Italy response was more subdued.

> The residents of Manhattan's Italian sections took the news of Mussolini's ouster without much show of emotion. They were happy about it and hoped it would mean that Italy would soon be out of the war. Along Mulberry Street, for example, women discussed the matter on the stoops or seated on chairs in the streets. From their appearance they might just as well have been talking about the weather. The men continued with their card games, smoking and sipping beer. The children showed no letup in their games of 'commando." In short, a stranger would never have known that an important news event had just occurred.[312]

The jaded *New York Times* reporter proceeded to describe the neighborhood people as slightly animated for a group photograph, but otherwise "reacted pretty much as did most Americans." With so many of their sons in the armed services, a reality evidenced by multitudinous large American service flags and numerous stars in the windows, it thereby rendered any suggestion or question of regret over Mussolini's demise as foolish. Because so many in the area were of Sicilian origin, they were particularly bitter at Mussolini for the destruction that their home region had suffered.

Like Americans throughout the land, their primary concern was the welfare of their sons in the armed service.

Following Mussolini's ouster, Italian King Emmanuel appointed Marshall Pietro Badoglio, premier. The former Chief of General Staff of the Italian Army tried to lead the nation in disengaging itself from Germany and the war, while simultaneously retaining international influence. An extremely difficult task, in the end, Badoglio had to accept the unconditional surrender theme pressed upon him by General Eisenhower.

HOME FRONT REACTION TO FALL OF ITALY

Following the September 8, 1943 announcement that Italy had formally joined in the war on the side of the United Nations, Italian American jubilation was much more enthusiastic. The event was likened to Armistice Day in 1918, especially in Italian neighborhoods as pictures of joyous lower East Side Italian Americans extending themselves from pennant-decorated windows or in the streets waving Italian and American flags in celebration adorned news accounts, while newspaper editorials predicted this development would inspire Italian Americans to greater efforts. As if to underscore the patriotic boost on that day, dozens of Italian American workers in Brooklyn's Beatrice Waist and Dress Company, purchased $4,100 worth of War Bonds with proprietor Dominick Azzaro, himself buying $2,500 of them.[313] Mayor LaGuardia voiced the view that the event would mark the beginning of a new Italy, while leading exile Carlo Sforza used the occasion to call for an end to the Italian monarchy. Brooklyn Assemblyman Charles Beckinella commented "It is a marvelous thing for Italians in the entire world. Italians did not want this war; they are a peaceful people." Other Italian American leaders, such as Judge Ferdinand Pecora and James J. Freschi, called for assistance to Italy, while renowned conductor Arturo Toscanini commented "Finalmente," as he announced he would conduct a "Victory Concert."[314] New York's Italian Americans were overjoyed because it would now mean that Italy was no long an enemy nation.

BATTLEFIELD ROLES

While Italian Americans were engaged in important home front activity, overall these accomplishments received limited attention in the English language press compared to conspicuous battlefront triumphs. Even battlefield roles in which Italian Americans played critical roles received inadequate attention—their place in facilitating the invasion of the Italian mainland at Salerno is a case in point. English Prime Minister Winston Churchill effectively described the difficulties confronting the Allied forces in the Salerno Campaign that began at dawn September 9, 1943, in which German forces disarmed Italian troops and undertook defense themselves. "Our men were met by well-aimed fire as they waded ashore, and they suffered heavily. It was difficult to provide proper air-cover for them, as many of our fighters were operating at extreme range from Sicily ... "[315] American forces found themselves under terrific punishment from German troops who held higher elevations while British forces, south of the engagement yet hoping to encircle the enemy, were unaware of the shortest route. At this juncture, Brennan and his Italian American component in the O.S.S., that had long prepared for this operation but had been given little cooperation, stepped in. The result was that contact was made with the Italian general, who agreed to lead the British on a shortcut to rescue American forces at Salerno.[316]

Although there was some mention of this episode among Italian American sources on the home front, it was deemed not sensational enough for ethnic group representatives who were constantly seeking out far more dramatic examples to demonstrate front line Italian American loyalty. They were, in other words, in search of battlefield heroes that could become household names on the home front. Tom Brokaw in his deservedly popular *The Greatest Generation* provides a useful commentary on the misuse of "hero" in our times, when it frequently is used as a synonym for "star" or "celebratory" status. The use of "hero" during World War II was markedly different—essentially it referred to ordinary Americans who performed in an extraordinary manner on the battlefront no matter what, even if it cost them their lives. Virtually all of those who performed so valorously would deny they were doing anything exceptional, yet that precisely made what they did so spectacular. In addition to those previously mentioned, others conspicuous for their bravery included some colorful and unmistakable flyers of Italian descent like Captain Allen V. Martini of California, and Captain Don Gentile of Ohio. Both of them received a fair amount of reporting in the nation's English-language press, and even more extended coverage in the Italian ethnic press.

It was with pride that Italian Americans on the home front read about the heroics of Captain Allen V. Martini from San Francisco, who dubbed his Flying Fortress "Dry Martini," and whose plane was credited with incredibly shooting down twenty-two Nazi planes in fifteen minutes, and who had taken part in over thirty combat missions in Europe that earned him the Silver Star, the Distinguished Flying Cross, and the Air Medal with three Oak Leaf Clusters.[317] Possessing indomitable courage and committed to an admirable sense of justice, the intrepid flyer was one of the few Italian American combat participants to write about his experience and have it published in the prestigious *Saturday Evening Post*. In his exciting account, Martini described the emotions bomber pilots experienced as they awaited attack by enemy planes.

> The pilots, having no guns, are the most helpless men on the bomber; moreover their spot is the most exposed. There is a certain fascination about watching jerry get ready for the attack ... A dozen to fifteen Focke-Wulf 190s swarmed in peeling off and turning upside down, their 20-mm cannon making a red line of fire along their wings as they got us in their sights ... their wings as they got us in their sights ... I lost control momentarily and the Dry Martini dived out of formation ... The enemy saw my predicament almost as soon as I realized it. I was now a straggler, and hence, as jerry thought, his meat ... The air was getting congested with twisting, flashing, yellow-nosed F-Ws, Herr Goering's

> crack spitefuls, and they were really eating us up ... The
> wings and the fuselage had been punctured many times ...
> it dawned on me that there must be a bigger Power up here
> in the sky carrying us through this one than just ourselves
> alone and the ship, stanch as she was.[318]

Somehow and by means of crash-landing, Martini got the stricken plane in and on the ground—after sustaining160 cannon and bullets holes. Italian American spokespeople were most enthusiastic in locating and publicizing those of their ethnic group who received wartime awards as live examples to impress the young that one can survive the evil of war and return a live hero. The ethnic press accordingly lauded him as one of their finest representatives. "We frequently followed his heroic deeds, happy that he is one of us, through the blood in his veins, through his traditions and aspirations, because the Italian people have remained traditionally in love with liberty and its major aspiration is dedicated to its material and spiritual future, Captain Martini has given therefore the same and that is being a great American, so that not only in the land of his birth, but that even in a land of liberty, that has his political foundation and his eminent Christian belief."[319]

War heroes like Martini served a larger purpose—they could help raise funds to fight the war. On June 2, 1944, Major Martini was the guest speaker at Tavern-On-The-Green in New York; before 1,000 members of the motion picture industry and film distributors, he warned against an attitude of complacency that he sensed around the country because, "there is no reason for over-optimism, as the war is not over yet, not by a long way." He also suggested that Americans should ask themselves a telling daily question, "What have I done today that a mother's son should die for me tonight?"[320]

DON GENTILE

Few Italian American heroes received so thoroughgoing publicity as did Captain Don Gentile. For nearly a two-week period in April 1944, *Il Progresso Italo-Americano* provided daily, abundant, front-page accounts

of Gentile's air deeds, replete with interviews and photographs. Gentile
had just become an Italian American household name by virtue of breaking the United States record of German planes destroyed in war, previously
held by World War I ace, Captain Eddie Rickenbacker. The son of poor
southern Italian immigrant parents who "came to this county in third class
[steerage], like other poor immigrants" and had settled outside of Dayton
in Piqua, Ohio, Don Salvatore Gentile was one of the most celebrated heroes that the ethnic community produced. Both an inspiration and a source
of pride for us, young impressionable home front Italian Americans, his
exploits received extensive coverage. That this was not unique to those
of us in Brooklyn was attested to by his biographer, Mark Spagnuolo of
Michigan, who writing in the mid-1980s, confessed that he first heard of
Gentile in 1944, essentially the same time when I also became familiar
with his name.[321] A genuine product of the Italian American ante-bellum
milieu, Don Gentile survived a near fatal childhood disease that his family
attributed to a miracle, and subsequently developed a life-long love affair
with flying. He exhibited such an astonishing facility in aviation that he
was considered a natural-born flyer, one who was able to overcome his
parent's initial opposition to flying to a point where they financed private
flying lessons. Impatient and unwilling to wait until the United States entered the conflict, he
was able to join the
British Royal Air

*For numerous Italian
American households
on the home front, the
achievements of air ace
Don Gentile, from an
authentic ethnic milieu,
was a source of enormous
pride. Here he celebrates
breaking Eddie Ricken-
backer's record of enemy
planes shot down.*

Force (RAF) where he served until this country entered the war, when the RAF Eagle Squadron unit was transferred en masse to the United States Army Air Force in 1942.[322]

Commissioned a second lieutenant, Gentile became an integral part of the Fourth Air Force where he flew a Spitfire fighter, and then a Mustang fighter assigned to protect bombers in their dangerous mission runs over Germany. A pilot with extraordinary expertise in manipulating an airplane, yet one who found the taking of life dreadful, he nevertheless transformed his dream of becoming an "ace" by scoring numerous hits on German enemy aircraft. Since it took five victories to become an ace, he had achieved that and more by March 1944. His achievements simply were stupendous as he proceeded to shoot down enemy craft in record-breaking fashion so that on April 1, 1944, he was credited with his twenty-second kill, thus bringing him to the verge of bursting the legendary Rickenbacker's World War I record. In the process, Gentile shot down out of the air Germany's top air ace Major Kirt Von Meyer, who was credited with 150 Allied "kills." Gentile's accomplishments also brought inordinate notice. News reporters frequented the air base to be on hand when and if Rickenbacker's total of twenty-six kills would be broken—a feat that had seemed unsurpassable until Gentile and a fellow pilot in the Fourth Air Force inched closer to the mark attracting a great deal of media attention. The unfortunate death of the other aviator left Gentile the focus of attention. That he was aware of the momentous record-shattering event was clear in the fact that, although more than eligible for leave, on at least three occasions, Gentile delayed his liberty. He continued to fly until a dangerous mission that left him in a state of shock and finally compelled him to enter a hospital for convalescence. Unwavering in pursuit of his dream to become an ace—it would thereby bring pride to his family and to Italian Americans as a whole. In view of the peril associated with his combat profession, his reaction as to how he regarded his exploits revealed the persona of a serious, religious individual rather than a nonchalant, casual performer. He maintained that, like every pilot, he experienced fear and the feeling of God's presence and that in the midst of mortal combat he prayed hard for deliverance thereby strengthening his own spiritual sense. "I am religious, I am a good Catholic ... now I assist at Mass every Sunday."[323]

> Having experienced anti-Italian discrimination earlier in life he was determined to demonstrate that his people had something of importance to contribute. April 5, 1944 saw an exhausted Gentile return to his air base following a grueling day of combat in which he was credited with five kills, thus exceeding Rickenbacker, however, the Fourth Air Force Command abstained from making the announcement until the flyer's claims had been assessed by the Claims Board. While that was transpiring he continued going on assignments and scored additional victories for a total of thirty, including eighteen in one month. He was the undisputable Ace of Aces whose name and exploits were transmitted on radio broadcasts, in newspapers, and magazine articles. He became the highest-scoring fighter pilot in American history up to that time.[324]

It was a time for honors, and Gentile received his share, highlighted by a ceremony on April 11, 1944, when Supreme Allied Commander General Dwight Eisenhower, accompanied by other celebrated generals, bestowed the Distinguished Service Cross on Gentile, calling him a "one man air force." For his exceptional performance, he received the Distinguished Flying Cross with seven Oak Leaf Clusters, the Silver Star, and the Air Medal. (He was honored by the other Allied nations as well but never was awarded the Congressional Medal of Honor.) The young Italian American flyer was acclaimed a national hero; and to Italian Americans, he was a towering champion. In the light of his accomplishments, it was inexplicable to us on the home front that Gentile never was awarded a Congressional Medal of Honor—an award that was proffered to Joe Foss who also broke the Rickenbacker record.

We were, of course, aware of many war heroes that the media proclaimed and that we joined in honoring, Colin Kelly, Audie Murphy, etc, however, it always seemed that they were "Americans" and somewhat apart from us by heritage and physical appearance—individuals who were clearly not of Italian extraction. But in fixing on Don Gentile, we were extolling the bravery of a person who did not possess an Anglo-Saxon name, who was not light, blond and freckle-faced, who did not worship in a Protestant church, and who did not salivate over meat loaf, mashed potatoes, and sliced white bread. Notwithstanding his astounding boldness on the field of battle, Gentile impressed us as a loving son with a sense of family, and a practicing Catholic. In addition, he was aware of his ethnicity, having experienced derision because of it, yet always proud of his ancestry and determined to prove that those of his background could make important contributions to the war effort. For young Italian Americans on the home front like myself, who longed to see heroes from our nationality—men who looked as we did with olive skin, dark eyes and brunette hair, and who spoke a dialect variation of Italian like us, whose name ended in a vowel, whose parents immigrants were armed with little formal education, who respected their hard-working parents, who enjoyed a cuisine of pasta and sauce or veal cutlets, and who were unashamedly Catholic worshipers as were we—Don Gentile was, in many respects, the embodiment of the Italian American serviceman. It was heartwarming to read his own words in which he admitted that although he was somewhat wild as a young man in Ohio, and did not go to church regularly, but thanks to the persistency of his mother, father, and sister, he now went to Mass regularly and faithfully. "I am religious. I am a good Catholic, now I assist at the camp Mass every Sunday."[325] We could relate to this religious commitment because we saw the same attitudes within the families of those around us. For several days in succession, *Il Progresso Italo-Americano* commissioned a King Features correspondent to tell Gentile's story in front page accounts, replete with photographs of his airplane, the award bestowed by General Eisenhower, and family members like his mother who resembled so many in our ethnic group.[326]

Asked why he chose to fight, Don's reflection on his ethnic background as well as his feelings about America stand as a summary and encapsulation of Italian American loyalty: Italian Americans on the home front could not fail to be stirred by Gentile's homage to his ancestry.

> There are my mother and father. They were born in Italy. They came to the United States in third class as poor immigrants. In Italy, they were poor. They could not be other than poor. Look at them now. My father is a person of substantial importance in Piqua, Ohio. We have a fine house and my sister Edith and I have had all we desired. My mother is smiling and happy, not a bowed woman, because she is American and resides in America. I have a debt toward America, isn't that true? I fight in part to pay that debt.[327]

Early in May 1944, Gentile was sent home on leave to be reunited with his family. First, however, he was taken to Washington to meet with the top Air Force generals and distinguished members of Congress. Piqua, Ohio celebrated "Don Gentile Day" with a parade as the governor of Ohio, military and civic leaders hailed their hero. On May 25, Don was the center of a special war bond rally that was the beginning of an extended war bond tour.[328] After the war ended, Gentile remained in the Air Force as a test pilot until he lost his life in a crash in 1950 while attempting to save the life of another person.

THE NATION'S HIGHEST HONOR

Although Gentile never received the nation's highest honor, the Congressional Medal of Honor that we thought he deserved, that distinction was conferred on thirteen Americans of Italian descent and thereby became a source of additional pride to us.[329] In March 1942, Willibald C. Bianchi of New Ulm, Minnesota, became the first of the ethnic group to earn the cherished citation for conspicuous gallantry and intrepidity above and beyond the call of duty in the Philippine Islands. In June 1942, Lieutenant Bianchi became among the very first in the nation to win the coveted medal for his courage, leadership, and indifference to wounds that he manifested in the Bataan jungle, in the face of Japanese machine-gun fire on February 3, 1942. That Bianchi's family resided New Ulm, a German farming community, might seem unusual; however, the explanation was that his grandparents were born in Schleswig-Holstein, although both were of Italian descent. William worked on the family farm, attended college, where he joined the Reserve Officers Training Corps and was commissioned a second lieutenant upon graduation. Soon assigned to the Philippines, he was part of the defense forces when the Japanese troops landed, and it was here that he fought so gallantly that he received his citation at the hands[330] of General Douglas MacArthur.

Notwithstanding Bianchi's partial German background and the fact that he did not hail from one of the more familiar "Little Italies" in the New York area, the Italian ethnic press expounded at length about his accomplishments via extensive narration, including photographs with his mother. The honor conferred to Bianchi was a conspicuous opportunity for Italian Americans to demonstrate their patriotism early in the war.

A product of an Italian enclave in Packville, a mining town in Pennsylvania, Pfc. Gino Merli won the nation's highest honors in Belgium in 1944 when his company was overrun by superior German forces. Feigning death twice, he remained at his machine gun post and was credited with killing over fifty enemy soldiers. Tom Brokaw, who met him on the occasion of a special NBC program on the 40th anniversary of the D Day invasion, wrote of him as a self-effacing man. "This quiet man stayed at his machine gun, blazing away at the Germans covering the withdrawal of his fellow Americans, until his position was overrun. He faked his own death twice as the Germans swept past, and then he went back to his machine gun to cut them down from behind.[331] Born in Decatur, Illinois, Master Sergeant Vito Bertoldi won the Medal of Honor for his awesome display of bravery in withstanding the attack of vastly superior German forces for more than forty-eight hours while aiding his men to escape. He was credited with killing at least forty enemy troops.

Closer to the New York City area was the wartime heroism of Peter J. D'Alessandro, born in 1918 in Watervliet, New York. He became the pride of large numbers of Italian Americans on the home front, in the vicinity of Albany, when he was awarded the Congressional Medal of Honor for his bravery in battle against an overwhelming enemy attack that saved his company from complete rout in December 1944. This courageous background figured prominently in his election to the New York State Senate in 1946. A measure of the esteem in which D'Alessandro was held by home front Italian Americans can be gleaned by a plaque in his honor prominently displayed in the headquarters of the Italian Center of Albany.

Although born in San Francisco, California, Ralph Cheli entered the Army in Brooklyn, New York. He became a Major in the Air Force, winning a Congressional Medal of Honor citation for conspicuous gallantry and intrepidity above and beyond the call of duty in action with the enemy in the Pacific. The frontline bravery for which he was hailed was his courageous decision, even as his plane was ablaze and a crash inevitable, to continue leading an airplane attack would cost him his life. Other Italian Americans who won the Medal of Honor posthumously were Joseph Cicchetti, Joseph J. Damato, Anthony Peter Viale, Frank J. Petrarca, and Arthur Defranzo.

JOHN BASILONE

Of all Italian American heroes in the Second World War or of any war, none was more highly regarded by Italian Americans than John Basilone. Born of immigrant parents from the vicinity of Naples on November 4, 1916, in Buffalo, New York, he grew up in Raritan, New Jersey. One of ten children of a tailor, he went to Mass at St. Ann's Church and also attended parochial school. After joining the Army for a three-year hitch in 1933, in 1940, he enlisted in the Marines and saw action in the Pacific in the early phases of the war, particularly as American forces went on the offensive in the steaming jungles of Guadalcanal on October 24, 1942. The Battle of

Guadalcanal was to mark the turning point of Japanese advancement in the Pacific, namely the taking back of territories previously overrun. Together with other marines of the 1st Marine Division, they participated in one of the fiercest and bloodiest battles of World War II. Basilone, in charge of a machine-gun section, showed his gallant resolve in the face of a devastating Japanese counterattack that endangered the entire American mission, running through a hail of deadly enemy fire, rescuing two Marines and killing numerous (thirty-eight) enemy soldiers.[332]

Back on the home front, we read with great pride the exciting accounts of the momentous battle that marked an end to Japanese forward aggression and the beginning of the road back toward Tokyo. Headlines of the major dailies kept us informed of the huge cost in men to both sides as the enemy hammered at the Marines' defensive position and threatened to overrun it. For seventy-two hours, Basilone manning several heavy machine guns, mowed down wave after wave of Japanese infiltrators, virtually annihilating an entire regiment.[333] So spectacular were his actions that General Douglas MacArthur called him a "one-man army."

On September 13, 1943, "John Basilone Day" in Raritan, New Jersey began with a Mass in which the priest held up its native son as a model to emulate. "His life will be a guide to American youth. God has spared him for some big. work." Wealthy socialite Doris Duke provided the grounds of her estate nearby for a celebration and his parents beamed with pride as 30,000 fellow townsmen accompanied by brass band and joining in a parade greeted the immigrants' son who had returned home a hero. "Basilone Day" continues to be a tradition in the community. Known as "Manila John," handsome with dark com-

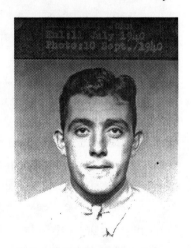

To home front Italian Americans, Congressional Medal of Honor winner Marine Sgt. John Basilone was the foremost hero within the ethnic group.

plexion and a wide grin, he was in demand for war bond drives, particularly in Italian neighborhoods where he was received as an indisputable hero. For example, a grateful New York City Mayor LaGuardia was effusive in his praise and warmly welcomed him as the centerpiece of a major war bond drive. "I know you must be good, I know you must have plenty of guts because that medal is not awarded lightly." The literature promoting the bond drive that culminated on Pearl Harbor Day 1943, highlighted him as the only living Congressional Medal of Honor Marine and featured his stirring words. "On that dark night at Guadalcanal, when I fought my way back through the Japs to get more ammunition for my machine gun crew, the ammunition was there. It was there because you folks bought war bonds." Basilone's exploits became well-known to us on the home front not only because of the ethnic press, but also because of widespread coverage in English language daily press and national media journals such as *Life*. Arguable one of the most popular journals of the day, *Life* provided all-embracing photographs of the hero, his family, townspeople and movie celebrities. It seemed that John's fame was contagious and everyone wanted to be associated with him. Hugely popular with the ethnic group, he was credited with raising nearly $1.5 million in ten days. In addition, for several successive months together with famed movie stars such as Martha Scott, John Garfield, Virginia Grey, and Gene Lockhart, he toured the country on a war-bond drive. In 1944, he married Lena Riggi, a sergeant in the Marine Corps Women's Reserve, and was offered a lieutenant's commission in the Marine Corps, an offer he refused because of the commitment he made to his men on the battlefield. Eschewing the shelter of stateside assignment, he requested return to action and on February 19, 1945, landed on the black sandy beaches of Iwo Jima. Engaged in some of the nastiest fighting of the war, it was while he assaulted a machine-gun pillbox that a mortar shell exploded nearby killing him instantly. This final demonstration of courage gained Basilone a posthumous Navy Cross.[334]

Basilone held the record for being the only enlisted man to earn both the Congressional Medal of Honor and the Navy Cross—a truly spectacular performance. Although his exploits were recounted in national magazines, it seemed that the appetite Italian Americans on the home front for more coverage could not be satiated. Subsequently, a naval destroyer was named after him, as was a Sons of Italy lodge, a river (Raritan) and American Legion posts. Into the 21st century, the service station on the New Jersey Turnpike that bears his name is a continuing reminder of the singular contributions of Italian Americans to the defense of the country, while in 2004, the United States Postal Service announced it will issue a stamp in honor of Basilone.

ANTHONY CASAMENTO

Corporal Anthony Casamento of East Harlem, New York—in keeping with the reputation of coming from one of the toughest districts in New York—joined the Marines in 1940, and would see action before the end of the first year of war. As a member of the 1st Marine Division that took part in the invasion of Guadalcanal, on November 1, 1942, he commanded a machine-gun section during a ferocious engagement with Japanese troops. Although every member of his unit was either killed or wounded and Casamento suffered fourteen severe wounds, he nevertheless managed single-handedly to deter enemy forces until the main American attacking force arrived.[335] Growing up in a rough neighborhood where he learned to fend for himself may have served Tony well—"Where I grew up a guy had to be on his toes. You had to know what time it was,"—his wounds were so damaging that he barely survived. Notwithstanding his obvious show of valor, Casamento did not then win the Medal of Honor supposedly because of the absence of an eyewitness to corroborate his heroics. Disappointed, he was not about to give up his entreaty for the nation's highest award, as he marched in front of the White House in an attempt to bring attention to his case. All told, he waged a thirty-eight year battle to receive the decoration, a campaign that proved almost as arduous as his struggles on the bloody island beachhead. With the help of Italian American organizations, which exerted pressure on important political figures, Casamento's heroism was finally recognized.[336] It was a belated but satisfying moment for Casamento and for those of us assembled at the National Italian American Foundation dinner in Washington D.C. in 1980, when President Jimmy Carter announced that Casamento finally was to secure the Medal of Honor.

DiMaggio and Sinatra

Given the reality that Italy, their mother country, was an enemy nation and that it perforce engendered mistrust, home front Italian Americans constantly sought out ways to counter suspicion. One unique means was to emphasize the accomplishments of superstars within the midst who commanded a following beyond the ethnic group. High on the list were Joe DiMaggio and Frank Sinatra.

Joe DiMaggio and San Francisco's southern Italian American communities were deeply intertwined. The DiMaggio family was part of the second wave of Italian immigrants to California that emanated from southern Italian provinces, a more commonly a proletarian movement. The typical southern Italian transplant was motivated by a conscious effort to recreate the way of life that he had known in Italy in a region of the United States whose land and climate closely resembled the land of his birth. For the DiMaggios who hailed from the Sicilian island Isola delle Femme, it meant to engage in fishing, an occupation which Southern Italians came to dominate in the California of the 1880s.[337] Their effectiveness as a work force was enhanced by a spirit of solidarity that bound them together in fishing specialties according to provincial origins that they plied in San Francisco Bay. It was within the hubris of that sub-culture that Joe DiMaggio was nurtured, and of which he became its proudest product. He was the eighth of nine children of Sicilian parents who forsook the populous eastern cities of the United States, the favored destination of most of their fellow countrymen, for the coastal regions of California. Joe's father was a fisherman, as were two of his brothers, a background that rendered Joe himself quite familiar with the trade.

Closely-knit but hard working Sicilian American families had so developed the fishing enterprise of San Francisco Bay that it was considered one of California's foremost industries by the early 1900s. The onset of the Second World War severely impinged upon the success of the enterprise since the United States Army took over operation of the main piers and wharves. In addition, restrictions prevented alien fishermen of a nation at war with the United States from further developing the industry. For San Francisco's Italian fishermen, the woeful wartime atmosphere was heavy with irony. Impeded by severe restrictions on employment, residence, and travel, thousands of them nevertheless were quick to aid the American war effort, even to the extent of donating thousands of square feet of fishing nets to army units near San Francisco. These nets were of finer interlaced pattern than those issued by the army and were extremely useful to combat troops for camouflage purposes.[338]

The fisherman background was to become a memorable DiMaggio reference point, especially after the publication of Ernest Hemingway's classic work, *The Old Man and the Sea,* in which the great writer describes the old fisherman fantasizing the dream of fishing with the great ballplayer. In reality, however, and much to the dismay of his father, Joe, like his brothers Vince and Dominic, and others of his ethnic ilk in the San Francisco of the 1920s such as Tony Lazzeri and Frank Crosetti, dreamt of nothing else but playing baseball, the traditional American pastime. The San Francisco milieu was to serve as the nexus of some of the most noted products of the Italian colony in the field of sports and other areas. The great financier A.P. Giannini who founded the Bank of America, the travel entrepreneur John Fugazi, and the politician Angelo Rossi, mayor of the city, are some examples.

Joe DiMaggio effectively began his professional baseball career in 1933 with the San Francisco Seals, a premier New York Yankee minor league team. Instantly, he excelled in batting, fielding, and base running, all with impeccable style that would become his trademark. As an eighteen-year-old rookie, his sixty-one game hitting streak stands as the Pacific Coast League record for that difficult achievement. In 1934, he was declared the league's greatest player ever—it was merely a matter of time before he attracted the attention of the Yankee organization. Heralded as the most anticipated major league rookie since Ty Cobb, he joined the big league in 1936, shortly becoming the star player of the storied Yankee ball club as a worthy successor to immortals like Babe Ruth and Lou Gehrig. He was an instant hero to New York's large Italian population—the largest of any city in the world outside of Rome—who traveled for miles to see him play. "Subway guards as far away as Coney Island were accosted by recent immigrants who wanted to know 'Which way da Yankee Stadium?' When DiMaggio made a hit, huge Italian flags, smuggled into the bleachers by his admirers, were unfurled and shaken."[339] His stellar batting average of .323 in his rookie year 1936, followed by .346 in 1937, and .324 in 1938, set the stage for 1939 when he won the first of his three Most Valuable Player awards as he hit his highest season average at .381. 1941, the year when the United States entered the war, was a history-making year for baseball—Boston Red Sox phenomenon Ted Williams hit an astounding .406 while Joe re-wrote baseball history by hitting safely in 56 straight games, thereby accomplishing what is considered one of baseball's greatest feats, one that still stands and one that many experts predict likely never will be equaled.

For young Italian Americans like me, Joe DiMaggio was our first and most undisputed hero. I was just beginning to understand the game of baseball and avidly joined in the inevitable arguments that youngsters engaged in over the best player. There were, of course, many outstanding players who figured prominently in a betting game that was a feature of life in the Brooklyn streets during baseball season. The idea was to bet on a combination of three players who would hit safely that day—with payoffs coming with combined hits. Along with favorites like Stan Musial and others, I inevitably selected DiMaggio as one of the three. No one even came close to the adulation he inspired.

Joe's outstanding talent, moreover, was matched by a gentlemanly demeanor, peerless grace, and admirable dignity—attributes for which he became legendary and whose relative absence in the contemporary sports world are widely lamented. The gifted columnist Murray Kempton captured the essence of his nobility of manner when he wrote, "For no figure abides in memory to incarnate that inner sense of peace and the instinctive awareness of its every mystery so perfectly as Joe DiMaggio did."[340] He was at the top of his game, easily winning admiration not only of baseball fans, but also by the general public. DiMaggio's heroics inspired bandleader Les Brown to write "Jolting Joe DiMaggio" which became popular in 1941, and years later, Paul Simon featured him in another tune "Mrs. Robinson"—a testimony to his enduring popularity. Joe won the esteem of his baseball colleagues as well.

Although these characteristics won the respect of the nation at large, they were even more noteworthy for Italian Americans during a wartime atmosphere because they were products of the country from which they or their parents descended that was an enemy nation. By the end of the 1930s, Italian Americans seemed to have been on the cusp of acceptability, after decades of enduring low esteem during which they suffered from unflattering characterization as superstitious, ignorant, unintelligent buffoons, or even worse as the personification of gangsters. Despite his evolving folk hero status, Yankee teammates referred to DiMaggio as the "Big Dago." A *Life* magazine article is even more revealing as it describes the casual bigotry that existed. While perhaps not meant to demean him as an Italian American, but rather to comment on his baseball achievements, the author nevertheless, indulged in the prevailing stereotype as he described the athletic son of Sicilian immigrants in his own hackneyed image. "Although he learned Italian at first, Joe, now twenty-four, speaks English without an accent, and is otherwise adapted to most United States mores. Instead of olive oil or smelly bear grease he keeps his hair slick with water. He never reeks of garlic and prefers chicken chow mein to spaghetti."[341] In other words, Italian American sports superstars could perhaps be acclaimed for their talents, but they could hardly be mistaken for the genuine, typical Jack Armstrong Anglo-Saxon-descended all-American citizen that was regularly regarded as the epitome of true Americanism. First and second generation Italian Americans were aware of the not so subtle distinctions prevalent in society. For the most part totally ignorant of the game of baseball, the first generation nevertheless boasted of DiMaggio as one of their own whose intrepid performance on the field brought them a degree of pride and success.

DiMaggio was even more meaningful to the second generation as one of the few in their midst that commanded the respect of the nation and even if only by osmosis, as it were, validated their own claim to Americanism. Teammate Lefty Gomez' pithy observation well captured his popularity when he observed "All the Italians in America adopted him. Just about every day in New York and on the road there would be an invitation from some Italian-American club for Joe to attend some dinner or something ... Everyone wanted to be Italian if they could get DiMaggio to come to their dinner."[342] In the tenements and congested ethnic neighborhoods of the teeming cities, he was their undisputed and abiding hero. California's wartime Italian American community was beset with an ambiguous situation. While those categorized as enemy aliens, on the one hand, endured serious restrictions, numerous products from these same families served in the nation's armed services. Joe DiMaggio mirrored this bewilderment as he along with many other Italian American ballplayers, such as Phil Rizzuto and Yogi Berra, interrupted their careers to serve. The government supported the idea of professional baseball players assigned to units that taught baseball and performed for the entertainment of other servicemen. It was part of an extensive effort to boost military spirit by providing various forms of enjoyment to distract men from frightening and frequently, fatal aspects of their time in service.

Although DiMaggio was not known for aggressively promoting his ethnicity, he was definitely perceived as an Italian American and was widely acclaimed by the ethnic group as its hero. Like many of us of that era, he was most at ease in the sheltered milieu of an ethnic community in which people looked, spoke, and dressed like him, one in which Italian, or a dialect thereof was the language of the home, and where Italian customs were the norm. Conversely, once out of the familiar cocoon, as for example when thrust into a high school outside the area, he experienced a discomfort that could only be countered by his prowess in baseball. A 1941 description further captures the perception. "Joe DiMaggio has been described as an essentially modest fellow with a sense of responsibility typical of his Sicilian-American upbringing ... His dark eyes, dark hair and prominent nose suggest his Southern Italian antecedents ... He is understandably, the idol of Italian Americans. Some 30,000 tried to crowd into the Cathedral of Sts. Peter and Paul on the occasion of his marriage..."[343]

Frank Sinatra was a second icon of the Italian American constellation whose career accelerated spectacularly during the Second World War, and who thereby fortuitously served as an intermediary for the ethnic group. Born to Genoa-descended Dolly and Sicilian Martin Sinatra in Hoboken, New Jersey, in 1915, he was the only child of a working-class family that resided in Hoboken's Little Italy, replete with its Italian grocery stores featuring provolone hanging from the window and suffused with pungent garlic aromas. Frank did not grow up in a slum, but rather in what might be called a lower middle-class neighborhood, like that in which I lived. Frank's mother possessed an aggressive personality and a penchant for local Democratic politics that found her presuming the dominant parent role in the family, while Frank's father was content to run a bar and remain unobtrusively in the background. Although Dolly was a Democratic ward heeler, in a demonstration of ethnic consciousness, on one occasion, the Sinatra family supported an Italian American Republican for mayor. Other Italian mores were readily reinforced by the Sinatra family through its active participation in organizations such as the local Sicilian Cultural League.

Formal education held limited interest for young Frank who after an undistinguished academic career, left high school. In the pre-radio days of Sinatra's youth, Hoboken residents could hear music occasionally in the church or at special social and political events. The advent of the radio transformed popular entertainment in ethnic neighborhoods, especially in summertime when windows were open wide, and strollers could hear the strains of familiar operatic arias and popular melodies suffusing city streets. It was during later teenage years that music began to attract Frank, who found in Bing Crosby his own singing model. In a short time, we members of the young generation became avid radio fans of programs like "The Battle of the Baritones," a New York radio program that my friends and I eagerly awaited every Sunday which regularly featured the two singers. Both Irish and Italian Americans could enter into friendly competition over who was the finest.

Not merely content to emulate Crosby, Sinatra was determined to inject his own style that was based on the bel canto repertoire then popular.

> It is easy to forget how omnipresent operatic singing was
> for a first generation Sicilian American growing up in the
> Italian neighborhood of greater New York in the 1920s
> and 1930s. Not only was opera the old-country music of
> parents and neighbors, however working class, it was also
> a regular feature along with comedy and popular music,
> on both vaudeville stages and radio variety shows.[344]

I recall operatic music emanating from the open door of barbershop around the corner during summertime and thought it remarkable that the medium was such an absorbing fascination for the barber—one of humble circumstances. Pete Hamill, a Sinatra biographer, opines that his voice was his finest accomplishment. It was "a combination of voice, diction attitude, and taste in music that produced the Sinatra sound. It remains unique. Sinatra created something that was not there before he arrived: an urban American voice. It was the voice of the sons of the immigrants in northern cities—not simply Italian Americans, but the children of all those immigrants who had arrived on the great tide at the turn of the century."[345]

Frank's career received a boost via his performance on New York radio stations. He came to the attention of big bandleader Harry James, who intrigued by his singing performance, signed him to a contract. It was merely a matter of time, when as lead singer for the James band in 1939, Frank began to draw critical scrutiny, receiving affirmative reviews. James soon discovered that his male vocalist not only regarded himself as the greatest singer in the business, but was also extremely sensitive to his ethnic origins. When James suggested Sinatra change his name to the less Italian-sounding "Frankie Satin", the Hoboken singer adamantly rejected the notion. "I said no way, baby. My name is Sinatra. Frank fucking Sinatra."[346]

A very different personality than DiMaggio, Sinatra was intensely aware of and keenly sensitive to slights attributed to his ethnic heritage. "Of course it meant something to me to be the son of immigrants. How could it not. How the hell could it not. I grew up for a few years thinking I was just another American kid. Then I discovered at—what? five? six?—I discovered that some people thought I was a dago. A wop. A guinea. You know like I didn't have a fucking name."[347] There is no question that anti-Italianism wounded his psyche; he became convinced he was the butt of insults simply because he was Italian. "Every once in a while, I'd be at a party somewhere, in Hollywood or New York or wherever, and it would be very civilized, you know, black tie, the best crystal, all of that. And I'd see a guy staring at me from the corner of the room, and I knew what the word was in his head. The word was guinea."[348] Thus along with others of his nationality, he bristled at the sting of ethnic prejudice; however, when the opportunity presented itself he would use this negativity to promote ethnic tolerance. The opportunity came very early in his career.

In January 1940, Sinatra joined the Tommy Dorsey band where he learned valuable singing techniques, especially breathing and phrasing from watching Dorsey's unique manner of playing a trombone. He recorded major hits including "Ciribiribin", "All or Nothing at All", "Night and Day," and "I'll Never Smile Again". At the end of 1942, he left the big band singer in favor of going solo—a move which gained him increased theater audiences and limited appearances in Hollywood movies. Sinatra, however, was more than merely a singer, he was a phenomenon able to inject a sexual element that was enormously attractive to young female audiences. An example was his Christmas 1942 engagement at the New York Paramount that was made legendary by the response of the bobby soxers—thousands of delirious young women for whom Frank served as a surrogate for their absent soldiers. He described it as follows: "It was the war years, and there was a great loneliness, and I was the boy in every corner drug store ... who's gone off, drafted to the war. That was all." However, he was not universally acclaimed. Indeed, for a time stinging insinuations buttressed by outright heckling that he was a draft dodger haunted him. His biographers explained his absence from the service al-though of draft age—he was classified as 4-F (deferred) because of basic ear problem attributable to a difficult birth.

By the end of 1943, Sinatra was recognized the nation's premier popu-lar male vocalist. Perhaps just as important as the popular acclaim was the recognition that he was setting the pattern that would become the model for a whole generation of singers. With his unsurpassed vocal artistry and his swaggering personal style, he was on his way to becoming the domi-nant presence not only in standard music, but in motion pictures as well. Although his early film roles were forgettable, in the post-war period, he began to perfect an acting ability that would win him an Academy Award. It prompted celebrated director Martin Scorcese to remember him as "an idol of mine and millions. A great Italian American, a great American, a great actor, by the way a great, great actor."[349]

Becoming a major national figure during the last two years of the war, Sinatra was also controversial, eliciting both negative and positive reactions. Columnists criticized his sometimes pugnacious attitude, his unabashed support of Democratic President Franklin D. Roosevelt and an unsupported claim that he had "bumped" a veteran to fly home at the conclusion of a USO tour. However, he was praised for his many appear-ances before high school groups to promote ethnic harmony and tolerance. Significantly a number of these visits were in predominantly "Italian" neighborhoods such as Benjamin Franklin High School in East Harlem, New York, where he was greeted by Principal Leonard Covello, the outstanding Italian American educator. Sinatra not only sang, but also was applauded for his exhortation to work together, regardless of race, religion, or national origin; he labeled anything less as anti-American.[350] "He had not forgotten the streets of Hoboken where epithets like 'guinea' and 'wop' had provoked him to reach for a loose brick."[351] Sinatra's anti-intolerance campaign was highlighted by a 1945 Oscar Award-wining movie short, "The House I Live In," that schools regularly utilized to encourage tolerance." As a young teenager then in a Brooklyn high school, I viewed the film in the school auditorium and was impressed with the toleration message from a favorite Italian American. As a member of the glee club at Brooklyn High School of Automotive Trades, I delighted in being part of the chorus that practiced that song pondering the message of tolerance it encompassed. I also joined thousands of others, some of who played hooky to go to the New York Paramount to see him in live performance. The fact that he and others associated with the film contributed their services underscores his commitment to ending prejudice. Frank received the American Unity Award for his effort.

Like DiMaggio, although Sinatra had a national following that transcended ethnicity, he became a special symbol for Italian Americans; namely that by 1942, a young Italian American singer suddenly began making headlines in every newspaper in the country. Whereas DiMaggio personified the image of a dignified, silent personage, Sinatra was much more aggressive, even combative in articulating his views about prejudice.

> "He arrived suddenly on the scene when DiMaggio was silent, when paisanos were mournful, were quietly defensive about Hitler in their homeland. Sinatra became, in time, a kind of one-man Anti-Defamation League for Italians in America, the sort of organization that would be unlikely for them because, as the theory goes, they rarely agreed on anything, being extreme individualists: fine as

soloists, but not so good in a choir, fine as heroes, but not
so good in a parade."[352]

By 1943, Sinatra had become the rage of the nation. Girls swooned just at his presence. Merely by listening to him over the radio, it was reported, young females sighed with love."[353] On one bizarre occasion, New York City detectives resorted to imitating Sinatra's voice in a successful effort to jog the temporary amnesia that afflicted two young bobby-soxers, following a Sinatra anti-discrimination appearance at Benjamin Franklin High School.[354] Granted Sinatra did not serve in the armed forces and that contention marked his early career, he nevertheless rendered genuine contributions. Working, often gratis, for tolerance and good will between ethnic and racial groups—this was not a trivial responsibility when one considers that racial relations in northern cities witnessed some of the worst race riots on record during the war. He also lent his talents to visit troops and sell war bonds. Along with the greater Italian American community, Sinatra was supportive of efforts to aid war-torn Italy in the period following Mussolini's ouster and Italy's re-alignment as an associated power with the Allies. Thus, in the waning days of the war and the immediate postwar period, as Italian Americans organizations undertook steps to raise money on behalf of Italy, they frequently called on Sinatra to headline the participation of well-known Italian American performers, including Perry Como, Lucrezia Bori, and Jimmy Savo.[355] In sum, via his recordings, movies, personal singing appearances, and his good will visits during the war, he had become an enormously popular icon that would endure for six decades of the century. "He had confronted bigotry and changed the way many people thought about the children of immigrants,"[356] and thus helped blunt what might have been egregious hostility to Italian Americans.

The significance of DiMaggio and Sinatra to the wider acceptance of Italian Americans on the home front during this trying time is perhaps better understood by an analogy with African Americans. A student of the 1940s acutely observed a phenomenon pertinent to African Americans as a minority people—that notwithstanding the respect merited by individuals such as statesman Ralph Bunche, heavyweight boxing champion Joe Louis was even more important for their prestige because sports involved such an enormous public. Likewise for Italian Americans, the genius and artistry of an Arturo Toscanini, the financial achievements of an Amodeo Gianinni, and even the highly successful public service of Fiorello H. LaGuardia, all elicited admiration. However, just as among African Americans, the careers of DiMaggio and Sinatra, since their activities rendered them much better known, may have had more meaning to the general public. Simply put, DiMaggio and Sinatra, because they became enormously popular icons, and because they were transparently of Italian heritage, were helpful to acceptance of Italian Americans. One can only imagine how much grimmer it could have been for Italian American acceptance had there not been individual sports and entertainment heroes such as DiMaggio and Sinatra, whose exceptional talents compelled admiration and respect.

CHAPTER VII
HOME FRONT RESPONSE TO
TRANSITION IN ITALY

POLITICAL TRANSITION PERIOD

The political evolution of Italian Americans on the home front during World War II was essentially that of a transitional phase in contrast to their impact a generation earlier in the pre-World War I period, when their influence was limited to the periphery where, with few exceptions, they held minor offices: coroner and assistant district attorneys being among the most prominent. Like other "new immigrant" people of peasant background possessing scant experience of participatory democracy, ignorant of the English language, understandably preoccupied with earning a living and, in contradistinction with other immigrant people, frequently intent on returning to Italy to settle permanently, their participation was slight. This meant for all practical purposes that they would have to be content to accept elective office primarily within characteristic Italian enclaves and to accept minor appointments. Thus, Michael Rofrano's elevation to the relatively modest post of Deputy Police Commissioner of New York City in 1914 was celebrated as an occasion of great moment to the city's Italian community. It is revealing to note that in communities outside New York City where they formed small but distinct minorities, deputy sheriffs—essentially to keep law and order within the ethnic communities—were the first public positions to which more than a few Italian Americans were appointed.

Despite their limited conspicuousness in public office during the earlier period, they were nevertheless acculturating American political practices including that of organizing the ethnic group. James March and Paul Vaccarella, even before the 1920s, for instance, achieved a measure of success and considerable clout by recruiting thousands of immigrants into political clubs within their New York Italian communities, thereby commanding attention of the major political parties. Sometimes supplanting other nationalities in extant organizations, by the 1930s, Italian American political clubs had grown to such proportions that their sway was becoming more visible. For example, Francis X. Mancuso's assumption of power of a Democratic club in East Harlem—the largest concentration of Italian Americans in the city—rendered him a political forces in Manhattan, while Jerome Ambro's success in ousting German American Henry Hasenflug in a Democratic club in Brooklyn likewise found him a force to contend with in that borough.[357] That organizing the ethnic group was necessary in Brooklyn was evident in the realization that although Italian Americans constituted a minimum of twenty-five percent of the borough's population in the 1920–1940 periods, their representation in elective office was considerably lower. In 1920, of 49 elected positions, including state assembly, state senate, United States Congress, city council, borough president, and district attorney, only one was held by an Italian American. In 1935, the figure jumped to six, while in 1945, it would total seven.[358] Albeit a gradual development, it nevertheless constituted a degree of progress.

The 1920–1940 decades were a time of classic ethnic politics during which the newer and growing ethnic groups—Jews and the Italians—sought to wrest power from the Irish, the old time power brokers. "Prior to this invasion," as Jerome Krase and Charles La Cerra point out, "Irish

Catholics had formed the bulk of the democratic voting population, and, long after the Irish lost their demographic hegemony in that borough, they continued to dominate in party leadership and high-level patronage appointments."[359] Of considerable aid to the Irish was their influence in the Roman Catholic Church. By contrast, although overwhelmingly Catholic, Italian American influence was on the periphery, not central in the religious institution. The tussle for power between ethnic groups manifest itself in the struggle to gain domination of the James Madison Club, perhaps Brooklyn's most powerful Democratic organization. The reality was that control of the club was tantamount to electoral victory in local and state elections, and on occasion, exercised considerable influence in national affairs. The Jews clearly won out in the contest to control the Madison Club, a fact reflected in the ascendancy of club product Irwin Steingut, to the position of Assembly leader.[360] Not completely shut out, Brooklyn's Italian Americans settled for less prominent satellite associations that were nevertheless clubs of some political clout. A case in point was "Pigtown," later called the Three Leaf Democratic Club that functioned effectively in the Crown Heights section of Brooklyn. Many Americans of Italian descent joined the organization through the efforts of Anthony Jordan, Sr., an Italian plumber who became captain of the "Pigtown,", and had created a valuable liaison with the Madison Club—the source of jobs. Accordingly, Jordan was instrumental in bringing out the Italian Americans vote.[361]

BROOKLYN POLITICAL PROGRESS

Ralph Foster Weld, the perspicacious reporter for the respected daily *Brooklyn Eagle* confirmed the progress of Italian Americans into the political arena in my home borough when he wrote that "they progressed from a state of political innocence to comparative sophistication." Weld also observed that growing political involvement occurred in accord with an acceleration of the rate of naturalization. "The racial boss was more or less common to all groups, but Italian bosses were among the craftiest of the genus." He cited the success of Brooklyn's Francis L. Corrao, who as president of the Italian American Political Union, inveigled his way into the county Democratic Party organization, as the beginning of a string of similar examples.

> As the Italian vote grew, the names of Italians began to appear on party tickets. Matthew T. Abbruzzo, a native of Brooklyn, became a Federal district court judge. Francis X. Giaccone, who been an assemblyman, an assistant district attorney, and Deputy Fire Commissioner of New York City, was made a city magistrate. Henry Ughetta was elected to the state Supreme Court. In recent years a number of Brooklynites of Italian blood have achieved party tickets.

> Matthew T. Abbruzzo, a native of Brooklyn, became a Federal district judge unusual distinction, but no one of them has been more conspicuous than Juvenal Marchisio, judge of Domestic Relations Court, who during the Second World War became national president of American Relief for Italy.

Simply put, the many shades of the political spectrum from the extreme left to the extreme right were to be found among Brooklyn's Italian Americans, with a small but articulate and colorful group promoting a radical / socialist tradition usually outside of the mainstream Democratic and Republican parties. Economic interest, as with most groups, was a powerful factor in political preference. The lower economic classes usually were Democrats while many of the more prosperous were Republicans.[362]

Weld's observation found affirmation in my neighborhood where most people were Democrats as were the majority of the elected representatives. To my young impressionable mind, it was the Democratic Party that was more supportive of deprived people—a fact underscored by the Christmas baskets that our family and other needy people received and appreciated from the local organization club; (to this day I am a registered Democrat) yet more than a few Italian immigrant apartment landlords identified themselves as Republicans. Although these landlords were really proletarian people who worked in factories and other non-professional occupations, and who lived in flats alongside their tenants, they regarded themselves primarily as property owners and thus of a somewhat upper economic class.

Coupled with increased sophistication by Italian Americans in politics were an expanded role in social, professional, educational, and especially the business world. Thus, organizations of Italian Americans in Brooklyn in various professions, such as an Italian medical society and an Italian pharmaceutical society, in numerous mutual aid societies and fraternal lodges, in charitable and religious organizations, underscored their growing prominence in society. "The reason that there were Italians of prominence and ability in nearly every field of activity in Brooklyn was plain enough. It was not simply that the Italians were a versatile people, it was because there were so many of them."[363] Clearly, the establishment of this groundwork would be of immense benefit to aspiring politicians—both Republicans and Democrats who reached the peak of their power in the next phase of political maturation—between the two world wars. The expanded nationality base was important to individuals affiliated with the Republican Party like LaGuardia and Marcantonio at least early in their careers, and those with the Democratic Party like DeSapio, Capozzoli, and Pope.

COMING OF AGE

Republicans LaGuardia and Marcantonio are examples of those who came of age politically in this period and whose sway extended beyond their ethnic enclave. By the outbreak of the Second World War, LaGuardia was firmly entrenched in a singular position as the most conspicuous and most influential Italian American elected to public office. Beginning with election to Congress in 1916, he was an exception to the general rule of lesser political posts, of course, and he would make the most of it by becoming President of the Board of Alderman of New York (the predecessor of the City Council) in 1919. He returned to Congress where he excelled and thereby was encouraged to seek nomination as mayoral candidate and finally voted in as New York City mayor in 1933, a post to which he was re-elected twice until he left office at the end of 1945. LaGuardia was exceptional in other ways as well—he was a Republican Italian American politician whereas the majority of New York Italian Americans then were Democrats, as was the party affiliation of most of their early officeholders. It is obvious that his hold on public office during the critical war years was especially consequential for the ethnic group.

The fiery left-winger Vito Marcantonio belied his Republican Party label at the beginning of his congressional career in 1934, becoming a factor in the leftist American Labor Party by the 1940s. Among prominent elected officials within the New York Italian community, his was the most unyielding voice in opposition to Fascism. Although he opposed the United States entry into the war before Germany invaded Russia in 1941, he immediately reversed course and became a strong proponent for military defeat of Fascist Germany and Italy. Notwithstanding his extreme left-wing philosophy, he emerged as the national legislature's most noticeable and consistent defender of Italian Americans. Eschewing the defensive, he objected to denigration of his ethnic group and through diligent research sought out instances of heroism by servicemen of Italian descent. He cited the heartening response of Italian Americans to war bond drives and recounted for his congressional colleagues many episodes of their wholehearted participation in defense work and other operations to win the war. Accordingly, he fought for the right of Italian Americans to work in defense plans, castigating discrimination against them as frustrating the full mobilization of American power.[364] With the fall of Italy's fascist government imminent in 1943, Marcantonio worked vigorously for a quick peace treaty and ready acceptance of Italy as an ally, as well generous aid to that country. One of the hardest working legislators, Marcantonio was the most constituent-oriented congressman of his time not only for his own district but far beyond—at one point, a family friend contacted the Manhattan congressman on behalf of my father when he was seriously ill.

Not as prominent of LaGuardia or Marcantonio during the war years, Staten Island Republican Joseph H. Palma nevertheless enjoyed the distinction of being the only American of Italian origin to serve as a borough President in New York City. A veteran of the First World War and the father of ten including two in the military services, Palma was proud of his borough that was home to probably the greatest percentage of inhabitants of Italian Americans ancestry in the entire city. He was lavish in his praise of their patriotism, which was manifest not only in the number who served in the armed forces, but also in their participation of other activities such as a scrap-metal drive, in which it was estimated that each individual contributed one hundred pounds, rendering it the highest percentage in the city and probably in the nation.[365]

Democrats Louis Capozzoli, Carmine DeSapio, and Generoso Pope are examples of Democrats who also became more prominent in this era. Capozzoli, along with Marcantonio, was the other New York Italian American serving in Congress during the war years. Representing the heavily Italian American Lower East Side of Manhattan, he was a typical politician who came to his position as the Irish American element began to decline. Capozzoli made few speeches in Congress, but when he did, he did not fail to pay homage to his ethnic compatriots. He condemned discrimination against Italian Americans and proposed a bill to remove the "enemy" designation attached to Italian aliens. In 1943, he also broadcasted messages to the Italian people, advising them to resist compliance with Hitler.[366]

Born of a second generation mother and an immigrant father in 1908 in Greenwich Village, Carmine DeSapio attended the local parochial school, Fordham Prep and Fordham University, while becoming active in the Huron Democratic Club, which was affiliated with the powerful Tammany organization. These political clubs then exercised considerable influence in the pre-welfare program days, especially at Thanksgiving and Christmas time when they doled out turkey baskets to the needy. I recall with conflicting feelings, that on one or two occasions, the local political club in my neighborhood provided my family with a food basket at holiday time. Indeed, it was on these occasions when DeSapio could work at the Huron Club, extending aid to women and children that he especially cherished.[367] DeSapio began to challenge the Irish hegemony in local Democratic politics in the late 1930s, and although he won district leadership in 1939, he was still denied recognition by the Irish leadership. By 1943, however, he had become the undisputed leader of the area and in recognition of the demographic shift that found more numerous rank and file Democratic members of Italian extraction, he was on his way to becoming Tammany Hall leader—a kingmaker whose enormous political clout was manifest in local state and even national affairs. Unfortunately, his association with mob boss Frank Costello tarnished his reputation, but he nevertheless is credited with engineering the election of a governor and a mayor, and even had access to the White House.[368]

These were also decisive years for Generoso Pope, who although never a holder of public office, nevertheless became a foremost power broker who wielded enormous political power. Emigrating from Italy as a poor teenager, his meteoric rise in business and political circles was accomplished through his ownership of *Il Progresso Italo-Americano* in 1928 as well as his proprietorship of *Il Corriere della Sera. Il Progresso Italo-Americano,* the largest Italian language paper in the country, with a 200,000 daily circulation, rendered it a potent force, especially within the Democratic Party throughout the 1930s, 1940s, and 1950s, and enabled Pope to exercise discernible impact in New York City as his newspaper endorsement could make the difference between victory and defeat for most Italian Americans candidates running for local offices. Notwithstanding Pope's favorable promotion of Fascism during the 1930s, because he was a major power broker within the New York Democratic Party, Pope's persuasion's extended beyond the city, indeed into the White House itself. As the nation veered closer and closer to war, Pope's earlier stance became more vulnerable, causing him to reevaluate his position. Under pressure from anti-Fascist elements now beginning to sway President Roosevelt, the chastised *Il Progresso* publisher reversed his earlier pro-Mussolini stance, and now used the pulpit of the largest Italian American daily to call for Mussolini's defeat. Reflecting this new posture, his newspaper printed "unadulterated denunciations of Mussolini in both [English and Italian] languages." Pope's explanation of his support for Mussolini acknowledged that although he had been beguiled, he had come to realize he had been misled.

> We can all look back at the early years of Mussolini regime and admit in all candor that like uncounted others we did not distinguish the Italian people from the Mussolini regime. The Mussolini myth was extraordinarily beguiling ...
>
> Frankly we too did not escape this insidious Mussolini spell. We too were blinded by the Mussolini bluster and sham ... "our awakening came in 1938 when Italy promulgated her first anti-Semitic laws. We were shocked by this deviation from the time honored Italian tradition. Italians have never known or practiced racial discrimination. It was our first intimation that Mussolini was falling under the influence of Hitler. Our suspicions were confirmed when, on June 10, 1940, Mussolini dragged Italy into war. We knew then that he had betrayed Italy, democracy and the world.[369]

This admission has led historian John Diggins to conclude that even though still regarded with suspicion, he deserved credit for

> ... his courageous stand against Italian anti-Semitism and continued support of Roosevelt attest. Moreover, as we shall see shortly, when Italy entered the war Pope made absolutely clear his undivided loyalty to the United States, though admittedly his position on Italy itself, like that of many Italian Americans was tortuously ambivalent."[370]

Mirroring the larger society, Italian American women while virtually absent from elective office during this period, were active in some pursuits that could have political consequences. Led by social worker Elba Fara-bogoli, a group that included the wives of Edward Corsi and Vito Marcantonio formed organizations, loosely linked together under the Council of Italo-American Womens Clubs, to promote Americanization among Italian women. The idea was to promote citizenship, as well as social and recreational integration with non-Italians.[371]

EXILES AND COMPETING POLITICAL PHILOSOPHIES

The war years found New York's Italian Americans animated politically not only within traditional party alignments, but also over the issue of Fascism. The incipient antifascist movement saw opponents of Mussolini come to this country to try to educate not only Italian Americans, but Americans in general about the evils of Fascism. While some of the individuals and groups involved in this movement were radicals, there were others from more traditional bases that also became active in the New York area. One of them was Luigi Sturzo, a Catholic priest from Sicily who was just as opposed to Fascism as those from liberal or left-wing hues, except from a more traditional viewpoint. Founder of the Catholic Popolare party, Sturzo lived for a number of years in Brooklyn, where he wrote books, articles, and letters denouncing the Mussolini regime and opined that "even the anticlericalism of Italian liberals was preferable to that of the Blackshirts." [372]

It was ironic that while living in Brooklyn, Sturzo felt compelled to defend Italy against perceived disparagement over the fighting quality of Italians, even as the war unfolded and liberated Italy joined the fight against Germany. Specifically, he took umbrage with Hanson Baldwin's denigration of the fighting aspect of Italians, who in his estimation "have been of very slight military value in the front lines and they have been of less value than had been hoped behind our line." To Sturzo, Baldwin contributed to "the all-too-frequent generic depreciation of Italy's efforts."[373] Although attracting limited attention from the intelligentsia and the elite, Sturzo's views received considerable notice within Catholic circles, including the Italian language weekly *Il Crociato* that was available in my parish and the other predominantly Italian parishes in the Brooklyn diocese. My recollection of *Il Crociato* is that of a four page weekly with, what was to my young mind, an arresting front page depiction of the cross, to introduce two English-language and two Italian-language pages. To Alberto Cupelli, prominent anti-Fascist, who criticized the paper for its pro-Fascist stance, the assertion that this publication was edited by Carlo Di Biasi, "brother to the notorious Black Shirt Agostino De Biasi ... " was a sham. "But Carlo de Biasi, as far as we know, has never been a writer, and so we seem to see the hand of Agostino ... "[374]

Better known among the intelligentsia was the Mazzini Society that inveighed against the Fascist regime until the end of the war when it continued to warn against a revival of Fascism.[375] Organizers of this society included a small but influential number of recent Italian political exiles like Salvemini, Ascoli, and Sforza as well as those who had come to this country in an earlier period such as Carlo Tresca. Members of this group interacted with Italian American antifascists in other circles, as for example, Antonini of the labor movement. The seemingly common bond of antifascism in reality masked a political scene that contained varying shades of the political spectrum. "From the start, despite a broad consensus on anti-Fascism and liberal democracy, *Nazione Unite's* writers and de facto editorial staff faced their own internal disagreements about the paper's objectives and editorial policy. Such differences reflected fundamental fissures within the Mazzini Society itself."[376] Salvemini, for instance, notwithstanding his genuine credentials as a sincere antifascist, nevertheless, took a rather doctrinaire stand adamantly opposed to collaboration with people who had previously been linked with the detested ideology. Virtually anyone of prominent political stature in attendance at any gathering in which a known fascist spoke, was branded with the pro-fascist brush or that of fascist sympathizer. The obstinate posture extended to those who otherwise also had strenuously opposed Fascism, such as Antonini whom he rebuked because the labor leader was willing to accept association with Generoso Pope following the publisher's denunciation of Mussolini. Even after Pope turned on Mussolini, Salvemini continued to judge him a Fascist tool—even willing to discount the fact that Roosevelt also had entered into a rapprochement with Pope; yet this was of no matter to Salvemini. For similar reasons, Salvemini likewise reproached Antonini for associating with Edward Corsi, former Commissioner of Immigration and LaGuardia's Relief Administrator. Salvemini's inflexible position is to be contrasted with radical Tresca, whose anti-Fascist credentials were never in doubt, while never reconciling himself with Pope, did reunite with Corsi.[377]

The exiles' activity operated against a background of United States government policy that was relatively ambiguous toward the political activities of foreign language groups within the United States. Two of the several agencies that had considerable say in the matter—the Department of State and the Foreign Nationalities Bureau—differed over what the government policy toward such groups ought to be, with the former less tolerant of political activities than the latter. "The State Department, along with the FBI, viewed America's ethnic population with suspicion and thought it essential to limit, or at least control, ethnics' political activities."[378]

SOLIDARITY TO DEFEAT MUSSOLINI

Despite bickering between various political elements in the early part of the war, they were of a similar mind when it came to use their positions to call for Mussolini's defeat. In his weekly broadcasts beamed to Italy, LaGuardia spoke out forcefully against Mussolini and his German allies. "He called for Italians to create ... trouble and incite ... to riot". He asked that Rome be declared an open city a save it from destruction and as liberation forces penetrated Italy, he appealed for food to reach the starving Italian people.[379] There is strong evidence that LaGuardia's broadcast encouraged Italians to hasten the defeat of Mussolini.

In addition to Italian American leaders, spokesmen for the United States government, in a move to further weaken Mussolini's hold in Italy, also emphasized that extensive help would be extended to Italians who surrendered. As a case in point, former New York Governor Herbert Lehman, now serving as Director of Foreign Relief and Rehabilitation Operations, announced that "Italian people would be supplied with food and other necessary items once the tyrants of overthrown."[380] Newspaper editorials chimed in with reminders of erstwhile amity between the American and Italian people. "We have a long tradition of friendship and fair-dealing with the Italian people to support our words." was the declaration in the June 15, 1943 editorial. Even more revelatory was the June 17, 1943 *New York Daily Mirror* statement:

> Our conflict with Italy has been unique in that Americans had never considered themselves at war with Italians.
>
> We have known them in this country, have seen them become good citizens, liked them for their gaiety and zest, respected them for their industry.
>
> There are still 1,223,580 persons in America who were born in Italy, 284,075 in New York State. Of the latter 248,134 are aliens. They have given us no trouble.
>
> There are countless other Americans of Italian strain, descendants of the immigrants who came here in the greatest numbers around the turn of the century—2,045,877 of them in the peak decade 1900-1910."[381]

DIVISION WITHIN POLITICAL SPECTRUM

However reconciled were the disparate Italian American groups working for the defeat of Mussolini's Fascist government, Left and Right wing factions were far from united with regard to the kind of government that should replace Il Duce. For example, there was a tiresome rift within the Mazzini Society over the role that Communist elements should play that was further complicated by the killing of fiercely anti-Stalinist Carlo Tresca in January 1943. In the end, the Communists were isolated. Meanwhile, the demise of Mussolini encouraged the Italian American Right to try to promote a traditional political approach in Italy.[382] However, most Italian American political leaders, midway between the Left and the Right, used their influence to pressure for immediate relief to war-torn areas of Italy.

Typical of many New York Italian American political leaders was the activity of Paul Rao, who in August 1943, broadcasted a shortwave message imploring Italians not only to abandon the Fascist government, but also to welcome American forces. He informed listeners that he was a son of Sicily, born in Prizzi, in 1899, immigrated to the United States as a child, and now held the important government position as Assistant United States Attorney General. In asking them to be open to American forces, he sought to jog their memories by recounting the remarkable aid Americans had extended to Messina, Sicily, in the wake of the calamitous earthquake of 1908, when United States naval vessels and the Red Cross brought extensive emergency help, and American personnel became noteworthy for efforts over four months to rebuild houses that were destroyed. In gratitude, the area of Messina in which the rebuilding activity took place had given American place names to two of its streets: "Rosuvett" (President Theodore Roosevelt) and "Brocchlin" (Brooklyn).[383] Rao, who had served in the American Navy in World War I, also reminded them that the United States and Italy fought side by side in that war, and also that American soldiers currently were fighting and dying in order to help them gain liberation.[384]

THE POLITICS OF AID TO ITALY

The grim reality was that Italy was faced with an economy in shambles, a chaotic monetary system, and a desperate shortage of food. Confirmation of the seriousness of the Italian situation was abundant. Both Colonel Charles Poletti, Allied Military Governor in Italy, and William F. O'Dwyer,

Chief of the Economic Section of the Allied Mission to Italy, attested to its gravity, as did New York Archbishop Francis Spellman who visited Italy in late 1944. Spellman's eyewitness account emphasized the utter devastation that that hapless nation faced. "Disillusioned, stunned and completely crushed the Italians ask now only the right to work to gain their daily bread."[385] To move the Roosevelt administration to deal with the situation was to prove an arduous and protracted campaign since the administration saw Hitler's defeat holding priority, rather than aid to a former enemy nation—a belief that undoubtedly reflected the views of most Americans. Although there some prominent Americans warned about the potentially catastrophic situation in areas of Italy, their voices paled in contrast to a solid and vociferous phalanx of Italian American leaders and organizations, who participated in a loud drumbeat of demands that the United States aid the stricken nation immediately. Italian American spokesmen on the home front reminded listeners and readers of the millions of Americans of Italian descent with relatives in Italy who looked to America to extend a hand of generosity. Prominent leaders within the ethnic group formed committees and organizations, such as the American Committee for Italian Democracy, with esteemed Judge Ferdinand Pecora serving as chairman, and Luigi Antonini executive vice-chairman. Notwithstanding the admiration of the individuals involved, the Committee unfortunately

Pictured here at a picnic in New Jersey are Italian prisoners of war. They were among the thousands who agreed to assist the American war effort after Italy became a co-belligerent power.

PHOTO COURTESY GIUSEPPE DELIGUORI

fell into the pitfalls of factionalism and personal jealousy that produced disunity within the ethnic community, with some critics objecting that it was extreme arrogance to try to foist a democratic system on Italy, while others denounced the exclusion of Communists by the Committee.[386] One example of the contretemps was described by columnist Drew Pearson, when he censured the Order of the Sons of Italy for its failure to cooperate, charging that while there was no question regarding the loyalty of rank and file members, the organization still maintained a pro-fascist leadership.

> Again I repeat that I am confident that many of the Sons of Italy are faithful, industrious and patriotic. But I also repeat that it is up to them to purge themselves of a leadership which has been definitely pro-fascist in the past, and which appears quite willing to sit on the sidelines waiting for the government to prod them into the war effort, rather than take the initiative like true "Sons of the United States," not men who live in the past as "Sons of Italy."[387]

For its part, officers of the national Italian fraternal organization retorted by adamantly rejecting Pearson's charges as utter falsehood, maintaining that the Sons of Italy had been cited for its efforts in support of the United States, including, for example, broadcasts to Italians to accept American forces not as conquerors but as liberators, and also by participating in War Bond drives. The pressure exerted on the Sons of Italy had a desirable effect—by the third week of July 1943, the fraternal order announced its willingness to handle and finance propaganda broadcasts to Italy, a move regarded even by Pearson as "one of most patriotic moves made by an Italian group to date."[388]

Still others in the ethnic community followed their own inclinations, like Marcantonio who notwithstanding his severe criticism of the American Committee for Italian Democracy and his participation in a rival left-wing movement that sponsored a large rally at Madison Square Garden to stress its case, nevertheless used his Congressional seat to promote the cause of better treatment for Italy.[389] "In Congress, Vito Marcantonio succeeded in getting the House Foreign Affairs Committee to open hearings on Italy's plight, while LaGuardia threatened to suspend his propaganda broadcasts to Italy; the Catholic hierarchy, spurred on by the Pope's plea for immediate aid, resorted to both prayer and pressure."[390] A staunch defender of Italian Americans, Marcantonio rebuked critics who demeaned the fighting quality of Italians by pointing out that Italians would fight strongly for freedom but not for tyranny. After Italy's surrender, he called for acceptance of Italian fighters as free men, rather than as prisoners of war.

In addition to internal division within the Italian ethnic group, attempts to expedite aid to Italy were frustrated by government inaction that elicited spirited criticism. In April 1944, *Il Progresso Italo-Americano* lamented the fact that ten months after Allied forces started to liberate Italy, aid for the suffering came excruciatingly slow, "many things have been left undone which could and should have been done some time for relieving their urgent wants and burning needs." The realization that Charles P. Taft, acting chairman of the War Relief Control Board, was opposed to the Italian American private aid effort earned an unsubtle rebuke to the red tape delaying tactics that had stymied sufficient as faintest excuse on earth for any government official holding up the formation of a relief committee genuinely representative of the entire Italo-American community in our country."[391]

The delay in bringing meaningful relief also was due in part to internal discord within the Roosevelt administration, namely brouhaha between Undersecretary of State Sumner Welles and Secretary of State Cordell Hull. In early 1943, even before Sicily surrendered, Italian American leaders had developed a "Bundles to Italy," relief project that then Acting secretary of State Welles seemed to support. Before it could be implemented, however, there occurred "the unfortunate personal feud between Mr. Welles and Secretary of State Hull, with the result that Welles resigned and Hull seemed to frown on anything which Welles had approved or initiated."[392] The end result was the harmful forestalling of meaningful aid for nine months.

Relying on their particular vocational and or professional interests, home front Italian Americans embarked on various programs. A significant undertaking was that of the medical profession which organized the American Medical Relief for Italy. With headquarters in New York and headed by Dr. Charles Muzzicato, this organization specialized in collecting and delivering sorely-needed medical supplies to stricken Italy. One of the most energetic individuals in this activity was Italian-born philanthropist, Dr. Augusto Rossano, chief doctor in New York City's Transit Division, and active in the development of Harlem Hospital. Within a few months, this organizations had expedited several groups of medical items valued at thousands of dollars. Noteworthy also was the creation of the God Parents for Italian War Orphans Committee in New York early in 1945, which devoted itself to raising funds to "adopt" and assist children orphaned by the war. In April 1945, committee chairman Margherita De-Vecchi announced a gift of $1,620 had been given to the Italian Red Cross to purchase scare items: linens, towels, soap, shoes, toothpaste, etc., for the maintenance of 180 orphans. Other Americans of Italian descent such as fraternal groups, ethnic organizations, and businesses in Trenton's Italian enclave did their part, responding to Judge Marchisio's call for aid to Italy by collecting funds to purchase ambulances.[393]

ITALIAN AMERICAN ALLIED MILITARY GOVERNORS

While Italian American political leaders vied with one another over the best approach to deal with Italy, we Italian Americans on the home front kept hearing the disquieting and dispiriting news that, in spite of steps taken by the Allied forces to regularize order in the defeated nation, conditions seemed to worsen. Presumably because of the ethnic root connection, the appointment of prominent Italian Americans as military governors over areas of Italy held out some hope. Since LaGuardia was indeed the most prominent political figure within the ethnic community, there was speculation that he would be appointed administrator of aid to Italy. Furthermore, LaGuardia's desire to obtain a military commission to help administer liberated Italy was an open secret, one that never came to pass however, as such commissions were extended to others.

In addition to the aforementioned Major Toscani, the naming of Frank Gulotta, Charles Poletti, and Michael Musmanno was welcomed since all possessed palpable Italian roots. The Gulotta family had emigrated from Santa Margerita di Belice, Sicily, to my community of Ridgewood, a heavily Sicilian enclave. Frank Gulotta, a product of this background, who understood Italian language and culture, moved to Nassau County where he became an Assistant District Attorney and volunteered for the service with the outbreak of war. By the beginning of 1945, Major Gulotta had been appointed military governor of Frosinone, a region of east central Italy, that had been heavily damaged as a result of the war and its aftermath. We became acquainted with the deprivation sustained by the local populace via the publication of Gulotta's accounts that were reported in the ethnic press. Italian Americans with close relatives struggling to survive in a war-torn country found some encouragement reading about how these people coped with their dismal situation with help from America. In one installment, Gulotta described the gratitude of a small town that he visited and to which he brought aid.

After his service as Military Governor of an Italian province during the war, Frank Gulotta went on to become the first Italian American elected to countrywide office. Here he is being sworn in as Nassau District Attorney. His youngest son Thomas eventually was elected Nassau County Executive.

Yesterday I visited a small town after a dangerous trip under a furious snowstorm. I was enthusiastically received by the people who improvised a triumphal procession for the townspeople, marching under the American and the Italian flags. I was made an honorary member of an association which has a chapter in the United States I attended a dinner "di onore" where the local theatrical group performed. I then appeared at the balcony where townspeople offered thanks to the accompaniment of a stanza of the Star Spangled Banner.[394]

CHARLES POLETTI

Born in Barre, Vermont, and the son of Italian immigrants, Charles Poletti had served as Lieutenant Governor and then Governor of New York. Indeed, besides his high profile political background, Poletti possessed excellent Italian credentials—including winner of the prestigious Eleanora Duse fellowship to study law at the University of Rome—he was also fluent in the Italian language and a recipient of a law degree at Harvard University. Notwithstanding this impressive pedigree, nevertheless we on the home front were apprehensive as we continued to read about problems experienced by disconsolate Italians and naturally were concerned about the welfare of our relatives. As the only member of her immediate family in this country, my mother understandably worried about her mother, her two sisters and two brothers, and their children who remained in the old homestead. She was constantly exchanging information with other relatives in the neighborhood to ascertain whether or not things were improving. Although not heavily emphasized at the time, the situation was further hampered by the persistence of a fundamental difference of opinion between Great Britain and the United States, the two major powers responsible for policy toward Italy. Generally speaking, Great Britain remained unsympathetic to the plight of Italians for the reason that the British had endured great suffering due to the actions of the Axis power, of which Italy was a partner. Great Britain, furthermore, felt it should have a major voice in the matter of Italy's disposition because of its historic role in the Mediterranean, in contrast to the United States interest which was temporary—only as long as the war lasted. The matter was further complicated by the appointment of British General Sir Harold Alexander as Force Commander of the "Husky" operation, which the British interpreted as making them the senior partner in dealing with Italy. The American attitude, however, was more compassionate in part because a large segment of its fighting forces were of Italian ancestry as well as the political reality that the ethnic group formed a significant voting bloc in major American cities in the eastern part of the country. Even before Allied forces landed in Italy, it was recognized that the liberated Italians would welcome Americans—these realities influenced military and political leaders.

> There are, for example, the strong pro-American feeling in Sicily and southern Italy; the surety as to American long-range sympathy because of the several million American citizens of Italian origin, and the close contact, in normal times, of these elements with their families in Italy; and America's historical detachment from questions involving the relations of European states with each other. The propaganda campaign of the Fascist regime against the United States has not been as bitter or as effective, nor has it left its marks on so many elements of the Italian population, as has the abusive campaign against England, which has continued almost without interruption since 1935.

> ROOSEVELT WANTS AS MANY AMERICAN APPOINTMENTS AS PRACTICABLE [Msg, Roosevelt to Churchill, 14 Apr 43, OPD files, 014.1, Security (1-38)]

> Replying to your telegram of April 13th, I have given my approval to appointment of General Alexander as the Allied Military Governor of HUSKY-land during occupation and under the Supreme Commander General Eisenhower. In view of the friendly feeling toward America entertained by a great number of the citizens of the United States who

are of Italian descent it is my opinion that our military problem will be made less difficult by giving to the Allied Military Government as much of an American character as is practicable.[395]

With Prime Minister Churchill's acceptance of the proposition that the Allies should fully exploit the advantage of American ties with Italy due to the large number of Italian American citizens, many of the ethnic group were appointed to play leading roles—Poletti being one of the most important and most distinguished. In his newspaper, Generoso Pope warmly endorsed Poletti's appointment, especially since the Allied Military Governor visited Pope's brother in Benevento, Italy, that incidentally revealed the existence of Fascist pressure on the Italian branch of the Pope family "because you in America were enthusiastically supporting the victory of the Allied cause"—an interesting insight into the antagonistic attitude toward Pope after he decided to denounce Fascism.[396] Declining a proffered commission as colonel until he had earned it, in April 1943, Poletti was made a lieutenant colonel, landed in Sicily a few days after the invasion and soon was appointed Allied Military Governor (AMG) of the island. Allied military progress was so swift that that it sometimes produced an awkward situation for Poletti. Thus as was the practice, within hours after combat troops took over towns, steps were taken to regularize civil affairs. In one case, the military left immediately after liberating the town of Favara, Sicily, leaving Poletti the sole American in a town that had been hostile only minutes before. It was with an eerie feeling that he went before the chief of police to issue orders to him. "Then I made a speech to the mass of people crowded around City Hall and explained that there would be no difficulty if they obeyed the military regulations. They applauded and cheered as I drove away. It was just like a political meeting back home."[397]

In February 1944, he was transferred to serve as AMG of Naples and subsequently of Rome and Milan. As Military Governor Poletti emphasized ousting Fascists from regimes, providing sufficient military police,

and control of civilian transportation—the key to the economy.[398] These
priorities were very important of course and under Poletti's guidance great
progress was made. There continued to remain, however, intractable problems regarding the issues of food, fuel, and clothing that Poletti acknowledged and attributed to "widespread corruption and dishonesty in the
Italian civil service ... aggravated by war conditions." Likewise "to oust all
Fascists meant sometimes to dismiss capable men ... " and thus place important civilian functions in the hands of people who were inexperienced
and inefficient.[399] In explaining the nature of the problems, Poletti offered
an instructive contrast between military and civilian administration.

> The problems of administering a region like the Campania
> are of course much more difficult than administration back
> home. There has been so much destruction of the vital ele-
> ments of the Italian economy by the unavoidable acts of war
> and by the unnecessary dynamiting by the Nazis that the
> struggle to rehabilitate is tremendously challenging. How-
> ever, the officials—I don't mean the Fascists ones because
> we threw them out—and the Italian people are cooperating
> magnificently and we are making great progress.[400]

In the conclusion of historian A. Russell Buchanan, Eisenhower insisted
on the imposition of military rule, officially called Allied Military Government of Occupied Territory (AMGOT), as a means of maintaining control
of areas formerly in enemy hands. These governments, moreover, were
"generally successful in maintaining law and order behind the fighting
lines. Military government officials administered justice fairly, recruited
labor, and tried to deal with such problems as divided command, looting of
food, and black markets."[401] However much progress was reported, home
front Italian Americans clamored for more.

MICHAEL MUSMANNO

Appointment to the position of Allied Military Governor of Sorrentine
Peninsula in liberated Italy was an especially fateful assignment for naval

officer Michael Musmanno. Born in 1897 in western Pennsylvania, he was the son of Italian immigrants, whose father worked in the coal mines. Experiencing a hardscrabble life as a youngster, he served in the military during World War I, became a lawyer who in 1927 served in the historic defense of Sacco and Vanzetti, an unselfish champion in the cause of the downtrodden, an author who saw one of his works, "Black Fury" become the basis for a Hollywood film, a jurist in the momentous Nuremberg War trials, and a prominent public figure and judge in Pennsylvania.[402]

During the course of the war in 1943, Musmanno became Allied Military Governor for an area of Italy, which included some 200,000 Italians who were confronted with the daunting challenges of survival in the midst of war, especially with regard to a severe food shortage. To alleviate the problem, Musmanno enlisted the aid of three Italian fishermen to salvage and repair an Italian schooner, and sail it to the port city of Bari to obtain desperately needed supplies. They arrived at their destination on December 2, 1943, and had just loaded the ship with olive oil when they were surprised by a ferocious German air attack that forced them to abandon ship, and placed him in imminent danger. "He was deep in the water. Above him on the surface a fire was raging, giving the blue waters of the Adriatic Sea an orange glow as he looked up ... He fought his way upward."[403] Musmanno and his three companions made it back to shore where they witnessed further devastation when several ships anchored at Bari port were hit and the harbor soon became an inferno of flames and smoke accompanied by violent explosions of the burning ships. It was one of the worst disasters inflicted by German adversaries and one of worst naval setbacks.

Musmanno was, in fact, in the midst of one of the most disastrous bombing attack against allied ships during the entire war—some analysts described it as the most punishing air attack since Pearl Harbor. Since the port of Bari was in the British theater of operations, many of the sunken vessels were British; however, the several American merchant ships in the harbor on that fateful day also were victims. The final tally was a total of seventeen ships sunk, including five American, and six damaged vessels. There was a huge toll in civilian and military casulties, including several hundred men who were smeared with mustard gas oil that had escaped from a destroyed British ship—many of whom would succumb in the weeks following the bombardment.

REMEMBERING THE OLD COUNTRY

That Italy was severely devastated and in need of substantial help was a propostion readily admitted by most observers, although there was considerable disagreement on the home front as to how the aid should be facilitated. In part, private resources undertook the task of succoring the afflicted old country as indicated in advertisments to which readers of the ethnic press were implored to respond. One example, featured a photograph showing the results of German destruction—rubble in the main street of the destroyed Sicilian village of Randazzo that illustrated the hellish impact of war. The nostalgic plea exhorted Italian Americans that the result of the war would hopefully call to mind their native village in their pristine days, realizing that these dear places that used to be their cherished home are now despoiled and not so beautiful. Americans of Italian descent were enjoined to recollect the former attractiveness of these beautiful mountain towns and realize that to ascend to these places now would be to travel along paths of devastation marked by jagged course stones and ugly tree stumps. Pulling out all emotional stops, the immigrants were reminded about the bell in the village square whose pealings customarily summoned towenspeople to festivals and funerals. They were asked to think about their homes, the small monuments at the fountain in the village square, and the public garden where they played as children. In this unusual appeal for funds, *Il Progresso Italo-Americano* called upon well-bred home front Italian Americans also to submit short accounts of what their villages meant to them. While ad hoc efforts of this type to rebuild Italian villages were helpful, it was apparent that a broader and more structured approach was needed. In calling for assistance to Italy, some spokesmen had the temerity to suggest that critical posts should go to Italian Americans in order to facilitate and hasten the desired result.

> Our country should strengthen the caliber and official rank of its representatives in Italy—with additional men of character and capacity ... More food, clothes and medicines should be shipped to the people of Italy. In recent months, the drive in our country to rush supplies to needy Italians has gained much momentum. Americans should have greater and truly adequate representation in the agencies distributing inside Italy the relief which, in the main comes from the United States. Our citizens of Italian descent can be of special service in this situation, since they know the people and the language of the war-stricken land better than the representatives of other nations.

> For the same reason, American military men—particularly those of Italian extraction—should be drawn much more into commissions helping to reorganize Italy's armed forces on a more effective and democratic basis.[404]

MARCHISIO AND AMERICAN RELIEF FOR ITALY

By 1944, the issue of adequate relief for war-torn Italy had become an overriding concern on the Italian American home front—notwithstanding the appointment of Italian Americans as allied military governors. Thus it was acknowledged that while competent administrators like Poletti, who were serving as representatives of the United States Army, acted from proper and necessary military impulses, nevertheless, deprivation and suffering remained. Accordingly, the home front, while accepting the necessity of additional military action to free northern Italy, and the further necessity of the military to establish governments for liberated areas, nonetheless concluded that to leave the situation unchanged would result in an even more critical state of affairs. Italian Americans became increasingly concerned over basic bread and butter issues that their relatives faced in Italy, and that unfortunately did not receive much priority. To that end, in 1944, New Yorkers of Italian ancestry along with others of like persuasion created the American Relief for Italy Inc. with Brooklyn Judge Juvenal Marchisio as its president. Obtaining a leave of absence from the Domestic Court of New York City, Marchisio endeavored diligently to create a network of relief organizations in an effort to find "the most efficient way of coordinating all the resources of Americans of Italian origin in this country who are so anxious to offer aid to their blood kin across the sea."[405] In the ethnic neighborhoods of Brooklyn and throughout the city, we read with interest about the fruits of these efforts. For example, we learned that by marshalling together various resources, on July 1944, the relief organization sent 1,000,000 pounds of clothing, $850,000 worth medical supplies, 50 tons of powdered milk and 10,000,000 vitamin pills to Italy. Such efforts, worthy in themselves, alas were not deemed to be adequate to alleviate the serious nature of the problem, thus calling for additional action including on the spot examination.

The Administration was undoubtedly motivated by political considerations. "Watch for F. D. R. to speed up aid to the Italian civilian population as the elections draw near. Worried about the Italian vote, White House advisors are preparing to move heaven and earth to aid Italian civilian population before winter," wrote a perceptive columnist. He emphasized that the Administration was "increasingly aware of fears being expressed by Italian-Americans as to the treatment their relatives are being accorded in their native land."[406] In reality, Roosevelt's motivation in this regard was his sense of the need to shore up his base amidst a perceived softening of the Italian American vote in the face of the approaching 1944 presidential election. Against this backdrop, Marchisio's organization was able to exert such extraordinary political influence as to be able to overcome formidable opposition from the military and their spokesmen. This pressure was evidenced in Roosevelt's rejection of the advice of his own cabinet member, Acting Secretary of War Robert Patterson, who opposed Marchisio's proposal to visit Italy in order to further implement relief work, arguing that relief matters should proceed along military channels. "I am fearful that to permit Judge Marchisio to go to Italy at this time as a representative of private American charity will jeopardize the success of the Army's efforts to obtain distributions in Italy of the relief supplies provided by Judge Marchisio's organization.[407] The record seems to demonstrate a major difference of opinion between the military and the civilian approach to the topic of administering aid. Thus, even while Poletti acknowledged that conditions in the Frosinone province "are bad, very bad," military authorities did not appreciate involvement of private civilian groups. Matters of relief should be placed under military not civilian jurisdiction.

Thus, it was revealing and momentous for Marchisio to depart for Italy in September 1944, when together with Myron C. Taylor, Roosevelt's ambassador to the Vatican, he met with Pope Pius XII to further coordinate relief efforts. That the Pope was extremely eager for additional aid for Italy is suggested by his approval of Msgr. John Patrick Carrol-Abbing's creation of Boys Town of Italy in 1944—a program that had strong support in the American Catholic Church, especially in Italian parishes. Upon his return to the United States, Marchisio reported that Italy was in dire straits, using descriptive terms that went beyond military reports. "Reduced to utter poverty and, in many cases, famine, the entire population is in a state of helpless confusion." He stated that the Italian crisis was a test for democracy and voiced hope that Americans would respond positively "in the humane and charitable spirit of their objectives, afford today to the unfortunate and misled Italian people an opportunity to receive relief from their sufferings: food clothing, shelter and aid ... " Over and beyond humanitarian concerns Marchisio spoke about the detrimental political consequences of inadequate and immediate aid "unless the American people wish Italy to be in a state of anarchy by February."[408] Although constantly decrying the insufficiency of relief provided his organization, Marchisio continued to promote campaigns for aid that resulted in reports that highlighted various home front contributions such as that of canned milk by Brooklyn Boy Scouts and other shipments of powdered milk, clothing, vitamins, first aid kits, needles, and thread. While we Italian Americans on the home front contributed to these campaigns via union, church, and organizational drives, we also undertook personal family efforts to bring solace and aid to stricken Italians. That this was a matter of great concern in my household was evident in the tasks my mother, sister, brother, and I undertook in sending private assistance.

MESSAGES FROM HOME FRONT TO ITALY

From the beginning of the war, home front Italian Americans played important roles in communicating messages to Italy via short wave radio. In their radio addresses, many an Italian American leader spoke to Italians in this manner urging them not to resist the Allies—appeals that were believed to have made considerable impact.[409] But it was not only famous political leaders who became involved in this form of communication, as illustrated in the remarkable example of Natalie Danesi Murray who broadcasted messages to the Italian populace three times a day via NBC station in New York, constantly articulating and lauding the great achievements of Italians—including the marvelous invention of the wireless system by their countryman Guglielmo Marconi—the very instrument of her communication. Utilizing a well thought out method, she brought news to Italians of their "blood relations" in America amply supplemented with their contributions to the fight against Mussolini. She carefully avoided any association of Italians with Fascism, and eschewed condescension by rejecting the notion of inherent inferiority as the explanation for Italian Army defeats on the battlefield, attributing the same to an unwillingness to fight for Nazi Germany. Italian American short wave radio speakers sought to sway Italian public opinion by using their ancient language and dialects, informing listeners in Italy about the patriotism of so many of young people of Italian ancestry in the armed forces serving to liberate them from a cruel and burdensome Italian Fascist dictatorship. To Italian Americans on the home front, such communications were hopeful signs that the end of the Italian Fascist regime was in sight and that substantial aid would soon flow from the United States to liberated Italy. They were heartened also by a more sympathetic stance on the part of the United States government, however, it would soon become a reality that assistance would be slow to develop. [410]

CHAPTER VIII
ITALY,
AN ASSOCIATED POWER

PROGRESS OF THE WAR

Decisions of significant moment for the prosecution of the war were made in 1943; these would have major consequences on the war front as well as the home front. Militarily, the decision arrived at by President Roosevelt and Prime Minister Churchill at the Casablanca Conference to invade North Africa in 1942, then to proceed to invade Italy in 1943, was moving apace impressively, although at great price. Paradoxically, the invasion of Italy that was of vital interest to Italian Americans was extremely costly—it was estimated to have resulted in over 300,000 American and British casualties, and ironically was subsequently judged by some to have been of dubious value. "The Italian campaign was a needlessly costly sideshow" is the conclusion of historian David Kennedy in recounting that the effort was proffered as a tactic to occupy large numbers of enemy troops, thus forcing Germany to transfer numerous divisions from the eastern front, thereby relieving pressure against the USSR. The upshot was that, in reality, a relatively small number of German divisions were all that it engaged.[411]

The decision to invade Italy had its genesis in the call for a second front after Germany invaded Russia in June 1941. The consequence of Hitler's action resulted in driving Communist Russia into an alliance with other major Allied powers: anti-Communist Great Britain and the United States. As a principal Allied partner, USSR Premier Josef Stalin argued that while Great Britain and the United States were relatively spared the worst of enemy attack, his nation alone was bearing the awful brunt of Axis aggression and that a true joint venture required the other partners to undertake meaningful steps to aid his nation. Simply put, he clamored for a genuine second front in Western Europe, not North Africa nor southern Europe. Military decisions were not made in a vacuum of course. To British Prime Minister Winston Churchill, for whom political issues always constituted an integral and indispensable part of wartime policy, Allied policy should be based also on the compelling need to prevent the Communist nation from filling a power vacuum in eastern Europe after the defeat of Germany. Unable to gain support for the second front to be launched in the Balkans in Eastern Europe, he then proposed the invasion of Italy. Also under consideration was the genuine desire to build Allied forces to a higher level of preparation before a second front in Western Europe could be launched successfully. Stalin accepted neither reason, letting it be known that he would not be satisfied with anything less than a cross Channel invasion. It was to be an uneasy alliance. "Unconditional surrender" or the absence of a negotiated settlement was the other critical decision decided upon at Casablanca. Regarded as a hard line policy, it alarmed noted anti-Fascist leaders who found this to be so rigidly inflexible as to discourage internal movements to oust the Mussolini regime. Even Churchill suggested alleviating the policy with regard to Italy.[412]

WELCOME AND REUNION IN ITALY

D Day was almost a distant year away from the July 1943 foray into Sicily, where the Americans and the British followed up initial success in Sicily by invading southern Italy, with corollary impact on Italy and home front Italian Americans. These moves served as coup de grace to Fascist Italy where the military leadership soon took steps to stop the fighting and secure peace. The warm reception accorded American troops, in contra-distinction to British forces, was for the most part extraordinary yet unsur-prising, given the existence of many ongoing ties between Sicilians and Americans because the former had numerous relatives in the United States. Not to be overlooked also was the extensive propaganda effort illustrated in the action of American planes dropping fifteen million leaflets among the Italian populace prior to the invasion, informing Sicilians why they should surrender and simultaneously trying to dispel fears over American occupation because in fact they would be treated well.[413] We on the home front avidly read letters and newspaper accounts, especially in the ethnic press about the happy surprises experienced by American servicemen that they encountered in small villages. We read, for instance, about a fifteen year old Sicilian boy—my age in 1943—born in New York, but had gone with his family to live in Italy before the war, earning a hero citation from Americans because of his service as an interpreter for the Fifth Army.[414]

Capturing the essence of this event and numerous similar incidents of encounters with Italians who were familiar with English, a journalist was inspired to write albeit hypothetically, but in reality mirroring an altogether commonplace occurrence; he iterated an account of an Italian American soldier upon entering a small town.

> Let us follow him down a street in a small Italian town. "Hello" someone calls to him. He looks about expecting to see an American. But the man who has hailed him from the doorway of a stone house, is obviously an Italian, dressed in the costume of the countryside. The American stops in surprise. "Come inside" the Italian urges hospitably. "Rest

a minute. I haven't got much to give you—but how about some of our own wine."?

The astonished soldier follows the Italian. He learns that his host had been in America, that some of his family is still there.[415]

Although imaginary, the account nevertheless struck responsive chords on the part of many on the home front where reports of such dramatic encounters were as soul-wrenching as they were abundant. One could only imagine the anguish and dilemma of a family whose members served with opposing belligerent powers possibly fighting against family whose members served with opposing belligerent powers, possibly fighting against one's own ancestral country, with the knowledge that they might well be killing their own flesh and blood. It could not help, but produce a sense of melancholy or fatalism, but it did not overcome the sense of American patriotism that was shared by American soldiers.

The juxtaposition between divided families and national loyalty was a common theme on the Italian American home front of my youth. It could not help to be a recurring consideration as we became acquainted with the accounts from newspaper correspondents and other media people who expressed their amazement at the warm hospitality extended to them in the English language. For example, a photographer for the African edition of *Stars and Stripes* wrote about the reply to his clumsy effort to use his limited knowledge of Italian to greet the first native of Sicily he came across, startled to receive "Hiya, kid" in response. The Sicilian was Tom Adamo, who had worked for eighteen years as a presser in New Jersey.[416]

Within weeks of entering Sicily, the home front began to learn about incredible family reunions such as those of previously mentioned Middletown, Connecticut Sicilian Americans Frank Tarallo, Max Corvo, and Louis Fiorilla, along with other soldiers, who met mother, father, brothers, sisters, aunt, uncles, and cousins in that island and nearby—encounters that tugged at the heart. Among these remarkable instances was that of Pvt. Anthony Pace, who left Malta to find his fortune in America, only to return as a soldier where he found his mother in Gozo Island near Malta. Writing home from Sicily about reuniting with relatives where he was part of the invading American forces, Sam Therina said "I saw the place where Papa was born and where he played hide-and-seek. Your sisters told me that never in their life did they think they would see one of your sons, and boy, were they glad to see me."[417]

Long Island airman Albert Romeo related the account of meeting his grandmother near Naples, while Pvt. Joe Gallo from Poughkeepsie was surprised when he went to his grandmother's house in Gela, Sicily, and found her fondly holding a picture of him on her lap. It was an exceptional moment for Captain Iovino of Lawrence, Massachusetts, to be reunited with an old aunt who before the war had returned to Italy after a stay of several years in the United States, and for two American soldiers, who were cousins, who went together to the Italian house where their mothers were born.[418] From the Italian enclave in Westbury, New York, Private Louis Pascucci met his grandmother and cousin in a town south of Naples, while the Cucchi brothers, one a sergeant in the American Army and the other in the Italian Army now a prisoner of war, were reunited after 23 years.[419] One can imagine the overwhelming emotions of Corporal Salvatore Di Marco who had left his Sicilian home and family when he was fifteen, now returning to Mezzojuso to embrace his mother, father, and sister who had remained in the old country.[420]

For some Italian American soldiers, assignment to duty in Italy was welcomed as an opportunity to fulfill long held desires to visit relatives. In the 1930s, the brother of Brooklyn's Phil Dario went to visit relatives in Italy and returned extolling the virtues of the country to such an extent that it instilled in Phil an urge to visit for himself if the opportunity came —the war provided him with the chance. As part of the American invading forces that landed in Salerno in 1943, and possessing fluency with the Italian language, he played a useful interpreter role in helping to facilitate the liberation of a number of small towns where he interacted with grateful Italian townsfolk—upon his return decades later, the townspeople continued to remember and honor him. As part of the invading forces, he was able to visit Nocera Inferiore, his family's ancestral town where he met his grandmother and other close relatives.[421]

AMBIVALENCE

It was clear that for more than a few Italian Americans, the prospect of taking up arms against Italy posed such a profound moral dilemma that they requested and were granted assignments to fight elsewhere than in Italy. The Capoferri family that had emigrated from a small town south of Rome and settled in Pittsburgh was one example. The call to the colors of two Capoferri brothers energized their mother to take prompt action—she was determined to influence Army policy by going in person to Washington D. C. in order to talk to military authorities and plead with them not to send her sons to fight in Italy because of a fear that they might end up fighting against their own blood relatives, some of whom were in the Italian army, while others were in the Resistance movement. The upshot was that the two brothers were not sent to the Italian theater of war. Whether this was result of mother's plea is unknown, but it is significant to note that a number of Italian Americans became very concerned about this potentially traumatic possibility of brother against brother or other close relatives.[422] The anguish of having to go to war against Italy was clearly reflected in the sentiments of an East Harlem resident, who when asked about the issue, responded that he prayed to the Madonna to ease the pain. "It covered a lot of hurts. The Italians were so proud of being Italian." When asked about their feelings regarding Italian Americans fighting Italians, the answer was, "Not too hot, no, because it was their own ... But we couldn't do anything about it."[423]

It is uncertain whether there existed a universal Army policy with regard to providing Italian American soldiers an option as to whether or not they would be assigned to fight in Italy. Based on a number of interviews, variations of policy were employed, with some apparently given the option, thereby reflecting an indication that the issue was of concern to military authorities. In his study on the war, Peter Belmonte found that the question came up in a number of instances. Belmonte cites Tony Pilutti, who while in training, actually had to sign a waiver stating that he would fight against Italy, if necessary. His cousin, who shared his birthday, was at the time, a soldier in the Italian Army. Although he had mixed feelings about the possibility of fighting against the Italian Army, Pilutti nevertheless signed the waiver, figuring that in any event Italy was almost out of the war at the time, and he would most likely be fighting only against the Germans. Bill Donofrio, an infantryman in the 70th Division, recalled that, during his induction physical, "I was asked if I would object to fighting against Italy, to which I answered no. That, and being asked if I liked girls were all I recall about any interview." The possibility of fighting against Italy was a potentially traumatic experience for Giulio Miranda, whose two uncles harboring strong sympathies for Italy, had returned to fight for the land of their birth at the outbreak of the war. "When I went into the army it was a heartbreaking experience, I specifically requested not to go to Italy. I had relatives there. This is an affirmation of the persistence of culture." Even though he harbored a deep aversion to Fascism and had a deep loyalty to the United States, given a choice since there were different theaters of war, Miranda sought not to go to Italy. "I would have found this very difficult to do and I am sure I would have been in trouble with the army. In fact, I was in trouble once because I fraternized with Italian prisoners and this was poorly looked upon."[424] Likewise, upon being drafted, Bronx immigrant Egidio Faustini requested that he not be assigned to fight in Italy since his brother Rocco was a soldier in the Italian Army.[425]

Dom Porcaro, born near Naples in 1922, came to the United States in 1931, and received derivative United States citizenship because his father was an American citizen. Inducted in 1943, and ordered to join the Marines, he managed to join the Navy and became an aviation machinist instead. Although he served in the South Pacific, he did not relish the possibility of fighting against Italians. "I did wish that I would not have to do

so. I was happy that I was sent to the Pacific Islands (instead of Europe),"
he recalled. Armand Castelli stated that his feelings were mixed at the
thought of having "to possibly kill my own blood, maybe my own relatives. I took a very detached view about the matter because they probably
felt the same way. [German Americans] felt the same way, but we were
Americans above all."[426] While Sgt. John Brinidisi from New York was
not interrogated on the matter of fighting in Italy, he was assigned to secret
work in the signal corps where apparently his Italian background was the
basis for suspicion.

> I was interviewed by about five officers including at least
> two full colonels. They asked me about my education and
> my training. Questions seemed routine until they asked
> about my family. Soon they concentrated on my father
> when I told them he was born in Italy. They asked what
> newspapers he read and if he belonged to any Italian
> organizations .I accept they were checking to see a pos-
> sible fascist connection. I believe they checked back in
> our community but have no evidence of that. I was quite
> embarrassed by the interview and never discussed it with
> my team mates none of whom were Italian-Americans.[427]

In one of his 1944 missives to his family on the home front, inveterate
letter writer Philip Aquila described his "washing out" of the Air Cadet
program, which trained pilots for the Air Force, that is revealing in its
perception that ethnicity may have been a factor. Although he was never
given the exact reason for his rejection, leading to a speculation that it
may have been due to a surplus of fliers, there was also a hint that his nationality may have played a role. "He recalled that during the interview he
was asked whether his ethnic heritage would prevent him from dropping
bombs on Italy or any of Italy's allies."[428]

For other Italian American servicemen, assignment to Italy provided an
opportunity to do some good in the midst of war. Dr. Joseph Nocentini, a
captain in the army occupying Sicily, wrote to his family that he regarded
it an honor to serve in the armed forces, and at the same time, to be able to

assist "blood brothers" who had experienced and resisted oppression and the suffering due to the invasion. A similar sentiment was expressed by pilot Gaspare Giunta from my area, who in letters to his father, expressed his joy at being in Italy where he fulfilled his dream of seeing the great monuments and marvelous works of beauty of the land of his ancestors. But he was also upset at the economic and political problems facing the wounded and impoverished nation, specifically the black market and the emerging but potentially damaging Communist party. He expressed the hope that Italy would recover quickly and begin anew.[429]

AMERICANS FIRST OF ALL

Repeatedly, newspaper accounts informed the home front that Italian American soldiers were first and foremost Americans, even if that meant fighting against Italians. Ethnic group members were reported to be eager to knock Italy out of the war—that was the essential priority. "There are thousands of doughboys of Italian descent who are eager and willing to knock Italy out of the war as quickly as possible," observed a war correspondent for the Associated Press accompanying the invasion of Sicily. As an example of a cross section of attitudes among troops of Italian descent, he cited Pvt. Jim Sangemino of Brooklyn, whose parents had been born in Sciacca, Sicily, and had immigrated to this country early in the twentieth century. "I hope they put up the white flag, but if they are really going to put up a scrap we'll give it right back to them and about ten times as hard. When I say that I am feeling as though I am speaking for just about all the Italian boys in our unit, and there are plenty of them." Even while expressing his willingness to fight against Italians, if necessary, Sangemino was very cognizant of familial ties. "If I ever get into Sciacca I am sure I have relatives there. You see my grandfather had thirteen brothers."[430] Hence, Italian American troops subordinated the anguish of violence against ancestral obligation to an unabashed identity that they were unequivocally Americans, and that whoever was an enemy of the United States, perforce was their enemy. They fought unstintingly when called upon to serve in Italy. The mindset of bombing enemy locations while disturbing was accepted as a necessity, as Albert Romeo of Patchogue explained, "We were bombing South Germany, Austria, Yugoslavia, but toward the end of the war we were bombing Italy in mopping up operations. But it was still Italy and it was a mixed emotional experience. We gave it a thought, but did not dwell on it. We had our mission."[431] Lt. Victor Coreno voiced a similar sentiment when he wrote to parents about a recent air strike in his Flying Fortress. "Recently, I flew over the beautiful hometown of Dr. Romano on a bombing mission. I was sorry to see a nice town like that be bombed but there was nothing I could do about it. I performed my duty as any American would do, dropped my bombs and with an aching heart observed the terrific blasting."[432]

ITALY'S STATUS AFTER LIBERATION

The question of Italy's status within the framework of belligerent nations was an issue that absorbed the home front in Brooklyn and throughout all the Little Italies, when on September 8, 1943, following Mussolini's resignation, the successor Italian government under Marshal Pietro Badoglio announced that Italians should cease all hostilities against Allied forces and prepare to confront the Germans.[433] Competing Italian American groups across the political spectrum differed sharply over the question of recognizing Badoglio's government, the place of the Italian monarchy, and the divisive issue of the extent to which fascists or former fascist still held influence in Italy, with some critics maintaining that because of Italian American influence they continued in power. "Officially they [Allied troops] arrived in order to eradicate fascism; however the measure of the eradication was determined by the powerful influence of the Italian Americans."[434] The slow pace in rooting out fascist officeholders was also in part due to a reluctance to remove them in the face of a serious shortage of experienced non-fascist replacements for administrative tasks. As

Poletti explained it, "One reason why the housecleaning job has not been thorough—and is virtually certain to be resumed soon to a degree affecting important officeholders is that it is easy to clean out incumbents but extremely hard to find satisfactory substitutes."[435] The sole area of agreement between the disparate Italian American political elements was over the question of admitting Italy to an allied nation status, which would render it possible to receive substantial lend lease aid to the liberated portions of the stricken nation. Within the Italian ethnic community, there was general consensus with the proposition that liberated Italy should be recognized as an ally because in fact its citizens were taking up arms against the Nazi war machine. Since the American government response to the suggestion was very slow in coming and ultimately unaccommodating, it led to a firming up of resolve among Italian American political leaders to continue to apply pressure throughout 1943 and 1944. Finally, Italy was accepted not as an ally, but as a co-belligerent nation—an uncertain status implying increased military cooperation for Italy with her former enemies, but no voice as a victor in the final disposition of the war. The situation remained muddled for some time. "Italy had little or no freedom under the Allies not only because Mussolini had brought the country virtually to ruin but also because his successors in their blundered surrender had incurred the distrust of the conquerors." The situation also reflected the difference in views between Great Britain and the United States—"The Americans were willing to make Italy an ally, in name at least, but not the British and other Allies."[436]

THE 1944 ELECTION

There was extensive interest among home front Italian Americans as to the kind of government that was to be installed in Italy after the fighting was over, with various factions attempting to influence the Roosevelt administration. For his part, President Roosevelt, whose political acumen was legendary, watched the situation carefully, always conscious of the political consequences that American policies might have upon the home front. This was of primary concern in 1944, with the looming critical presidential election that by the summer saw New York Governor Thomas E. Dewey emerge as the Republican candidate. That the Republican candidate had received the support of large numbers of the state's Italian American voters in winning the New York governorship in 1942 is the conclusion corroborated by recent research that shows large Republican gains in 1942, when contrasted to 1940. In addition, lower voter turnout in recent elections also worried Democratic leaders who concluded that the 1944 election would hinge on a large voter turnout in the great cities, especially New York, where there was discernible dissatisfaction among various nationality groups.[437] Recent research confirms that Italian Americans continued to be offended over Roosevelt's "stab in the back" speech in 1940, as did resentment because the administration linked the ethnic group with the offensive "enemy alien" designation in 1941.[438] Added to this political mix was the divisive infighting between various elements in the normally pro-Roosevelt labor movement, including Sidney Hillman and David Dubinsky, that found the latter breaking with the American Labor Party and forming the Liberal Party, and it was understandable that the climate became worrisome to Democrats. For Italian Americans, however, political ideology was secondary to Italy's desperate humane necessities –needs that were succinctly summarized in a May 1944 Foreign Nationalities Branch memorandum:

> Italy, according to most Italian Americans, is being treated as a conquered country under secret armistice terms; a government not of her choosing has been forced on her; her status in the war against Hitler is that of an inferior; her armed forces are humiliated; her cities bombed; her people hungry; imperialistic powers are plotting to despoil her, rightful protector, the United States, has not intervened to defend her ...

> The high hopes for Italy's speedy liberation aroused among Italian-Americans by the armistice gave way first

to a state of troubled confusion and then, during the long
Italian stalemate to bitter disillusionment."[439]

The somber political mood created not only an ominous portent for
the Democratic Party, but it also served to affect Roosevelt's thinking as
he considered United States policy toward Italy. Overriding all considerations was the President's determination not to alienate the rank and file
Italian American leadership, even if some of that leadership had previously been favorable to Mussolini's government and would continue to
retain its influence within the community. To some scholars, such a course
delayed fundamental changes in the future makeup of Italy's government.
"The painful process was determined by many factors, among which the
necessity to avoid worsening the delicate quality of the relations with the
heads of the Italian-Americans was one of the more paralyzing."[440]

During the early months of 1944, Roosevelt was uncharacteristically
indifferent to the upcoming presidential election; he was understandably
concerned with issues other than where the Italian American vote would
go. Preoccupied with the indispensable role he was playing in directing
the Allied nations to victory, he also initially downgraded the challenge
represented by Dewey. Ironically, even the highly successful D Day invasion which would now bring Allied power into Germany itself, had the
unintended but nevertheless unwelcome result of diverting attention away
from the Italian situation. For the next couple of months, all the headlines
reported on the progress of the war on the western front –news about Italy
became secondary. However, by the fall of the year, the President realized that his opponent was making such important strides that he would
need to ratchet up his campaign against Dewey. Reports circulated that
some prominent Italian Americans like famous banker and philanthropist Amodeo P. Giannini, who had backed Roosevelt in prior elections,
was now supporting Dewey. Edward Corsi who had been successful in
bringing an end to the schism within the Order of the Sons of Italy, leading to dubious claims that he represented the views of millions of Italian

Americans, was also touting Dewey.[441] Clearly, Roosevelt was compelled
to pay serious attention. "When he began to get reports from the field that
Dewey was gaining, he changed his mind about the necessity for cam-
paigning and announced one day at cabinet meeting that he was going
to make an old-fashioned rough-and-tumble campaign."[442] In Roosevelt's
analysis, the election would hinge on the swing vote—those independent
voters who were subject to persuasion during the course of the campaign,
and it was to these that the strongest appeal must be made."[443] In other
words, he realized that he would need to bring to his side the significant
ethnic groups in states with large electoral votes like New York where the
Italian American vote could be pivotal. A realist, Roosevelt was aware
that his support within the Italian ethnic group had declined sharply in
1940 and would likely remain low without some meaningful action.

This was the backdrop to the presidential election of 1944 as each
candidate sought to outdo the other in expressions of good will toward
Italy, aimed principally at pleasing the Italian American electorate. When
discussing Italy, for example, Dewey carefully crafted his speeches that
were extensively reported in English language newspapers as well as the
ethnic press and on ethnic radio, to enunciate pro-Italy proposals while
simultaneously chiding the Democratic administration for ignoring the
serious problems Italy faced. "Now look in Italy. Some fifteen months
have passed since Italy's surrender. "We have sent over a batch of al-
phabetical agencies. They took with them invasion currency bearing the
legend, 'Freedom From Want. Freedom From Fear.' What a mockery that
must be to the Italian people today."[444]

His call for Italy to be accorded status as an ally, accordingly, found
such eager acceptance with home front Italian Americans that even those
elements normally opposed to the left wing, such as Congressman Vito
Marcantonio, supported his congressional resolution to resume diplomatic relations with Italy and recognize her as a genuine ally.[445] That the
Republican presidential candidate's position was making an impact with
Americans of Italian descent is clearly discernible in Luconi's study of

the Philadelphia ethnic community that showed a 52.8% plurality for Dewey in 1944 because "Dewey seemed more concerned about Italy than Roosevelt."[446]

Dewey's proposals also forced Roosevelt to make even friendlier overtures that were well-received by traditional ethnic group leaders, often at the expense of Italian political exiles. It was this reality that prompted the Roosevelt administration to announce full diplomatic relations with Italy and an exchange of ambassadors, only weeks before the presidential election. This policy "helped the Democrats to retain their normal heavy majority among Italian voters."[447] With the war still raging, Roosevelt urged voters not to "change horses in mid-stream." He carefully courted the Italian ethnic vote as could be seen in a major address shortly before the election, in which he hailed their wartime service as in the tradition of Americanism. "Today, in this war, our fine boys are fighting magnificently all over the world and among those boys are the Murphys and the Kellys, the Smiths and the Jones, the Cohens, the Carusos ... " In a further attempt to link up with Americans of Italian descent, now that Mussolini had been overthrown, he declared, "We are made happy by the fact that the Italian people—our longtime friends—are started once again along the paths of freedom and peace."[448] The pro-Italian gestures found favor with a number of prominent Americans, such as publisher Generoso Pope and singer Frank Sinatra, who promptly endorsed him.

Roosevelt did more than give speeches; he wisely enlisted the aid of Antonini, LaGuardia, and Earl Brennan to curry favor with New York's Italian Americans. Both Antonini and LaGuardia were already very well-known and had considerable influence within the ethnic group. One election analysis opines that by 1944 there were signs that among the electorate "Depression psychosis" over postwar jobs was a growing concern. To the extent that was prevalent among Italian Americans, Antonini and LaGuardia could promote Roosevelt's re-election as a symbol of job security.[449] Roosevelt's reliance on Brennan was on a different level since

Brennan's expertise was via involvement with Italian American affairs in the Office of Secret Service (OSS). This background enabled Brennan to procure the cooperation of prominent New York Italian American John Montana, a Buffalo city councilman with considerable influence in the community. Montana's questionable reputation because of Mafia connections, that surfaced years later, apparently was not an impediment. Brennan also succeeded in improving relations with the Sons of Italy inviting Republican Judge Felix Forte, Grand Venerable of the Sons of Italy, to the White House to discuss affairs regarding postwar Italy. Forte gladly accepted and thereby provided Roosevelt favorable publicity within the order to balance Corsi's supposed influence.[450]

As the election approached, polls showed that even though Roosevelt's support among New York's Italian Americans had eroded, he still maintained a slight edge. One study reported that Roosevelt had the backing of 54.8 % of the Italian American vote in the city in mid-October, while another analysis stated that the results of Roosevelt's importuning of the New York Italian American vote in 1944 seem to have succeeded even though "the vote as a whole did not reflect overwhelming confidence in the administration as a sizeable portion went to the Republican candidate."[451] Newspaper scrutiny indicated that Dewey made significant inroads within traditionally Italian neighborhoods, with one report suggesting, "The vote for Governor Dewey was in his favor or close where Italians predominated in population."[452] The fundamental point, however, was that the hemorrhage of Italian American voters was staunched. More pertinent than the actual number of votes for each candidate perhaps was the fact that politicians thought that it was worth courting the Italian American vote. By 1944, Italian Americans had arrived at that political point where they had achieved greater access to the president and his close advisors, while simultaneously obtaining considerable hearing in the highest levels of the Republican Party.

RESUMING CONTACT

For several months following the deliverance of Sicily from Fascist and German control, Italian American spokesmen on the home front exerted pressure for mail resumption and economic assistance. Finally in February 1944, Roosevelt informed Generoso Pope that mail between the United States and Italy would recommence by the middle of the month. While many Italian American leaders, responding to pleas from home front Italian Americans, had contacted Roosevelt on the matter, Pope boasted that it was his newspaper's importuning that finally brought it about—an invitation to the White House to discuss the matter bolstered the strength of his claim. Although it was obvious that the humanitarian aspect of mail resumption was a gesture deeply appreciated by the home front, it was also a movement pregnant with political possibilities in a potentially tight presidential race. Thus, in addition to the civilized aspect of mail communication, Roosevelt extended the call to the White House also in part due to the importuning of Bronx Democratic Party Boss Ed Flynn, who argued that conferring approval of Generoso Pope would go a long way toward mollifying New York's Italian American electorate. In other words, what was involved was cold political calculation—namely the belief "in Pope's ability to deliver the Italian-American vote."[453] It was the realization that Pope would reciprocate to the president's gesture by emphasizing Italian American gratitude to the president in his newspaper.[454]

In the midst of these developments, the civilian population of liberated Italy suffered from a multitude of problems: insufficient food, clothing and other basic goods, a chaotic monetary system and mammoth inflation—in effect, a lower standard of living. On the home front, we Italian Americans were undoubtedly more sensitive to Italy's trials and tribulations than the general public. We heard with pain and anguish about the desperateness of the land of out forbears that faced stark famine and eagerly welcomed opportunities to assist by sending packages to relatives. Some responded to advertisements from private delivery companies that specialized in transmitting packages to the stricken country, now increasingly featured in the Italian ethnic press. In my young mind's eye and with only old photographs to guide me, I tried to imagine the looks on the faces of relatives whom I had never met: my grandmother, aunts, uncles, and cousins my age to their seemingly hopeless circumstances. To us on the home front, there was little doubt about the severity of the hardship Italians suffered; we read about it in letters and newspapers, learned about it from friends and relatives and heard it from appeals in churches and from Italian ethnic organizations. It was heart wrenching to read a report about a newly liberated town in Italy and the unpromising reaction of a "spindly legged boy of four [who] looked up wonderingly at uniformed Americans who had just filled his hands with candy. The child just stood there and finally repeated "Pane, pane."[455] That these experiences deeply seared victims is evident in the testimony recorded many years later in the memoirs of individuals like Mario Macaluso, a sensitive and perceptive individual who vividly recalled his childhood years trying to survive the war in a small Sicilian town.

> Growing up in Polizzi, my playmates and I had plenty of time, but very little to do. The American invasion of Sicily in 1943, had inflamed our youthful imagination. We loved to play that event in the narrow, twisting streets of our medieval town. American soldiers had been kind and friendly to us, and we remembered also the candy they had tossed in the air from their moving jeeps.

> Our parents had warned us to stay away from "American soldiers" for fear that they would kidnap us and take us away to a faraway land. We did not listen to them, and came close to the soldiers with instinctive curiosity and fascination ...

> One day,—I still relive it, as if it were yesterday—American soldiers gave us an aromatic bowl of beef stew when they stopped to have dinner. They must have felt sorry for us children who were staring at them with eyes wide-open, twitching noses, and tinkling hunger pains for that delicious food.[456]

Liberation of Italy beginning with Sicily was indeed welcome news for the home front. One almost instant reflection of the changed status was the resumption of letter writing by Italian Americans, who had been deprived of contact with loved ones for years, but could now re-establish communication. Not atypical, my mother now felt some relief from the anxiety of an extended absence of communication with her family, and the anguish of not knowing about their health and their survival in the midst of war. The only one from her immediate family in America—her mother, brothers, sisters, nieces and nephews all living in Italy, it was a source of not a little happiness to enjoy the recommencement of mail service with liberated Italy. Many neighbors and relatives in the neighborhood likewise experienced renewed joy as they exchanged news of relatives with each other. It soon became a normal Sunday morning ritual in my household when my mother's cousin, Ciccio Nurrito, who was close to my mother's family, come by to exchange news contained in letters each had received from members of the family in Italy, and to discuss their needs that could soon be met by sending aid packages of clothing, medicine, and non-perishable food.

In support of exhortations to help the old country by press, pulpit, and personal letters, were Italian language movies that focused on the liberation such as "L' Italia Non Muore Mai." (Italy Will Never Die). By January 1944, advertisements that that film was playing in New York Italian language movie houses, was accompanied with a blurb describing it as the first complete cinematographic history of Italy's liberation including the part played by "your sons, brothers and husbands." It also emphasized the heroism of the Italian people, and their love of peace and liberty.[457]

POST OFFICE SATURDAY MORNINGS

For a number of weeks following the re-opening of mail to Sicily, I physically carried bulky cartons to the post office a few blocks away. Usually discarded by grocery stores, the cardboard cartons that my mother lovingly and carefully packed with hand-me-downs from myself, my brother, sister, along with a few newly-purchased items were put in my charge. After making certain the containers were properly sealed and secured with strong rope around them, and after carefully printing out names of relatives and street names—I distinctly remember my grandmother's address on Via Provinciale in Pioppo, Sicily, Italy—I made my way to the local post office where I was confronted with long lines before the overseas postal express counters as numerous neighborhood people were engaged in the same works of corporal mercy to their relatives. One was bound to meet many friends and neighborhood acquaintances on line and compare notes with them as to specific Italian package destinations and names of relatives. In addition to sending packages at the end of March 1944, the government permitted us on the home front to send money to relatives in a further effort to alleviate distress in the lands of their birth. One imaginative New York financial institution, the Sterling Bank, claimed expertise in the matter of remission of money to relatives in Sicily and liberated Italy, by advertising that its mid-town Manhattan branch was conveniently available to the large number of Italians Americans who worked in the garment center.[458]

It was an intriguing situation—dozens of people who normally did little parcel post business in post offices, dutifully assembled with securely tightened brown cartons addressed in large, crude letters to relatives in Italy. While Congress debated the issues of whether Italy's official status as a co-belligerent entitled the former Axis nation to special favors, tens of thousands on the home front provided the kind of assistance that could be rendered long-distance—dispatching clothes and medical supplies. Once mail resumed between Italy and the United States, missives sent by Italian mothers, fathers, brothers, sisters, aunts, uncles, cousins, etc., told the similar sad tale of dire physical and economic circumstances they faced, and pleaded with their American relatives for food and clothing. While few food items could safely be sent across the ocean, clothing was accumulated and sent in huge volume: discarded garb from various family members were mended, cleaned, and carefully packed in heavy cartons saved from supermarket discards. Catholic churches, unions, and Italian American organizations conducted clothing drives that were perhaps an inconvenience to the populace, but to which they responded splendidly. Indeed, it was an act of responsibility that brought the war closer to many an Italian American home. It also marked a very different response to the war on our part when contrasted with non-Italians on the home front for whom such concerns were either trivial or, at best, peripheral matters.

While many Italian Americans sent packages to Italy, few could match the ardor demonstrated by Mrs. Rose Maglio of the Williamsbridge section of the Bronx, who responded abundantly to pleadings in her sons' letters. Stationed in Rome, Captain Louis A. Maglio of the American Air Force was so profoundly affected by the poverty and desperateness of the Italian people that he asked his mother to send packages that he could distribute and thereby alleviate the suffering. Calabria-born Rose Maglio who came to this country in 1903, reacted with admirable alacrity on her own and not as a member of an organization, she collected goods from relatives and friends and filled packages with children items, soap, candies, etc., along with thread that Italian mothers could use to repair clothing. Averaging more than one a day, in a span of six months, she sent 200 packages,—perhaps a record in this type of individual philanthropic endeavor.[459] Although the accumulation of items for shipment to Italy was a chore, Italian Americans responded splendidly.

PRISONERS OF WAR

The presence of prisoners of war in our midst was another tangible evidence of war to us on the home front. I can still vividly recall a warm summer day in 1944, walking down my block in the middle of the street. Because of wartime rationing that placed stringent restrictions on pleasure driving on the relatively few car owners on the block, few vehicles traversed the streets on Sundays. Advancing up the block on the other end were three men in summer khaki uniforms bereft of insignias, except for green brassards marked "Italy" who we realized upon coming closer were

Italian prisoners of war. My astonishment increased as I saw them enter my building, and I was further flabbergasted when they went to my flat, knocked on the door and entered. The mystery was soon solved when I went inside and learned that one of them was my mother's godson whom she had not seen since she left Italy. He and his comrades were Italian prisoners of war on leave—thus my first personal encounter with former Italian soldiers now prisoners. (My last encounter was in 1969 while riding from Florence to Rome in an Italian railroad car—a compartimento that accommodated six people. One was a former prisoner of war who recalled his time in the United States positively.) Italian prisoners of war were for a time housed in Brooklyn's Ft. Hamilton. Its proximity to Bensonhurst, enabled some of the interned Italian soldiers—originally with United States military escort and subsequently, on their own to visit his aunts, uncles, and grandparents.[460]

Italian prisoners of war were not universally welcome. Some Americans on the home front were critical of tolerance extended toward them equating that behavior with coddling former enemies. Not fully aware of the substantial assistance that cooperating prisoners rendered the American cause, these civilians emphasized the negative. They complained that it was wrong for these prisoners to be treated with generosity, as for instance, being granted leave to travel and consume precious fuel, being entertained by American women at dances, and being provided with recreational activities as if they were "honored guests" while their own sons serving in the American Army were facing deprivation and death. There was particular concern over a number of liaisons between them and American women. Notwithstanding the exaggeration that frequently inhered, nevertheless this kind of criticism had the effect, at least in some quarters, of causing military authorities to limit privileges. "Treatment of Italian POWS was one of the numerous wartime problems which had no simple or satisfactory answer. Americans who had husbands, sons, or brothers, fighting and dying overseas, were understandably angered to see POWs enjoying themselves at social events."[461]

For African Americans, it was a bitter irony in that they continued to suffer discrimination, even though they had served loyally in the American army while their own government extended considerably more freedom to people who had fought against the United States. On at least one occasion, African American soldiers were so upset that in their frustration, they lashed out at the Italians. "Apparently in retaliation for the favored treatment of Italian war prisoners, black soldiers in Fort Lawton, Washington, attacked the POWs, seriously injuring thirty of them."[462] Although virtually absent in my neighborhood, it seems that some Italian Americans resented treatment accorded Italian prisoners of war, as indicated by Charles Ferroni in his research on the ethnic community of Cleveland in which prisoners housed in a nearby prisoner of war camp were hosted by local Italian parishes. Cleveland newspapers reported that a few Italian American servicemen "expressed general displeasure because these men had fought against the United States. The fact that they were Italians did not seem to make the least bit of difference now." Ferroni analyzes this "as a classic example of the degree to which these young Italo-Americans had been Americanized."[463]

By early 1944, there were approximately 50,000 Italian prisoners of war in dozens of camps throughout the United States. Captured in North Africa, Sicily, and southern Italy, the first captives were sent to the Great Britain, but when the prison camps in that country began to overflow, the rest were sent to the United States. When Italy became a co-belligerent in October 1943, it tried to get them back in order to strengthen its armed forces now engaged against Germany. The Allies refused because they regarded the prisoners as a potential labor force; American farmers in particular saw them as critical in filling the chronic shortages they encountered in running their farms, readily acknowledging the value of their labor Although American attempts to obtain Italian prisoners of war as laborers were stymied for a time, over provisions of the Geneva Convention rules of war that prohibited use of prisoners for war work purposes, by May

1944, many were in fact so employed via the creation of Italian Service Units (ISU).[464] Studies indicate that essentially those prisoners who were recruited to join these units were, in effect, agreeing to follow orders from American military authorities to help America win the war against Germany working in numerous activities such as assignment to auto pools where they greased army vehicles, loaded supplies onto military trucks, repaired vehicles, etc. Recruits received $24 a month, eight of which was in cash and the balance in canteen coupons. They enjoyed other privileges, such as leaving bases on weekends sometimes, but apparently not always accompanied by a military escort. At times, the presence of prisoners of war in New York attracted such widespread attention that leading newspapers provided extensive coverage as in the case of 165 "former prisoners of war, now volunteers in the Italian Service Unit" that went sightseeing on June 18, 1944. The *New York Times* account featured a photograph of awestruck Italian prisoners viewing the wonder of the Empire State Building, among the sights they saw while visiting the big city. Led by Major Peter Cascio, they also went to St. Patrick's cathedral, visited a radio broadcasting station, and attended a surprise dance sponsored by the Italian Welfare League which featured 200 hostesses. They were treated to food at the famous Automat Restaurant that dispensed culinary items after coins were placed into glass containers that showed the food contents, and they were also entertained by Metropolitan Opera singers like the great basso Salvatore Baccaloni.

> They asked guides to point out the Statue of Liberty and Brooklyn, and bought souvenirs to send home. They talked admiringly of the city and of the United States. "We feel as one of you and could cry with joy at being here and at the way we have been treated," commented one Italian officer. "I met a girl who used to live near me in Brooklyn," announced Tony from Brooklyn, handsome 24-year-old tank corporal who had served forty-eight months in the front lines. He had lived in the Greenpoint section until he was 15, he said.[465]

It may have seemed unusual to Americans as a whole to find numerous references to Brooklyn in movies and other popular literature, however, it was an authentic aspect of the ethnic experience—indeed, the Brooklyn mindset extended even deeply into Italy. "Brooklyn is a magic word in Italy" wrote a *Brooklyn Eagle* correspondent who related the warm reception Italians extended to American soldiers once they learned the latter were from that borough. This was true not only of Brooklyn soldiers who spoke fluent Italian like Pfc. Anthony Caminiti, but also those whose ancestry was not Italian. Brooklyn's Pvt. John J, Fallon marveled at the response of an Italian woman, "On learning that Brooklyn was my home town, there was no end to one signorina's joy. She had a sister back there whom she had not heard from in four years ... Brooklyn has been a charm word all over Italy."[466] To those back on the home front, this phenomenon only underscored the significance of Brooklyn that we assumed probably had more residents of Italian background than any other county, not only in New York, but also throughout the nation.

As a teenager who frequently went bathing at Brooklyn's Coney Island, I saw many of prisoners of war walking along the boardwalk, enjoying the ubiquitous "fun" parlors, eating delights at the numerous food courts, and flirting with agreeable young women. I was not overly aware of the military escorts—either they consciously assumed a less conspicuous role or we were more focused on the prisoners. In any event, the arrangement allowed for them to see relatives as in the case of my mother's godson. A June 1944 statistic showed that 34,764 out of 47, 613 Italian war prisoners, almost three of four, who became "volunteers"—a rather impressive number. Of those who refused, approximately 2,000 were considered "Fascists." Those prisoners who declined to volunteer were not necessarily anti-American, but rather men who legitimately feared endangering their families in northern Italy or compromising their standing in the Italian army.[467] An additional curiosity revolving around prisoners of war was the fact that in some, undoubtedly few instances, the prisoners included men who claimed American citizenship on the grounds they had been born in the United States, but whose families had immigrated to Italy before the war, and thus now found themselves unwittingly in the Italian Army.

FAMILY REUNIONS

On the home front, an unplanned and unusual outcome of the Italian prisoners of war incarceration in the United States was that it led to a number of family reunions—members of the same family who had been separated and had not seen in each other in years. Among these dramatic encounters that were reported were those of Italian American Michele, who upon learning that his brother was a prisoner of war in Camp Clark, Missouri, left from his east coast home together with his wife who had made sfogiatelle (pastries) for a special visit. Even more poignant was that of an Italian American mother who went to the same camp to visit her prisoner of war son whom she had not seen in 19 years.[468]

Home front Italian Americans generally were positively disposed to prisoners of war of their ethnic background. Many Brooklyn residents hosted lavish dinners in their homes or joined in planning community banquets, dances, etc. This was the case in our parish of St. Joseph that held dances in which Italian prisoners of war were entertained that impressed young people in the neighborhood like my sister who recalled seeing the men as she passing by the church hall. "I would look in the school yard, I was too young to go in. They all seemed to be having a good time."[469] There were similar scenes in other Little Italies in Brooklyn and beyond. Apprised of the loneliness and disorientation of Italian "ex-prisoners" of war in a nearby camp, the pastor of Our Lady of Mount Carmel in East Harlem preached to his congregation for forgiveness of the men –a step that elicited approval and cooperation in bringing 500 of them to the parish's annual festa. Further emphasizing the theme of forgiveness, Fr. Fiore then asked the people to take the men to their homes to share Sunday dinner. Although the experience was awkward because "they were enemies –we come from the same home town, but they were enemies," they overcame their self-consciousness and enjoyed "a beautiful day. Friendships were formed, and some of the Italian men married neighborhood women."[470] On June 18, 1944, 400 New Brunswick, New Jersey Italian Americans sponsored a picnic for 114 former war prisoners who were in engaged in war work at the Raritan Arsenal. It was noted that the men were under the command of their own noncommissioned officers.[471] In sum, our home front view regarding Italian prisoners of war, or at least those who had volunteered to work for the United States, was different from that of many Americans whose ancestry was not Italian. We were perhaps more aware of the important work they did—some of which was top secret and never publicized—such as cooperation in broadcasting instructions to Italian underground operatives, thereby facilitating defeat of German strongholds in Italy. We were naturally sympathetic to the many prisoners who were related to people in the community, and to their seeming willingness to learn English.

It was ironic that when the war ended and the prisoners of war were preparing to be returned to Italy, they were required to place patches on their uniforms designating their prisoner of war status. The action was not well received by the Italians who considered themselves allies, had volunteered to assist the Allied war effort, and had been open to the benefits of democracy. However, the authorities believed it was a prudent move for a return to their homeland where they might have been regarded as traitors.[472]

ATHLETES SERVE: BASEBALL

Even as the war progressed inexorably toward its conclusion and Allied success appeared increasingly inevitable during the last two years of the war, we were still sensitive to the many militarily dangerous and difficult days that lay ahead. Aware that Americans looked favorably to participation of prominent athletes who were in the armed services, Italian American newspapers provided extensive coverage to a similar part played by members of the Italian community. It was a source of pride and inspiration for us young Italian Americans to point to such athletes, which included some of the most famous names among the entire Italian American athletic constellation. In my neighborhood, the three main sports of interest were baseball, football, and boxing—basketball attracted slightly lesser interest. Baseball, the national pastime and arguably the most American game, was the number one sport, and among New York Italian Americans, it was the astounding New York Yankee lineup that by far commanded the greatest pride. Replete with the esteemed Yankee great Joe DiMaggio and emerging stars Phil Rizzuto and Lawrence (Yogi) Berra, this team elicited exceptional recognition. The city's ethnic group could heartily concur with Michael Musmanno's memorable assessment of what those names meant to an Italian American coming home from the war.

> It was one of the happiest days of my life when I disembarked in New York from the ship that brought me back to America ... we motored to Yankee Stadium to watch the mighty Yankees perform. Here my yearning to see Americans of Italian lineage recognized for demonstrated merit obtained thrilling realization. Four of the redoubtable Bronx Bombers were full-blooded sons of parents hailing from the Italian peninsula ... "[473]

Other prominent Italian American professional baseball players who served in the armed forces included Harry (Cookie) Lavagetto, Dolf Camilli, Johnny Rizzo, Sam Gentile, Dom Dellasandro, Dom DiMaggio, Marius Russo, Dario Lodigliani, Al Brancato, Johnny Berardino, and Johnny Lucadello.[474]

FOOTBALL

From the college football and basketball worlds, we lauded notables like Angelo Bertelli of the University of Notre Dame, Al Ratto, Paul Reginato, Ray Pucci, John Podesta of the University of St. Mary, Tony Minisi of the University of Pennsylvania in football, and Angelo (Hank) Luisetti in basketball. A great innovator, Luisetti who came from the Italian area of San Francisco, joined the Navy during the war, after earning three All American designations at Stanford University. Regarded the second greatest basketball player in the first half of the twentieth century, he is credited with introducing the one-hand shot, the precursor to the one hand jump that revolutionized the game.

Even though I did not then know all the techniques and intricacies of football, I recall the thrill of reading the Bertelli name in the sports section and cutting out his action pictures from the newspaper. His prowess with the "T" formation was so formidable that the entire offense of the team revolved around it. Bertelli was the standout player for the University of Notre Dame who won the coveted Heisman Trophy as the best all-around college football player of 1943. At the time of the award, he announced that he had joined the Marines and was in boot training. He subsequently saw action in the ferocious battles of Iwo Jima and Guam. "Jumping" Joe (Giuseppe) Savoldi was another Italian name with which the ethnic group identified. Born in Milan, Italy, he came to the United States in the early 1920s, attended the University of Notre Dame where he played under the renowned Knute Rocke and became famous for his "dropkick" plays during the 1929–1930 seasons. During his brief professional football career, he played alongside of legendary figures like Red Grange and Bronko Nagurski before he turned his talents to professional wrestling. With the outbreak of the Second World War, he joined the Army and became an important secret agent in the OSS under Max Corvo. In that capacity, one of Savoldi's assignments was that of being a bodyguard to an important Italian admiral who had been imprisoned.

Charley Trippi was another star football player with whom many Italian Americans on the home front identified. Like most immigrant families who had to work hard, he was the son of a Pennsylvania coal miner, who went on to a stellar collegiate career at the University of Georgia where he won many awards and which he temporarily left to join the Army Air Force. Upon his return, he continued his sensational career and for a time, also played baseball. Considered by many as the greatest all-around football player, he was one of the most versatile players ever and is enshrined in the Football Hall of Fame. John Ferraro grew up during the Great Depression, and attended Bell High School where his excellence on the football field led to a scholarship at USC. Although his studies were interrupted by service in the Naval Reserve during World War II, upon his return, he was named All-American twice and played in three Rose Bowl games; he also played professional football and was inducted into the National Football Hall of Fame. Subsequently, he became a respected Los Angeles City Council member. From New York's Columbia University, the name of Paul Governali struck a responsive chord with the ethnic group who responded positively to athletes in the service—in his case, the Navy. A standout football quarterback, playing for coach Lou Little (Piccolo), in 1942 he became the top passer in college ranks and was chosen an All American three times.

BOXING

The realm of boxing saw Italian Americans such as Fred Apostoli, Marty Servo, Steve Belloise, Lenny (Boom Boom) Mancini—father of Ray—, and Lou Ambers (Luigi D'Ambrosio) in American uniforms. Fred Apostoli, who served in the Army, was a foremost contender for the World Middleweight title. During his long ring career, Willie Pep (Guglielmo Papaleo) was called pound for pound the best boxer in the game, and among the top five greatest boxers of the century. He was World Welterweight Champion, and had an exceptional wartime career serving a hitch in the Army and another hitch in the Navy.[475]

GOLF

Names of Italian American servicemen from the game of golf included Tom Strafaci, and most especially the Turnesa brothers. The saga of the seven Turnesa brothers: Phil, Frank, Joe, Mike Doug, Jim and Willie were unique and especially edifying. A large immigrant family, they were children of Vitale Turnesa, who had come to this country in 1904 from Potenza, Italy, and found work cultivating the ground that was to become a major golf course. His children became caddies on this course and then by the late 1930s, they had advanced to become such exceptional golfers that their names became household bywords to golf enthusiasts during their ascendancy in that sport. "For years, one Turnesa brother or another seemed to contend for whatever New York area or national tournament was on that week."[476] For example, in 1942, they won or were near the top in many golf events: Mike was second in the Hale Amateur National Open (a wartime substitute for the U.S. Open), and Jim was the runner-up in the P.G.A. They were so popular that they appeared in a Hollywood short. What rendered the role of athletes in demonstrating their American patriotism was that their exploits attracted the attention not only of the ethnic press, but also of the English language media. Although some complained about the incomplete coverage regarding the contribution of Italian American athletes to the war effort, it was heartening to us on the home front to be aware that members of our ethnic group received a degree of acknowledgement. Although the relationship with athletes for the ordinary American of Italian descent on the home front may have been tenuous, it was nevertheless a further validation that our ethnic group was doing its share in the great crusade.

CHAPTER IX
THE END OF
TESTING TIME

THE METTLE OF THIS GENERATION

Decades after the end of the Second World War, a number of books appeared that evoked numerous gallant efforts amidst the throes of the conflict and celebrated the action of America's fighting forces. One of the most widely read tomes of this nature was Tom Brokaw's *The Greatest Generation*, a popular book that recounted the remarkable story of individual Americans who had led ordinary lives, but responded to the call of their nation to make the transition from civilian to military life, and in the process, helped bring victory for this and other Allied nations in this the most colossal of wars. As a young teenager on the home front, I too was awed by the overwhelming enormity of the event, its unmitigated totality, and the grand challenge it represented, and with every fiber of my soul, I supported the crusade. But I was also conscious of my Italian heritage—the heritage of those closest to me and that shared by most of my neighbors. I yearned to see the ethnic group more conspicuously acknowledged as vital actors in the drama, and was equally anxious that native-born Americans also be aware of and accept their story as an indispensable element in the saga. Specifically, should not Italian Americans be acknowledged for their part in this awesome historical event? Should not their admirable participation render them not merely tolerated but accepted as "real" and genuine Americans? Should not their authentic contributions be a major part of the legacy of those Americans of Italian ancestry—indeed should it not also be a cherished part of the greater American heritage? My sense was that their story was far from told, that it was at best known only in bits and parts, and it was this unrelenting awareness that constituted the reason for this account—to demonstrate that in their own way Italian Americans contributed exceptionally and extraordinarily to the outcome. This is not about bragging, boasting, or bluster; it is not about being chauvinistic because in truth, credit goes to so many people of so many varied backgrounds, nationalities, religions, and races that all played fundamental roles. My motivation is, however, to shed light on the role that Italian Americans played because this is largely an untold story—even some of the best read people in the field of immigrant and ethnic history have limited knowledge of the subject. It is also a largely untold story because of the peculiar reticence of most World War II servicemen who were reluctant to tell their stories in part because millions of people were doing the same and also because they regarded participation as their duty. If it is too extravagant to proclaim that this was the greatest Italian American generation, it would not be excessive to view Italian Americans of the World War II generation as possessing a special resolve, a fortuitous fortitude, and a singular reservoir of courage that enabled them to overcome the unusual obstacles and hindrances of being closely associated with America's foe in the greatest of all wars. They were challenged to go beyond the disapproving enemy label and demonstrated by their actions on the battlefield and the home front that they fully merited being linked to those Brokaw called the greatest generation. If not the greatest of the Italian American generation, they were a major element in the ranks of unsung heroes of the war. This was the mindset of Italian Americans on the home front as we lived, worked and sacrificed during the war years. For me and many others of my background, it was critically important that we were doing our share. For my fellow ethnics in Brooklyn, it meant a great deal to see those of our nationality performing the essential services that earned the respect of the nation.

The Seventh War Bond Loan Drive was the biggest single fund-raiser to support the cost of fighting during the war. It was estimated that it generated pledges of over 26 billion dollars to pay for the guns, ammunition, airplanes, naval vessels and other essential instruments of war.[477] The degree to which Americans supported the drive is an indication of the determination to place its monetary resources in the center of the war effort—a campaign that Italian Americans passionately endorsed. For instance, in the spring of 1945, *Il Progresso Italo-Americano* promoted the drive by invoking the memory of hero Marine Sergeant John Basilone, who had just lost his life in the bloody Battle of Iwo Jima. Readers saw full page ads with the memorable photograph of the flagraisers on Mount Suribachi, it also showed the picture of Basilone and reminders that, from beyond the grave, the Marine hero called upon them to buy bonds and thereby not abandon America's fighting forces. War bond rallies took place in ethnic neighborhoods like my own, where a Central Ave. fraternal lodge several blocks away sponsored a rally with a projected goal of selling $20,000 worth of bonds, in order to purchase ten ambulances—and actually exceeded its goal by selling $54,000 worth of bonds.[478]

THE COURSE OF THE WAR

As 1944 diminished, it seemed to us on the home front that the course of the war was moving inescapably toward a successful conclusion. On the western front, the Allied forces were advancing inexorably into the heart of the enemy, Germany; while on the eastern front, after withstanding all that the German military machine could inflict upon them, Russian forces had recovered all lost territory, entered Poland and were moving toward Germany. Just as it appeared that that war in Europe was entering its final phase, we learned of the Battle of the Bulge, the huge German counterattack in Belgium that had caught Allied forces off guard and threatened a breakthrough that could send Allied forces in the west reeling backward. The Movie-tone news on cinema screens showed scenes of grim and gaunt Americans troops menaced by unforgiving cold and snow as well as a rejuvenated German advance that indicated a bleak outlook for American forces. To us on the home front, this was mildly upsetting news, however, even at that time I thought that while the adverse turn of events was a shock that could delay the final result, it could not change the final outcome. By the spring, the bulge had been arrested and the push against Germany continued relentlessly. War news from the Pacific front gave every indication of extremely tough fighting that Americans faced. The horrendous battle of Iwo Jima, on February 23, 1945, for example, would claim over 25,000 American casualties, including 7,000 dead. Despite such military engagements that demonstrated an alarming suicidal enemy resolve, nonetheless, American forces were defeating the Japanese Army and Navy while retaking numerous islands, even while absorbing egregious casualty rates. It was merely a matter of time before the collapse of Japan.

In February 1945, newspaper accounts informed us on the home front of still another wartime meeting of the Big Three: Roosevelt, Churchill and Stalin at Yalta. While few details of the conference were made public at the time, it appeared that the Allied partners were further planning to squeeze the German forces. There was also talk about how poorly President Roosevelt looked—it seemed that the robust, energetic, and happy leader of previous years had aged noticeably, leaving us with the visage of an old and sickly avuncular-looking head of state. The visual impressions were indeed borne out by his death only two months later. On the evening of the announcement of his demise, my friends and I entered into animated discussions about his passing as if we were losing a member of the family. The realization came that my generation never knew anyone but Roosevelt as president, and we wondered what the future would bring; however, there was no concern that the death would affect the outcome of the war. We were further stirred by newsreels that showed large crowds on the streets openly grieving for the deceased president as his funeral cortege wound its way through the avenues of Washington, D.C. I was vividly moved by the sight of a middle-aged African American woman, standing among the sidewalk throngs in a black dress, with tears welling in her eyes behind her eyeglasses, waving a white handkerchief while bidding him farewell.

Although Harry S. Truman was an unknown quantity, we were assured that he would continue to prosecute the war as his predecessor had done. Indeed, on April 30, 1945, the war news was that Hitler had committed suicide and that resistance had ended. A week later, May 8 was V-E Day; in a somewhat muted celebration, we hailed the defeat of Nazi Germany as the culmination of a long and bloody war in Europe, realizing that Japan persisted in carrying on the fight in the Pacific and that that effort required continuing heroism on the part of all members of the armed forces. According to one estimate, the thirty-day phase that stretched from February and March 1945, encompassed a period "when the dying in WW II reached its climax."[479] The closer American forces approached their homeland, the more would Japanese forces fought tenaciously even fanatically. Clearly, there would be much hard fighting ahead that would require additional sacrifice. While we were grateful to the sacrifices made by Americans of all nationalities, on my block and in my Italian American neighborhood, the extraordinary activities of those of our background had special meaning.

SERVING WITH DISTINCTION

Albeit it is not known for certain how many Italian Americans reached the ranks of general during the war, there were at least two that the home front learned about via coverage in the ethnic press. Born in the North End, Boston's Little Italy in 1895, Brigadier General Robert V. Ignico attended local public schools before he went to Washington and Lee University in Virginia. He demonstrated bravery even as a youngster when he rescued two young boys from drowning. He began his military career during the First World War, remaining in the army where he specialized in aviation, developing an expertise in supply and transport—activities for which he was awarded the Legion of Merit.[480] Frank Milano, whose ancestors emigrated from the Italian Lombardy region, was born in San Antonio, Texas, in 1892, and served in the army with valor in the First World War. He was promoted to the rank of Brigadier General in the spring of 1943 while stationed in New Delhi, India.[481] Some Italian Americans World War II servicemen achieved the rank of general in the years following the war. Such was the case of Andrew J. Malatesta, born in Albany, New York, in 1911, who served with distinction as an officer from 1943 to 1945, and then completed a number of years in the Army Reserves and the New York National Guard. He eventually was promoted a Major General in the Guard.[482]

HENRY MUCCI

On the home front in early 1945, we were absorbed by exciting accounts of the freeing of Allied prisoners of war who had been unmercifully tortured and maltreated. It was further inspiring to read about the part played in liberating them by Italian Americans such as Lt. Col. Henry Mucci. A West Point graduate who had spent a few years in military service prior to the war, Mucci hailed from the Italian American enclave of Bridgeport, Connecticut. In late January 1945, he was placed in command of 107 Rangers and 286 Filipino guerillas who were directed to free 512 prisoners of war—survivors from the terrible battles of Bataan and Corregidor, who were barely surviving in a Japanese camp near Manila. Triple barbed wire fences surrounded the enclosure that was under heavy guard, thus requiring minute planning and the element of surprise to achieve a rescue. While reticent about his military activity to his family who complained that he "hardly tells us anything," Mucci later wrote a couple of accounts for publication where he detailed the operation.

> One of the first things I did was to tell all the men going
> on this expedition that we would all go to church. When
> I got there, I made a little speech in which I asked every
> man to swear he would die fighting rather than let any
> harm come to the prisoners of war under our care. I did
> that because I believed in it. Everybody on that mission
> took that oath.[483]

What followed was a remarkable episode in which Mucci's forces engaged their Japanese adversaries, inflicting huge casualties upon them and rescuing the 513 prisoners, some of whom were barely alive. Altogether, 532 Japanese were killed in the rescue effort at the cost 27 Allied deaths. Pleased at the results, General Douglas MacArthur noted: "The mission was successful. The Japanese guards were completely surprised and were annihilated. I have awarded the commanding officer [Mucci] the Distinguished Service Cross ... "[484] The heroism exemplified by Mucci's mission elicited enthusiastic acknowledgement not only from the highest military levels, but also from a grateful public as evidenced by a turnout of 50,000 Bridgeport residents, replete with dignitaries and band on hand at the city's railroad station. Greeting their home town hero with choruses of "Hail, Hail, The Gang's All Here," and salutations of "Welcome Home Henry" were his family, the city mayor, representatives of Italian American organizations and ordinary friends and neighbors. That night, he was honored by the principal of the local school he had attended as a youngster.[485]

ORDINARY MEN, EXTRAORDINARY DEEDS

As recounted previously, there were multitudes of unsung Italian American heroes on the home front: uniform clothing workers, war plant employees, inventors, blood donors, promoters of war savings bond drives, civilian defense workers, etc. But in spite of government exhortations that there was no difference between the home and the battle fronts since both were critical, surely we recognized that at the top of list were the service-men and women on the battlefield, many of whom paid with their lives and whose story was partially mentioned earlier. The public at large was aware of some of them: Congressional Medal of Honor winner, John Basilone, and intrepid air ace Don Gentile whose wartime exploits received wide coverage in contemporary popular newspapers and whose stories were familiar. There were also other narratives of Italian American war heroics, in some instances of individuals who had achieved some pre-war renown such as Louis Zamperini, while others would become celebrated national figures in the postwar period like Jack Valenti.

LOUIS ZAMPERINI

Born in New York in 1917 of immigrant parents, Louis Zamperini and his family moved to California where Louis entered school, humiliated because originally he only spoke Italian. He had a troublesome youth—he called himself "a social misfit," who engaged in cheating and stealing—but he also had an exceptional knack for running, focusing on that sport in high school, where he set an interscholastic record for the mile. Selected for the 1936 U.S. Olympic team, Zamperini joined his teammates in Germany, and while he failed to win his event he finished the final lap in an astonishing 56 seconds, a record. It was a performance that drew attention—he actually met Adolf Hitler who attended the event and expressed a wish to meet the young American.[486]

Graduating from the University of Southern California (USC), in World War II, Zamperini joined and became a captain in the Army Air Corps, when while on a search-and-rescue mission, he ran into difficulty after his aircraft developed engine trouble and crashed into the Pacific. Zamperini got tangled up in cables and started going down with the sinking aircraft. "I felt this was a hopeless situation and I knew it. This was it," he said. "My life didn't pass before my eyes, but I knew I had had it." Fortunately, he extricated himself and frantically swam for the surface and life raft. He then helped the plane's tail gunner and pilot, both injured, and got them aboard the raft. Since rescue was not imminent, they learned to survive by killing fish by jamming their eyes with a screwdriver. On the 27th day in the ocean, a Japanese dive bomber strafed the hapless raft but amazingly, no one was hit. The situation remained desperate until finally, after forty-seven days, they were rescued by a Japanese patrol boat and put into a prison camp on a Pacific island. Zamperini had lost 100 pounds and now weighed only 65 pounds. "I lay down and looked at my body. Just six weeks before I'd been a vigorous athlete who could run a mile in just over four minutes. Now I was fleshless, skeletal ... I broke down and cried."[487] After six weeks, Zamperini was sent to a prison in Japan, having been spared execution apparently because a officer Japanese friend from USC, convinced his leaders that Zamperini would be of better value if he was used as a celebrity on the radio. Meanwhile, since he was missing for 18 months, the United States government presumed him dead. However, he was taken to Tokyo, fed an American-style meal and read a brief statement telling listeners he was alive after being rescued by the Japanese. He spent two-and-a-half years in a Japanese prison camp, and was repatriated in late 1945.

After the war, Zamperini had a difficult time making peace with himself and became an alcoholic until his conversion to Christianity. He subsequently became a renowned motivational speaker and even conducted a missionary tour of Japan in 1950, where he was forgave a guard who had treated him cruelly. Years later, he came full circle and returned to Kwajalein Island—the place for much of the ill treatment. "Yet on April 10, 2001, when my flight from Hawaii to Manila landed for a routine refueling stop, "chills went up my spine and it was tough to control my emotions."[488]

JACK VALENTI

Sicily was the Italian background of Jack Joseph Valenti, who was born in Houston, Texas, in 1921, the grandson of an immigrant and the son of a father who held a clerical job with the Houston city government. Jack attended local schools graduating high school at age 15, the youngest ever to accomplish that education feat in Houston. He then worked in the daytime while attending night school at University of Houston. He also received an MBA degree from Harvard University.

A lieutenant in the Army Air Corps, Valenti saw extensive service during Second World War as fighter pilot-commander of a B-25 attack bomber with the 12th Air Force stationed in Italy, where he flew fifty-one combat missions. He won many awards, including the Distinguished Flying Cross, the Air Medal, the Distinguished Unit Citation, and the European Theater Ribbon with four battle stars. In addition, France awarded him its highly prized French Legion of honor. In 1952, he co-founded an advertising and political consulting agency that in 1955 led to a meeting with United States Senate Majority Leader Lyndon B. Johnson, who upon becoming president appointed him his press secretary. From 1963 to 1966, Valenti served as First Special Assistant to the President, actually lived in the White House and became the first Italian American to have such a close advisory role. In 1966, Valenti resigned in order to assume the position of president of the Motion Picture Association of America.

While the general public was aware of a few acts of heroism on the part of Italian Americans, it was unfamiliar, however, with role of many others who either received little or no coverage in English language newspapers or whose careers were reported primarily in the ethnic press that we on the home front either read or heard about. For the most part, participants in these deeds remained anonymous and spoke little about their astonishing actions, yet they were truly a cross-section of the rank and file achievements rendered by these servicemen. They were in the words of Brokaw, ordinary men whom the government turned to when the war began "ordinary Americans and [the government] asked of them extraordinary service, sacrifice, and heroics."[489] A sampling of the latter group may be instructive.

SAM MAURIELLO

The son of immigrants—his mother from Florence, father from Naples, Sam Mauriello was born in Manhattan in 1905, lived for a time in the mid-west where he became interested in motors and aviation. He returned to the east where he talked his way into becoming a test pilot, and in 1926, at age eighteen, Sam made $10 for his first parachute jump—it was the beginning of a career with airplanes that included working as a mechanic, a stunt pilot, a parachute jump specialist, and the proprietor of an aviation school. In January 1941, Sam, along with another Italian American, was one of twenty-one Americans to join the Royal Air Force that was begin-ning to form its famed Eagle Squadron that escorted British bombers. On one occasion, he fought it out with German planes shooting five of them out of the sky, a feat for which he was decorated by the king of England with the Distinguished Flying Cross. When the United States entered the war, he became part of the American Army Air Corps, participated in many low level bombing raids, saw additional combat against German planes and was then assigned to the home front to survey United States airplane manufacturing plants where he encouraged workers to increase production. "We need more of those airplanes up there ... Sure our boys are just as good as the Nazis, in fact they are better. But that kind of superior-ity won't mean much if we haven't a superiority in numbers of airplanes going up there. I know. I have been up there ... " This assignment brought him into contact with representatives of the ethnic press, enabled him to tell his story to the home front, and thus bolster morale.[490]

PETER BRESCIA

A native of Brooklyn, Corporal Peter Brescia, the son of Potenza-born Pasquale, and Sicilian-born Elizabeth, went on to a superb military career in North Africa. Albeit it did not seem so promising after he had been captured by Axis forces and was en route to possible internment in an enemy concentration camp. Upon reaching the city of Tunis, Brescia and another prisoner sprang into action after obtaining two discarded poles that they wielded into weapons, promptly seizing one hundred surprised Nazi soldiers, who now became their prisoners. It was seemingly impossible, yet they pulled it off, in an achievement that brought joy to his proud father and mother, five sisters and two brothers, including fourteen-year -old Johnny who boasted of his brother's heroics to his classmates. It was encouraging episode of valor to home front Italian Americans.[491]

ALFRED LONGO

In their hometown newspaper, Brooklynites read about the daring exploits of Elmhurst, Queens resident Lt. Alfred Longo, who had attended Grover Cleveland High School near where I lived and where I went to many dances. Longo, a flight leader in the famed 865th Hell Hawk group, found himself in a desperate spot when his plane was shot and heavily damaged while in action over Leipzig, Germany. Seemingly faced with disaster, Longo was able to belly land the plane in a field and then run for cover into the nearby woods. While the plane exploded and burned, Longo headed for the American lines by "borrowing" bicycles and discarding them when he approached towns. A slow operation, at one point, he decided he would need another bicycle when he spotted a German boy riding one.

> He was traveling in my direction so I put him on the seat behind me and he held on to my waist while I pedaled off in a standing position. We came to one town and I pedaled like mad right through the place and the boy shouted in German as we passed but I figured no snipers would dare fire a shot for fear of hitting the lad. We passed through a second town in the same manner and half a mile beyond I saw a column of Sherman tanks and other American vehicles. It was a Ranger battalion getting ready to move into the town ...

For the next three days the flyer manned a 50-caliber machine gun on one of the Ranger battalions on patrol, on one occasion rounding up thirty German prisoners.[492]

Flying 45 combat missions, he earned the Air Medal with four oak leaf clusters. His later career included years as a pilot and teaching.

JOHN CAPUTO JR.

By the middle of 1943, two New York airmen of Italian descent were emerging as military heroes. Described as a "compact, soft-spoken young man of Italian descent—who was born on St. Patrick's Day ... ," and whose home was in Jackson Heights, Queens, John Caputo Jr. enlisted a few days after Pearl Harbor, entered the Air Force, and saw air combat in the skies over Sicily, Italy, and Germany. While flying bombers over Naples—his father's birthplace—he was aware that he might be inflicting harm on his own kin. "I may have had some fifty second cousins down there. I don't know. Anyway it was part of my job." By the time he came home on leave in August 1943, he had seen extensive combat that included flying his two-engine plane on fifty missions over enemy territory, shooting down enemy planes, and more than once, bringing his plane back only on one engine following extensive enemy damage to the other engine. He received the Distinguished Flying Cross, Air Medal and seven oak clusters.[493]

VINCENT PUGLISE

From 86th St., Brooklyn, Vincent Puglise went from college into the Air Corps in 1939. Unable to become a pilot, he became a navigator and saw extensive service—over fifty missions—over North Africa, Italy, France, and Eastern Europe. On one occasion, when his flying fortress bomber was hit dozens of times by enemy anti-aircraft fire that seriously wounded two crewmen, Lt. Puglise demonstrated his mettle, by applying a tourniquet and giving morphine to one, and bandaging the wounds of the other. He received the Distinguished

Flying Cross for this feat, in addition to the Air Medal, and eleven oak clusters, thereby becoming one of Brooklyn's most decorated servicemen.[494]

MARIO GABRIELLI

Mario was a son of Italian immigrants who worked the coal mines and steel mills in the vicinity of Avella in the southwestern part of Pennsylvania. A superb athlete, tough and always in shape, Mario won renown in local schools that earned him a coveted football scholarship to Waynesburg College; however, with the coming of the war, he left college for the Army. He and his comrades were hauled long distances in ships and crowded cattle cars first to Africa, and then to partake of the invasion of Sicily, Italy, where his company was pounded by heavy German artillery.

> "Sitting there in a bobbing tub of a boat with water lapping the sides, I remember looking up at the blue sky ... sporadic shelling in the distance ... the cold fear in the pit of my stomach ... I didn't permit myself to feel any more ... I felt for nothing, cared for nothing ... nothing except the ninth Infantry Division, sixtieth Regiment Headquarters Company ... it rolls off my lips with pride" Mario was then assigned to England where he prepared to take part in the D Day invasion. At 7:00 a.m., June 15th, 1944, he was "squeezing a few more moments of sleep" when the shelling started. Before nightfall, his life would be changed forever. He was riding in a jeep full of ammunition that was to establish an ammunition dump when his vehicle ran into a hail of fire from snipers in the trees, as well as machine-gun emplacements. This was followed by heavy land artillery that hit right on top of him and sent him flying through the air.

> I remember hitting the ground ... I felt no pain. I opened my eyes to see that I was under a tree. My glasses were still on my nose and I was thinking about a Humphrey Bogart movie I had seen recently. I thought, 'This is it! I am dying.' I said aloud, 'GOD, DON'T LET ME DIE ... '

I yelled, 'MEDIC.'" The Medic arrived in a flash. He was the same one who had tended to the boxers. "Mike, will I lose my leg? He never looked at me ... just straight ahead, saying nothing." "My right leg was gone. It had been blown off by the 88 mm shell. From then on it seemed that I kept dreaming of running. I could not stop running. Run. Run. Run!

Mario returned home to Avella with a wooden leg and to heartfelt sympathy from his family and friends; however, he always maintained pride in what he had done for his country and assumed responsible civilian positions: one in the town postal department where he became postmaster, and the other as Pee Wee football coach.[495]

FRANK FUOTO

The Volturno River campaign, which unfolded in late 1943 and stretched into early 1944, found the American Fifth Army under considerable stress due to horrendous weather conditions and stiff German resistance as it tried to reach the East Coast of Italy. It was also the campaign that saw Brooklyn's Lieutenant Frank Fuoto playing an idiosyncratic role in San Vittore, a town near San Pietro, which the tenacious German forces had taken and who now sought to invest themselves in and around San Vittore in a determined effort to make a "Stalingrad," non-surrender type of resistance, and where three hundred of them were entrenched in a high observation tower determined to stop American advances. Intent on their mission, German forces accordingly occupied San Vittore, but they immediately incurred the wrath of townspeople because they forcibly commanded them to aid in setting up defenses. Although most townspeople fled for the mountains, those who remained were compelled to dig trenches and other impediments. Those who could also hid themselves from the Germans in a store basement where they awaited the Americans.

Although his infantry platoon was numerically smaller than the Germans, the undaunted Lt. Fuoto resolutely attacked, forcing the enemy to retreat from a large portion of the town; he then proceeded to lead his soldiers to search out and round up scattered enemy pockets that enabled them to surround German troops holed up in a group of thirty stone houses near the center of town. It was at this juncture which the Germans expected to defend to the utmost but where Fuoto demonstrated his distinctive leadership ability by forcing them out after a hard battle. The town suffered much devastation, but it was finally liberated. Overjoyed, the troops under his command responded by naming Lt. Fuoto mayor of San Vittore by acclamation, and further celebrated by killing and roasting a young bull that had evidently fled from the Germans.[496] Fuoto's parents had emigrated from Sorrento, Italy, in 1908, and still had many close relatives in Italy whom Ft. Fuoto was able to visit. And in an ironic twist of wartime fate, the thirty-year old Fuoto, who took pride in his Italian heritage, by dint of his extraordinary intrepid battlefield leadership, was now honored by the land of his ancestors.

DE VITTO FAMILY

The De Vitto family of five sons and three daughters was the product of Italian immigrants Raffaele and Luigia De Vitto who settled in Brooklyn. Typical city youngsters, the sons played games with which I was familiar, such as stickball using sewer covers for bases. The older brothers also began to obtain work in ordinary neighborhood occupations, such as barbering to which Fred was attracted. With the outbreak of the war, they were drafted and began their seemingly routine military careers. For example, despite his request for something more exciting, Fred spent most of his military career cutting officers' hair. On the other hand, Pasquale (Pat) saw his share of action when his infantry unit was pinned down by Japanese troops in Luzon, Philippines. Twice he was hit by bullets as he hurled grenades at the enemy, earning a Silver Star and two Purple Hearts. Liberty De Vitto, the athlete of the family, was killed in a German ambush in France, shortly after D Day. Luigia De Vitto's pride in her sons was tinged with sadness. "I gave five sons and four came back."[497]

SAM BERTUZZI

The son of an Italian immigrant who lived briefly in New York City before moving to Oneonta, New York, Sam Bertuzzi underwent a harrowing front line experience as a naval combat pilot in the South Pacific. On September 14, 1943, he was on a mission to escort a bomber fleet en route to Bougainville in the Solomon Islands, when he was hit by Japanese enemy planes swooping down on him for the kill. "I was prepared to die. Then I started to pray. I could feel my own mother at that instant praying for me, too. Whoever or whatever, I wasn't alone in that cockpit. That helped me focus. Maybe I could get past this." Although shrapnel had severely damaged his right arm and he had nearly lost consciousness, he was able to make a crash landing in shallow water. He was taken to a hospital on Guadalcanal where surgeons considered but decided against amputating the shattered limb, and he underwent extensive medical treatment. A grateful Bertuzzi was so determined to proclaim his thanks at being saved that he paid for a newspaper advertisement that stated "God flew my Hellcat for 150 miles."

Ironically, although Bertuzzi received a Distinguished Flying Cross and Purple Heart, and despite important service to his community as a city council member and city postmaster following his combat period, he still experienced ethnic prejudice. But "it didn't make me bitter. It only made me more determined. I began to explore my heritage."[498]

NICK NUDO

With the outbreak of war, rough and cocky Long Islander Nick Nudo, left his home in Patchogue, became a paratrooper, and subsequently a major participant in the fighting in the Pacific. He was one of 400 troops General Douglas MacArthur ordered to hold off and divert 20,000 Japanese soldiers concentrated near a prison at Los Banos, Philippines, that was twenty-five miles deep into enemy territory. When intelligence informed Americans that the Japanese were digging large numbers of mass graves, it appeared almost certain that the 2,100 men, women and children in the prison faced death. The diversion plan was intended to occupy the large enemy forces while an American parachute division would swoop down and free the prisoners. Although outnumbered fifty to one, five-foot-seven Sergeant Nudo and his men performed their assigned task at the Battle of Los Banos that enabled the paratroopers to rescue thousands of prisoners of war. This raid, which was considered one of most successful airborne operations in history, earned the parachute division the sobriquet "angels." For his role in the combat, he was awarded the battlefield Bronze Star medal.[499]

FRANK FAZIO

A product of Bronx 's Italian American enclave, Sergeant Frank Fazio entered the army in January 1941, was sent to North Africa, and subsequently saw action in Sicily, Anzio, and France. His battlefield performance in Barneville, France, in June 1944, —in which he volunteered to undertake dangerous front line reconnaissance, which left him exposed and without cover, in order to gage accurate location of German heavy cannon that had prevented further advance—earned him a Bronze Star and various citations. While these were in themselves admirable accomplishments, it was Fazio's refusal to accept promotion to a lieutenant's rank that made him stand out. He spurned personal advancement because he did not want to leave his comrades on the battlefield.[500]

ANDREW MAIELLO

For Brooklyn-born Sergeant Andrew Maiello, the North African campaign was the setting for his laudable front line accomplishment. He and his men were assigned the unenviable task of taking Gafsa, an enemy post that was protected by fields of treacherous land mines. To clear the field required nerves of steel, resolute fortitude, and unbending determination, attributes possessed by Maiello as he led the way carefully removing one hundred concealed weapons, thereby making it possible for the infantry to penetrate the area and capture the town. Coincidentally, it was another Brooklyn Italian American, Captain Richard Ciccolella, Maiello's friend, who led the penetrating infantry troops. Describing the episode to family back home, Maiello wrote, "We attacked a town the other day and I was in the lead taking out mines and traps. With me was my squad of men. We had a lot of fun playing with the high explosives and had no casualties." Unfortunately, not too long after writing the letter, he was killed in action.[501]

THE FARAONE BROTHERS

Their five sons in the armed services were the pride of the Faraone family of Corona, Queens, whose delight was mitigated by the family's anxiety that the war end soon, an apprehension evident as the family consented to being interviewed in mid 1944. In civilian life, one son, Ben, had worked and performed as a singer in Jack Dempsey's New York restaurant. By the time of the local newspaper interview, Ben, who was a member of General Patton's famed mechanized cavalry, had been wounded in France while another son, Louis, a lieutenant of the Army Transport, experienced his ship "blown up from under him and he and his shipmates floated on the cold water for several days on a life raft before they were finally saved."

Asked about her feelings regarding the war and her sons' participation, the Italian American mother, with tears welling in her eyes as she looked fondly at pictures of her sons, voiced the view of most mothers when she stated, "I am proud, but I would be much happier if the war were over and they came home again ... This is a terrible war. There is not a home in the neighborhood that has not been touched. My boys were born and brought up in Corona, and all the friends they played with and went to school with are fighting too. Do you think it will be over soon?"[502] A few weeks after the interview, the Faraone family received the tragic word that Ben had been killed in action.

THE PRIANTI BROTHERS

Stories of heroism and bravery were always tinged with the poignant and the heartrending—such was the case of the Prianti family of East Northport, Long Island, that provided five sons for the service during the Second World War. (A sixth Prianti sibling became a soldier during the Korean War.) They were serving in both the Pacific and the European theaters of war when telegrams started to arrive informing the family of devastating casualties. Twenty-one-year-old Peter was killed in the Normandy invasion, while four months later, nineteen-year-old Frank suffered the same fate elsewhere in France. The overwhelming tragedy prompted the mother, Caroline Prianti, to write a letter to General George C. Marshall, Chief of Staff, asking that the Army send home her three sons still in service, since she already lost two sons. Her request was denied, although the three surviving Priantis in the Army no longer saw combat. A third son was wounded, while a fourth contracted malaria from which he would die two years after the war ended. Caroline Prianti arranged that Masses be said for her sons every Friday, a devotion continued decades later by her daughter who recalled:

> Our family went through an ordeal no one can possibly imagine. I recall my parents not sleeping at nights as my mother would sit up in the chair all night saying her Rosary. My dad would stay by her side, both crying. It seemed the telegrams would not stop coming—who would be injured, who would be missing in action. I relive this over and over again.
>
> My mother buried five sons—the ones who survived came only to die from illnesses of the war ... If anyone should be honored it should be my parents for giving up the most precious things in life.[503]

FRANK FARANDA

Brimming with loyalty and determined to get back at the Japanese, Frank Faranda, whose parents were Sicilian-born, left Pratt Institute to join the Marines a month after the attack on Pearl Harbor. After basic training, he was sent to the Pacific, where on August 1942 he was killed in combat. The saddened family tried to keep the news from his mother who was ill, but who nevertheless sensed that something was grievously wrong. After obtaining additional information, the mother was informed of her son's death and of the deep impression he had made on his commanding officer who cited his splendid military record and death while fighting the enemy in the Solomon Islands. Frank's younger brother, seventeen-year-old Salvatore, was so moved by his brother's sacrifice that he also tried to enlist in the Marines. Having lost one son and with another one in the service, his parents prevailed upon young Salvatore to wait a little longer.[504]

The pithy summary of the war's impact on the Maiello, Faraone, Prianti, Faranda, and other households serves to underscore and affirm the authentic suffering experienced by home front mothers, fathers, and siblings. It simultaneously rendered valid President Roosevelt's reminder about the congruence between the battle front and the home front. Roosevelt embraced the total war concept, constantly linking the home front and the battlefront, while decrying as artificial the drawing of a line between the two fronts. There is one front and one battle where everyone in the United States—every man, woman and child—is in action ... That front is right here, in our daily tasks.

> To build the factory, to buy the materials, to pay the labor, to provide the transportation, to equip and feed and house the soldiers and sailors and marines, and do the thousands of things necessary in a war ... "When we send an expedition to Sicily, where does it begin? Well it begins in two places practically; it begins on the farms of this country, and in the mines of this country. And then the next step in getting that army into Sicily is the processing of the food, and the

> processing of the raw material into steel, then the munitions plants that turn the steel into tanks or planes or the aluminum ... And then a great many million people in this country are engaged in transporting it ... we have to remember that there is just one front, which includes home as well as abroad. It is all part of the picture of trying to win the war."[505]

That genuine suffering afflicted the home front, especially the women left behind, was a solemn consequence of the war that should be abundantly evident in the battlefield instances cited above. But it was not only those who lost loved ones in the service who would undergo heartache, it was also those who had to face the heavy and sometimes terrible burdens of life alone. Overlooked because their sagas received less attention than battlefield events, they were nevertheless, a critical part of keeping the home front together. "I too was a victim of the war," stated Jennie Immordino, a half century later. Knowing of her suffering and agony after losing a baby in childbirth and a miscarriage, her husband Robert heartily concurred. After Robert was inducted into the Navy in 1943, her trial became even more cheerless and dispiriting—she had to carry on alone. But she endured and went to work in a defense plant seven days a week, helping to build torpedoes for the Navy. Many years later, Robert asked a telling question, "Will an appropriate national, state or local memorial ever be created honoring the untold numbers of unsung Homefront [sic] Heroines of World War II?"[506]

SHIELDED HOME FRONT PERSPECTIVE?

In his study of the war time home front, John Jeffries maintained that there existed a considerable gap between home front and battlefront perspectives—that is, the government controlled news availability to the home front if it deemed such news as potentially detrimental to morale. "Home front views of the war often differed sharply from battlefield realities. The armed forces kept what was termed their "Chamber of Horrors"—photographs they would not release for publication because they seemed too grisly or otherwise inappropriate." Thus photos of dead GIs deliberately were not publicly shown until 1943, that is, not until the favorable turning of tide became clear.[507] It is an interesting question to speculate about whether the visible revelations of grim and ghastly scenes early in the war would have affected our thinking on the home front. On the one hand, it is true that enthusiasm for support of war on my part and that of others of my generation may have been our response only to more heroic aspects of battle, those incidents that extolled bravery and sacrifice while avoiding much that was gruesome and macabre. On the other hand, even after we did see more horrid war scenes that were shown in newspapers, magazines and movie news screens: frozen corpses in the unforgiving snow of Russia or the piles of emaciated Jewish bodies in hastily built graves or of the gaunt and pitiful survivors of concentration camps, we remained fervently loyal. For us on the home front, World War II had such stark moral clarity that there could be no mistake between the good side and the bad side. We did not see this as a conflict against vagueness, indistinctiveness, ambivalence, or uncertain perspective. For us on the home front, the mindset was certain and sure—this was a good war. Thus in retrospect, I do not believe that revelations about the more grisly aspects of war would have produced hesitancy on the home front.

VJ Day

During the three-and-a-half months that separated VE Day (May 8) and VJ Day, I, along with many on home front contemporaries, waited with growing anticipation for the conclusion of the war. New York Italian American clothing workers took note of the end of the war in Europe by proclaiming their pride in the troops on the fighting front, and simultaneously linking efforts undertaken on the home front to the victorious conclusion. " ... our workers in all industries, have been industrious, faithful, and enthusiastic in creating the arms necessary for victory by military

manufacturing uniforms, by contributing the their maximum, the victory
of this grand republic.[508] Once Germany had surrendered, Japan's fate
seemed inevitable, regardless of the enemy determination to fight to the
utmost. Although I would not become fully aware of the awesome power
of the atomic bomb until later, I accepted the government's explanation
that dropping the weapon on Japan was necessary to hasten the conclusion
of the war; the paramount priority was the end of the conflict—that was
the home front preoccupation. I do not remember any serious discussion
in my neighborhood revolving around the morality of using the terrible
bomb on civilians at the time, although seeing the ruin and desolation it
wrought in motion picture house newsreels did make one uncomfortable.
Furthermore, it all seemed to happen so rapidly—hardly had we digested
the enormity of the atom bomb, when within days, a second bomb was
dropped, leading to rampant rumors that Japan was ready to capitulate.

The skepticism that first greeted the announcement on the morning of
August 14, 1945, that Emperor Hirohito accepted surrender terms, yielded
to a joyous realization that it was true—the war that been so prominent, so
all-encompassing, and so much a preoccupation of my early teenage years
had ended. It was a heady feeling to realize that this critical, mind-forming
reality of these formative years, this defining period in my life as well the
rest of us on the home front, was finally over. It would be vastly different
in the near and distant future. But there was no time to dwell on that during
that hot August day—it was time to celebrate.

I happened to be preparing to go to work in a small machine shop in
Manhattan that summer morning, when the radio station I was listening
to broadcasted the anticipated announcement that war had come to an end
and that impromptu celebrations were beginning in various part of the
city—it was reason enough not to report to work that day. It was the same
in every city neighborhood: horns blared loudly, people called up relatives
and friends with the happy news, residents still in their pajamas came out
of their apartments shouting and singing "God Bless America." What was
unfolding was an atmosphere that reeked with unmitigated happiness and

revelry. Although it was a hot, sultry, and an otherwise dog day of summer, V-J Day was going to be different and special, and despite egregiously uncomfortable weather, it would not deter us. In our celebratory mood, my friends and I decided to take the subway to Times Square, the epicenter of the merriment where we joined in the festivities. But even in the short two-block walk to the subway station, one could already see unmistakable signs that a gloriously happy, congratulatory temper was suffusing the environment: smiling old people, middle-aged people, and young people, were coming out of their homes greeting each other and all passers-by with words of praise and congratulations. More than one older Italian man around the corner proudly put out his barrel of homemade red wine, together with glasses handy and ready to share with anyone who came along. Not accustomed to alcoholic beverages that early in the day, I nevertheless must have had at least two or three glasses of the cool but vigorous drink before reaching the subway station. We experienced additional scenes of happiness among the subway riders, all of whom apparently were heading for the same party on Times Square. Once arriving in the world-famous crossroads about which so much had been written and sung, we found ourselves in the midst of an unbelievable scene. It seemed to me that I was involved in a historic moment—the cheerfulness of two million people celebrating in a way that the nation had never rejoiced before or since.

Along with several friends, I tried to move along Broadway but quickly realized it was impossible to determine which direction we would follow. Realizing the futility of trying to traverse the avenue in solo fashion, we grasped each others arms and moved essentially in the direction that the twisting, weaving, moving, happy crowd was going; we simply went along thanking servicemen, hugging and kissing girls, all strangers who kissed back as lively as the were kissed. "And they went to Times Square," was one description of the event.

> All through the day the crowds flooded the once neon-lit heart of New York City. Milling around aimless, there were 200,000 of them by early evening, watching the

news ticker and grouping around radio blaring the latest: ... Japan accepts surrender terms. It was finished. It was done.

The cheers swept up the avenue and the side streets. It continued rising and falling, for twenty minutes. Ships whistled in the harbor, along the docks and in the rivers.

Now grinning citizens climbed out of the subways and off the buses and beheld a sight they had not seen in several years: All the Broadway theaters blazed with light ... And everyone was kissing everyone else, passionately, furiously ... By 10 p.m. more than a million partygoers filled the square—seething, rollicking, screeching, crying, kissing, laughing, By midnight there were 2 million of them.[509]

Nor was that the end of our celebration. People on our block organized a party with food, drinks, jitterbugging, and music—since we lived in the middle of the block where the bandstand was placed, my mother supplied an electric cord from our apartment for the music amplifiers below.

It was a similar scene in other heavily Italian American areas of Brooklyn as, for example, 74th Street, where a committee of volunteers took it upon themselves to decorate the block with American and Italian flags,

and thousands of colorful banners, topped off with a large poster across the street with the message: "For the Boys of this block, God bless them." An enthusiastic crowd of 3,000 people were entertained by ten musicians and singers, who performed a combination of popular American tunes

Home on leave from the Army and pictured here with the author is Epifanio (Farney) DiGiovanni, of the Himrod St. Brooklyn. His brother Anthony was killed during the invasion of Europe.

along with older Italian favorites, atop a hastily constructed bandstand. A block party organizer used the occasion to read the names of sixty-five block members who served in the armed forces during the war, introduced twenty who were present, and expressed pride in the role they played in bringing about a great American victory.[510]

Even as we rejoiced the return of young men from the service, we were aware of the bittersweet feelings in some households whose sons would never come back, such as Anthony DiGiovanni, brother of my good friend Farney, who had been killed in France. The DiGiovanni family lived across the street from us. There was even more mourning a few blocks away where my aunt Fifi and my cousins lived. Two of my cousins were killed in 1945. One was army soldier John Gorgone killed in Leyte during the invasion of Philippines, and the other sailor Joseph Gorgone. Joe's death was even more poignant since it took place a month after Japan signed surrender documents when on October 9, the island of Okinawa was visited by what was considered the most lethal storm ever to batter the United States Navy, one that inflicted more damage on the United States Navy than any other natural disaster.[511] My cousin perished in the hurricane. The terrible pain of the double tragedy was more than my aunt could bear—she would never be the same.

While we were celebrating V-J Day on August 14, it was not until September 2, 1945, on the deck of the battleship Missouri in Tokyo Bay, that the war officially ended. It was

We on the home front were pleased to share in the national patriotic fervor. Madeline LaGumina is pictured with Joe and Tony Gorgone. Tragically sailor Joe was killed in a hurricane off Okinawa at the end of the war, while another brother lost his life in the invasion of Leyte Island.

heralded with an official government holiday, and with appropriate ceremonies of thanksgiving and reflection in churches. Cessation of the war was acknowledged in small Long Island villages such as Port Washington, where auto horns, fire sirens, and church bells sounded the good news as elated residents lined the streets in a writhing dance. In Glen Cove, shopkeepers went home early, hanging out signs that read: CLOSED FOR PEACE. In other locales, there were block parties and a few small parades. That weekend, people relaxed at the beaches or traveled to New York to see the Brooklyn Dodgers and New York Giants split a doubleheader. People also could relax by going to see movies such as ``The Corn Is Green'' with Bette Davis, ``Thrill of a Romance'' with Van Johnson, and ``Son of Lassie'' with Donald Crisp and Peter Lawford, while Broadway, theatergoers could choose among ``Carousel,'' ``Life With Father,'' and ``Oklahoma.'' The government announced an increase in supplies of butter, canned salmon, ice cream, and whipping cream, but meats would continue to be rationed. For the first time since 1941, there was plenty of gasoline, and the highways were filled with Sunday drivers on the first weekend of peacetime. Throngs went to Jones Beach and other Long Island beaches, and huge crowds enjoyed racing at Belmont Park. It was the beginning of the end of rationing, and the onset of an optimistic era, a new hopeful future.

What About the Future?

In reality, there were numerous momentous questions to ponder for my ethnic community in general and for me in particular. Would there be a return to normality regarding continuity of cultural life in an ethnic enclave? Would things ever really be the same? In actuality, it was apparent that fundamental changes were inevitable. The massive mobility that was the concomitant of travel necessitated by military requirements, bringing many young neighborhood Italian American servicemen to distant places in the nation that they were unlikely to travel to otherwise, and where in many instances, they married women of different nationalities and religions, would serve to presage enormous change in the offing. Likewise, participation in wartime economic prosperity, distant employment opportunities, and the G.I. Bill of Rights that provided exceptional prospects constituted additional evidence of imminent alterations. Although we were aware of the irrevocable changes that had taken place, such was not our preoccupation as we continued to celebrate the end of the war, and the return of servicemen on Himrod Street and the neighborhood. Notwithstanding the potential for fundamental change that the war had wrought, for me and my friends, the portended adaptations seemed to be gradual rather than abrupt. Historian Tuttle attributed the changing mindset to peculiarities of Italian Americans that was bound together during the war by a combination of negative stereotyping from outsiders, and the force of family and ethnic ties. He cites the prevalence of three-generational households that were common in Little Italies, even while they were fading elsewhere—indeed, there were examples of three-generational households among my friends on my block.[512] Virtually all my friends had grandparents either living with them or close by. It was different for me since three of my four grandparents were deceased and my surviving grandmother lived in Italy. I felt so deprived that I did not have a grandparent to talk about that in my mind's eye, I looked upon Zia Concetta, my father's older sister, as a grandmother.

While it may have seemed gradual, nonetheless, unbeknownst to us, ethnicity had undergone a massive transformation—one mirrored in name changes, in the elimination or curtailing of Italian language education, and in the cessation of Italian American newspapers. For example, notwithstanding the name change of *L'Eco d'America* to the *Rhode Island Echo,* the newspaper ceased publication in May 1942, as the publisher acknowledged "that a newspaper which has recourse to a foreign language must necessarily be scrutinized by government agents in order to properly safeguard American interests at a time of national peril."[513] Thus, after Pearl Harbor, Mussolini Street in Providence, Rhode Island, became Russo Street, in recognition of an early casualty Albert Russo, while the Vittorio Emmanuel Lodge of the

Sons and Daughters of Italy, in Milford, Connecticut, changed its name to the Milford Lodge. In Cleveland's Little Italy, "When the public schools dropped the Italian language, the Sons of Italy did not complain. Lodges that had been named after Italian royalty were renamed Abraham Lincoln, Betsy Ross, etc. Membership declined. The junior lodges were closed ... "[514] Perceptive observers of Italian American life could not fail to see that the war had expanded social horizons and fostered assimilation. For Leonard Covello, this was a welcome development because it served to weaken a rather stifling insularity while it increased contact with other Americans that would result in a lessening of prejudice.[515] Writer Mario Puzo also saw the war as a liberating experience. "But I was delivered. When World War II broke out, I was delighted. There is no other word, terrible as it may sound ... My country called. I was delivered from my mother, my family ... and delivered without guilt ... And what an escape it was."[516]

With memories still fresh of the harshness of life during the worst of the Depression, many of the older generation were concerned about the post-war economy. Since it seemed that the war was the instrument that finally lifted the country out of the depths of economic doldrums, would its termination mean a return to bad times? Would there be enough jobs? Would there be a resumption of high unemployment? Because we were basking in the glow of being part of the world's greatest power and confident of the future, these issues were only of mild concern to me and my contemporaries. In reality, from the outset of the war, we were certain that the United States would win, even if must come at great cost. This view is confirmed by students of the subject. "Pearl Harbor brought shock and anger and often persistent anxieties, especially about loved ones; but there was little real fear about the eventual outcome and much national resolve and confidence." In our youthful enthusiasm we felt we were participating in a "common cause, of contributing to victory in a just and necessary cause."[517] We were part of a generation that found much in wartime life enormously fulfilling, one that derived enormous satisfaction in vicariously walking with the victorious American forces. Of course, we on the home front were removed from the horror and ugliness of the battlefront. "Removed as they were from the battlefronts, prospering during and because of the war, home front Americans seemed to be fighting the war on 'imagination' —an imagination shaped by Washington, Hollywood, and Madison Avenue."[518] We were part of a generation that was beginning to experience and enjoy a modicum of prosperity, and had soaked in the wartime propaganda that informed us we were fighting the good fight.[519]

Although we did not explore deeply the ideological meaning of the war, aside from the necessity of defeating fiercely totalitarian systems determined to enslave the world, we were certain that we had been on the good, right, decent, and moral side of the war. We were ready to go back to the way we were, minus economic depression. As for my erstwhile desire to be a member of the armed services, that I had so admired—a yearning that had been so much part of my mindset on the home front during the war and which my adolescence precluded, that too diminished—with the war over and the boys returning home, it became a fading dream.

REFERENCES

Introduction

[1] Tom Brokaw, *The Greatest Generation*, Dell Publishing, New York, 2001, p. 87.

[2] A.A. Hoehling, *Homefront, U.S.A.* Thomas Y. Crowell Company, New York, 1966.

[3] Richard Wrightman Fox, *Journal of American History*, 77 (Sept 1990,) pp. 553-593. Among the illustrious historians engaged in this discussion were David Brion Davis, Bradford Perkins, Carl Degler, John Hope Franklin. Miskio Hane, and Gerda Lerner.

[4] George E. Pozzetta, "My Children are My Jewels,' Italian-American Generations during World War II," p. 63, *The Home-Front War*, (edited by Kenneth Paul O'Brien and Lynn Hudson Parsons,) Greenwood Press, Westport, Connecticut, 1995, pp. 63-82.

[5] Bill Tonelli, *The Italian American Reader*, New York, 2002, p. xviii.

[6] Pozzetta, "My Children are My Jewels,' p. 75.

Chapter I

[7] John Fante, *The Wine of Youth,* Black Sparrow Press, Santa Barbara, 1985, p. 40.

[8] Pecorino, "The Italians in the United States," *Forum*, Vol. 45 (January 1911), pp. 15-29, reprinted in *The Italian Americans, Social Backgrounds of an American Group,* (editors Francesco Cordasco and Eugene Buccione), Augustus M. Kelley Publishers, Clifton, 1974, p. 153,

[9] Joseph Velikonja, "Italian Immigration in the United States in the Mid-Sixties," *International Migration Review*, Vol. I, No. 3.1967, pp. 25-37.See *The Italians of New York*, Arno Press, New York, 1969, p. 218 and Edward J. Miranda and Ino J. Rossi, *New York City's Italians*, 1976 p. 18.

[10] Pecorino, "The Italians in the United States," p. 155.

[11] Salvatore J. LaGumina, "Paul Vaccarelli, Lightning Change Artist of Organized Labor," *Italian Americana*, Vol XIV No. 1 Winter 1996 pp. 24-45.

[12] Jerre Mangione, *Mount Allegro*, Boston, 1942, p. 225.

[13] LaGumina, "American Education and the Italian Immigrant Response,"pp.61-77, *American Education and the European Immigrant: 1840-1940,* Bernard Weiss, edit., 1982.

[14] Leonard Covello. *The Heart is the Teacher*, McGraw-Hill Book Company, New York, pp. 150-51.

[15] Sr. Mary Fabian Matthews, "The Role of the Public School in the Assimilation of the Italian Immigrant Child in New York City, 1900-1914," *The Italian Experience in the United States*, (Editors, Silvano M. Tomasi, Madeline H. Engel, C. M. S., Staten Island, New York, 1970, pp. 125-141.

[16] Irwin L. Child, *Italian or American, The Second Generation in Conflict*, Russell and Russell, New York, 1943, pp. 40-41.

[17] Leonard Covello, *The Heart is the Teacher*, p. 129.

[18] LaGumina, *The Immigrants Speak*, Center for Migration Studies, Staten Island, New York, 1979, p. 72.

[19] Luciano J. Iorizzo and Salvatore Mondello, *The Italian Americans*, Twayne Publishers, New York, 1980, p. 118.

[20] Ralph Foster Weld, *Brooklyn in America*, AMS Press, Inc., New York, 1967, p. 141.

[21] Mario Macaluso, *Prickly Pears and Oleander*, 1st Books Library, 2002, p. 126.

[22] New York *Times*, March 14, 1986. The article described the extraordinary number of judges and lawyers who claimed the Sicilian town of Santa Margherita di Belice as their ancestry.

[23] Interview Mary LaGumina, 1974. My mother then went to services at non-Italian St. Barbara's Catholic Church.

[24] See Gaetano Salvemini, *Italian Fascist Activities in the United States*, Center for Migration Studies, 1977, pp. 228-229.

[25] Nat Scammacca, *Bye Bye America, Memories of a Sicilian American*, Coop. Editrice Antigruppo Siciliano & Cross-Cultural Communications, Trapani, Italy, 1986, p. 41.

[26] Donald Tricarico, *The Italians of Greenwich Village*, CMS, NY, 1984, p. 34. See also Eric Amfitheatrof, *The Children of Columbus*, Little, Brown and Company, Boston, 1973, p. 236).

[27] John W. Jeffries, *Wartime America,* Ivan R. Dee, Chicago, 1996, p. 122.

[28] Interview, Salvatore Finazzo May 31, 2003.

[29] Francois Avenas, "Changes in the Italian Neighborhoods of Queens Between 1920 and 1990: Citizenship as One Facet of the Assimilation Process," *The Italian American Review*, Vol. 5, No. 2, (Autumn/Winter 1996/1997), pp. 55-69.

[30] Scammacca, *Bye Bye America,* p. 23.

[31] Weld, *Brooklyn in America*, p. 137.

[32] Humbert S. Nelli, "Italians in Urban America: A Study in Ethnic Adjustment," *International Migration Review*, Vol. No. 3 pp. 38-55.

[33] Weld, *Brooklyn Is America*, p. 136.

[34] Vincent Schiavelli, , *Bruculinu, America*, Houghton Miflin, New York, 1998, p. 9.

[35] Schiavelli, *Bruculinu, America* pp. 186-191.

[36] See *Italians of New York*, United States Federal Writes Project, New York, 1938,.in passim.,.

[37] Frank J. Cavaioli, "Returning to Corona's Little Italy," *Italian Americana*, Vol. XV, No. 1,Winter, 1997, pp. 31-50. See also Amfitheatrof, Children of Columbus, p.238. Similarly the sense solidarity has been well described by many others including Irwin L. Child, *Italian or American*, who focused on the Italian immigrants in New Haven, and Virginia McLoughlin whose study *Family and Community*, University of Illinois Press, Urbana, 1982, centered on Sicilians in Buffalo.

[38] *Il Progresso Italo-Americano*, October 19, 1941.

[39] LaGumina, "Cesare Sabelli: Italian-American Aviation Pioneer," *La Parola del Popolo*, (May-June 1979), Vol. XXIX, No.148, pp. 49-64.

[40] Rockaway *News*, July 29, 1933.

[41] Louis Pierini, *Interview*, April 28, 2003.

[42] LaGumina, *The Immigrants Speak*, Center for Migration Studies, New York, 1979, p. 23.

[43] Ronald Bayor, *Neighbors in Conflict*, New York, pp. 18-19.

[44] LaGumina, *Vito Marcantonio The Peoples Politician*, Kendall Hunt, Dubuque, Iowa, p. 28.

[45] *La Gazzetta Di Syracuse*, August 19, 1938, author's translation.

[46] Weld, *Brooklyn Is America,* p. 150.

[47] Emelise Aleandri, *The Italian-American Immigrant Theater of New York City,* Arcadia Publishers, Charleston, SC,1999, p. 101.

[48] LaGumina, *The Immigrants Speak*, pp.91-92.

[49] LaGumina, *The Immigrants Speak* p. 138.

Chapter II

[50] Hannah Arendt, *The Origins of Totalitarianism*, World Publishing Book, New York, 1962, p. 257.

[51] Luigi Barzini, *From Caesar to the Mafia*, Liberty Press, New York, 1971, p.191.

[52] John Diggins, *Mussolini and Fascism: The View From America*, Princeton Univ. Press, 1972, p. 17.

[53] Diggins, *Mussolini and Fascism,* p. 231.

[54] Winston S. Churchill, *The Gathering Storm,* Houghton Mifflin Company, Boston, 1948, p. 187.

[55] See Arrigo Petacco, *Dear Benito, Caro Winston*, Arnoldo Mondadori Editore, Milano, 1985.

[56] Alexander DeConde, *Half Bitter, Half Sweet*, Charles Scribner's Sons, New York, 1971, p. 212.

[57] Diggins, *Mussolini and Fascism* p. 279.

[58] Diggins, *Mussolini and Fascism* p. 59.

[59] Nassau *Daily Review*, November 13, 1934.

[60] Hugh Johnson, "NRA Ballyhoo," in *The New Deal, A Documentary History*, edit. by William Leuchtenberg, Harper Torchbooks, New York, 1968, p. 47.

[61] Patchogue *Advance*, March 16, 1923.

[62] John Higham, *Strangers in the Land*, Atheneum, New York, 1971 p. 247.

[63] "Julian E. Miranda," *The Immigrants Speak*, edit. LaGumina, pp. 134 and 140.

[64] Stanislao G. Pugliese, "The Culture of Nostalgia: Fascism in the Memory of Italian American," *Italian American Review*, Vol. 5 No. 2, Autumn/Winter 1996/1997, pp. 14-26.

[65] *The Italians of New York*, WPA, New York, p. 224.

[66] Philip V. Cannistraro, *Blackshirts in Little Italy*, Italian Americans and Fascism 1921-1929, Bordighera Press, West Lafayette, Indiana, 1999, p. 10-13.

[67] "Joseph Zappulla," *Immigrants Speak*, p. 84.

[68] See Josephine Rossi, *Immigrants Speak*, p. 162.

[69] Diggins, *Mussolini and Fascism*, p.84-85.

[70] Diggins, *Mussolini and Fascism,*pp. 342-343, 348.

[71] Vanni B. Montana, *Amorostico*, U. Bastogi Editore, Livorno, p.164.

[72] "La Fede E La Mia Forza," *Il Carroccio*, Anno XIV No. 1 Gennaio 1928, pp. 10-11.

[73] Teresa Cerasuola, "The Arthur Avenue/Belmont/Fordham Neighborhood of the Bronx, New York," *Italian Americans in Transition*, edit. Joseph V. Scelsa, Salvatore J. LaGumina, Lydio Tomasi, American Italian-Historical Association, Staten Island, New York, 1990, pp. 75-78. See also Diggins, *Mussolini and Fascism*, pp. 94-95.

[74] For extensive background see Mary Ann DeNino, "Ethnic and Political Consciousness in the New York Italian American Community, 1940-1944," thesis, San Diego State University, 1980, p. 81.

[75] See Charles Killinger, "Nazioni Unite and the Anti-Fascist Exiles in New York City, 1940-1946," *The Italian American Review*, Vol 8, Number 1, Spring/ Summer 2001, pp. 157-195.

[76] DeNino, p. 88. See also Killinger, "Nazioni Unite and the Anti-Fascist Exiles in New York City, 1940-1946," pp. 168-169.

[77] David M. Kennedy, *Freedom From Fear*, Oxford University Press, New York, 1999, p. 395-7.

[78] Charles Callan Tansill, *Backdoor to War*, Henry Regenery Company, Chicago, 1952, p. 239.

[79] Fiorello B. Ventresco, "Italian Americans and the Ethiopian Crisis," *Italian Americana*. Vol. 6 No 1, Fall/Winter 1980, 4-27.

[80] Eleanor Clark. "The Italian Press in New York,: *The New Republic*. November 6, 1935, 356.

[81] DeConde, *Half Bitter, Half Sweet, An Excursion into Italian-American History*, Charles Scribners Sons, New York, 1971,p. 219.

[82] DeConde, *Half Bitter, Half Sweet,* pp. 218-219.

[83] Sando Bologna, letter to Salvatore LaGumina, June 19, 1995.

[84] Ventresco, pp. 14-16, 18-19, 20.

[85] Robert A. Divine. *The Illusion of Neutrality*. Chicago: The University of Chicago Press, 1962, 132.

[86] Tansill, *Backdoor to War*, p. 246.

[87] Divine, *The Illusion of Neutrality,* pp.150-151, Nadia Venturini, *Neri e Italiani ad Harlem*. Roma, Lavoro, p 129.

[88] Arnold Schankman, "The Image of the Italian in the Afro American press 1886-1936," *Italian Americana*. Vol. 4 No. 1, Fall/Winter 1976, 30-49.

[89] New York *Daily News*, October 4, 1935.

[90] New York *Times*, October, 4, 1945.

[91] John Diggins. *Mussolini and Fascism*, p. 288.

[92] Charles V. Hamilton. *Adam Clayton Powell Jr.,* New York: Macmillan Publishing Co., 1991, 90.

[93] Thomas Kessner. *Fiorello LaGuardia and the Making of Modern New York*, New York: Penguin Books, 1991, 373. At the time Powell was on the verge of inheriting leadership of Harlem's influential Abyssinian Baptist Church from his father, then serving as pastor. It is fascinating to note the Ethiopian origins

of this church which was created in 1808 by Ethiopian merchants in New York who were offended by the discrimination to which they were subject at the white Baptist Church in an earlier period. This unique background renders it more understandable that congregants and church supporters took particular offense at Italy's invasion of the African country. It is not surprising therefore, to learn that in 1954 Congressman Powell arranged for the United States State Department to encourage Emperor Haile Selassie, to visit Powell's Abyssinian Baptist Church in Harlem, on which occasion the Ethiopian emperor presented the congressman with a gold medallion that he wore and displayed constantly for the rest of his life. See Hamilton, 73, 208, for more on this matter.

[94] Venturini. *Neri e Italiani ad Harlem*. 115-116.

[95] Diggins. *Mussolini and Fascism*, 306.

[96] LaGumina, *Vito Marcantonio, The peoples Politician*. Dubuque, Iowa, Kendall/Hunt, 1969, 36.

[97] Gerald Meyer. *Vito Marcantonio Radical Politician 1902-1954*. Albany: State University of New York Press, 1989, 119.

[98] Hamilton, *Adam Clayton Powell Jr.*, 66.

[99] Covello, *The Heart is the Teacher*, pp. 188-189.

[100] DeConde, Half Bitter, Half Sweet, p. 240.

[101] Roy V. Peel, *Political Clubs of New York City*, I.J. Friedman Publishing Co., Port Washington, New York, 1935, p. 186.

[102] A Republican Party organ, L'Aurora sought to wean the Italian ethnic vote away from the Democrats in favor Republicans. "Italian Politics and Political Leaders, " *L'Aurora*, October 12, MCMXII.

[103] Doris K. Goodwin, *No Ordinary Time*, Simon and Schuster Inc., New York, 1994, pp. 67-68.

[104] Stefano Luconi, "World War II and Italian American Voters," *Italian Americans A Retrospective on the Twentieth Century*, Paola Sensi-Isolani and Anthony J. Tamburri, editors, American Italian Historical Association, 1999, p.54; New York *Times*, June 4, 1940.

[105] Examples of stiletto-induced violence attributed to Italians can be found in *WOP, A Documentary History of Anti-Italian Discrimination in the United States*, Straight Arrow Books, San Francisco, 1973, pp. 31 and 126.

[106] Gay Talese, *Unto The Sons*, Alfred A. Knopf, New York, 1992, pp. 579-580.

[107] John Blum, *V Was For Victory*, Harcourt, Brace, Javonovich, New York, 1976, p.150.

[108] Louis Adamic, *From Many Lands*, Harper and Brothers Publishers, New York, 1940, pp. 336.

[109] Jeffries, *Wartime America,* p124.

[110] Interview, Joseph Corso October 17, 1963. See also Bayor, *Neighbors in Conflict,* p. 147.

[111] Simon W. Gerson, *Pete, The Story of New York's First Communist Councilman*, International Publishers, New York p. 111.

[112] See Gerald Meyer, *Vito Marcantonio*, State University of New York Press, Albany, 1989, pp. 115.

[113] Roy Hoopes, *Americans Remember the Home Front*, Berkeley Books, New York, 1992, p. 152.

Chapter III

[114] Hoopes, *Americans Remember the Home Front*, p.33.

[115] Scammacca, *Bye Bye America,* pp.66-67.

[116] Susan M. Hartmann, *The Home Front and Beyond. American Women in the 1940s*, Twayne Publishers, Boston, 1982, p. 32, 39. Jeffries. pp. 100-101.

[117] Pozzetta, "My Children are My Jewels,' p. 78, f. 33.

[118] *La Vigna* (newsletter, Lawrenceville, New Jersey), Vol. XII, Issue 3, Fall Harvest Issue, September 1995.

[119] New York *Journal American*, September 5, 1943. *Il Progresso Italo-Americano*, March 15, 1944.

[120] *Interview,* Adeline Vicario Hillman, December 12, 2003.

[121] *Il Progresso Italo-Americano*, January 30, 1944.

[122] Sadie Penzato, *Sicilian and Female*, Bedford Graphics, Inc., Publisher, New York, 1991, p. 308.

[123] *Il Progresso Italo-Americano*, February 2, 1945.

[124] Weld, *Brooklyn in America,* p. 145.

[125] Luconi, *From Paesani to White Ethnics*, p. 98.

[126] *Interview*, Francesca Magliochetti, December 13, 2003, and May 10, 2004.

[127] Tuttle, *Daddy's Gone to War*, p. 142.

[128] Queens *Gazette*, February 25, 2004, *Il Progresso Italo-Americano*, September 9, 1944.

[129] *Interview* Joseph Nastasi, June 11, 2004.

[130] New York *Times*, February 15 and 24, 1942. On the heels of the Normandie disaster, news that Nazi warships had eluded the Allies caused Mayor LaGuardia to warn New Yorkers about the increased danger that port cities like New York City faced.

[131] Daniel Petruzzi, *My War Against the Land of My Ancestors*, Fusion Press, Irving, Texas, 2000, p. 26.

[132] Richard Aquila, *Home Front Soldier*, State University Press New York, Albany, 1994, p. 26.

[133] New York *Post,* May 14, 1943.

[134] *Interview* Frank Sutera, 2003.

[135] Gary R. Mormino, *Immigrants on the Hill*, University of Illinois Press, Chicago, 1986, p. 219.

[136] *Il Progresso Italo-Americano,* December 17, 1944; February 20, 1945.

[137] *Il Progresso Italo-Americano*, September 6, 1944.

[138] Brooklyn *Eagle*, May 6, 1945.

[139] Brooklyn *Eagle*, May 20, 1945.

[140] *Il Progresso Italo-Americano*, July 8, 1942.

[141] LaGumina, *From Steerage*, p.156. Peter L. Belmonte, "Italian Americans in World War One and World War Two: An Overview," *Italian Americans A Retrospective on the Twentieth Century*, editors Paola Sensi-Isolani and Anthony J. Tamburri, American Italian Historical Association, Chicago Heights, Il, 2001, pp.29-71.

[142] *Il Progresso Italo-Americano,* June 14, 1943.

[143] *Il Progresso Italo-Americano*, March 29, 1942.

[144] *Il Progresso Italo Americano*, January 25, December 13, 1942.

[145] Edwin Granai, *Letters From Somewhere*, Burlington, Vermont, 2000, pp.3-4.

[146] LaGumina, *From Steerage*, pp.156-157.

[147] Glen Cove *Record*, November 25, December 3, 1942.

[148] Robert Anthony Orsi, *The Madonna of 115ᵗʰ Street,* Yale University press, New Haven, 1985, p. 67.

[149] For fuller explanation of attitudes of Italian Americans based on ethnicity and social class, see Tuttle, *Daddy's Gone to War*, pp. 102-103.

[150] *Il Progresso Italo-Americano*, April 9, 1942.

[151] New York *Daily News*, 1945; Glen Cove *Record*, June, 1999. *Letter* from Lt. Lawrence Switzer to Alfred Carbuto, June 21, 1950, in possession of Carbuto family of Glen Cove, New York.

[152] Diary of Antonio Cesare, LaGumina, *From Steerage to Suburb*, p. 76. I got to know Antonio Cesare who was my barber years after the war and still recall the immense pride he took in his nationality and American citizenship.

[153] Jerry Della Femina and Charles Sopkin, *An Italian Grows in Brooklyn,* Little, Brown and Co., New York, p.11. Particularly revealing is Della Femina's boast

that he has not delved into most of the serious writing on Italian American history.

[154] *Il Progresso Italo-Americano*, January 25, 1942.

[155] *Il Progresso Italo-Americano*, January 17, 1943.

[156] Frank J. Cavaioli, "Returning to Corona's Little Italy," *Italian Americana*, pp.31-51, Vol. XV, No. 1, Winter, 1997, p. 38.

[157] Jeffries, *Wartime America*, p. 48.

[158] Kennedy, *Freedom From Fear*, p. 644. The full employment phenomenon impacted virtually all Italian American enclaves as, for example, Providence, Rhode Island, which prompted the following observation, "Bread lines and soup kitchens became a memory." Luconi, *The Italian American Vote in Providence, Rhode Island 1916-1948*, Fairleigh Dickinson University Press, Madison, 2004, p. 113.

[159] *Il Progresso Italo-Americano*, July 18, 1943.

[160] *Il Progresso Italo-American,* November, 26, 1943.

[161] Kennedy, *Freedom From Fear*, p. 644.

[162] *Il Progresso Italo-American*, May 9, 1943.

[163] *Il Progresso Italo-American,* March 21, 1943.

[164] *Newsday*, September 29, 2003.

[165] Hoehling, . *Homefront, U.S.A.*, pp. 13, 43, 45.

[166] Richard R. Lingeman, *Don't You Know There's A War On?,* G.P. Putnam's Sons, New York, p. 182-184.

[167] Lingeman, , pp. *Don't You Know There's A War On?,* 180-181.

[168] Schiavelli, *Bruculinu,* p. 29.

[169] Lingeman, *Don't You Know There's A War On?,* 279-280.

[170] Edward Marrugi, *Italian Heart, American Soul, An Anthology*, Winston Publishing, Pittsford, New York, 2004, pp. 210-211.

[171] Lisa Scottoline, *Killer Smile,* Harper Collins Publishers, New York, 2004 p.353-359.

[172] Richard Polenberg, *One Nation Divisible*, Penguin Books, New York, 1980, p.57.

[173] Lawrence DiStasi, edit., *Una Storia Segreta, The Secret History of Italian American Evacuation and Internment During World War II*, Heyday Books, Berkeley, California, 2001.

[174] DiStasi, edit., *Una Storia Segreta*, p. 10-11.

[175] DiStasi, edit., *Una Storia Segreta*, p. 13.

[176] Stephen Fox, The Relocation of Italian Americans in California during

World War II," *Struggle and Success*, (edit. Paola A. Sensi-Isolani and Phyllis Martinelli), Center for Migration Studies, Staten Island, N.Y., 1993, p. p. 199.

[177] DiStasi, edit., *Una Storia Segreta*, p. 33.

[178] William C. Richardson, "Fishermen of San Diego: The Italians," *Struggle and Success*, pp. 84-94, p.85.

[179] *Il Progresso Italo-Americano*, March 21, 1943.

[180] www.house.gov/judiciary/pinz1026.

[181] Jeffries, *Wartime America,* p. 30.

[182] Hoehling, *Homefront, U.S.A.*, p. 72.

[183] *Il Progresso Italo-Americano,* May 16, 1943.

Chapter IV

[184] William S. Tuttle, Jr., *Daddy's Gone to War*, Oxford University Press, 1993, p. 100.

[185] Blum, *V Was For Victory,* p.149. The 1942 Gallup Poll that elicited answers to the question as to which nationality groups "were as good as we are in all respects," is most revealing. Italians ranked among the lowest –of sixteen groups. See. Lingeman *Don't You Know There's A War On?*, p. 333.

[186] ."The War of Nerves: Hitler's Helper," *Fortune*, Vol. 22, November, 1940, pp. 85-87 +.

[187] Luconi, *From Paesani to White Ethnics,* p. 98-99.

[188] Diggins, *Mussolini and Fascism*, p. 399.

[189] New York *Times*, February 21, and June 29, 1942. In explaining its stand the government took a contradictory position by affirming the validity of habeas corpus on the one hand, yet asserting on the other hand, that the court would accept its limitation of civil rights in the light of the national emergency.

[190] Tuttle, *Daddy's Gone to War*, pp.164 and 181.

[191] Helen Barolini, "How I Learned to Speak Italian," *Italian Americana*, December 1998, Issue 3,4, pp. 12-15.

[192] Kessner, *Fiorello LaGuardia*, p. 518.

[193] Louis Adamic, *What's Your Name?*, p.xii.

[194] Adamic, *What's Your Name?,* p. xiv.

[195] DiStasi, *Una Segreta*, p.xi.

[196] Richard W. Steele, "No Racials: Discrimination Against Ethnics in American Defense Industry, 1940-42," p.67, *Labor History*, Vol. 32, Winter/ 1991, pp. 66-90.

[197] Dominic J. Capeci, Jr., "Fiorello H. LaGuardia and Employment Discrimination, 1941-1943," *Italian Americana*, Vol. VII, Number 2, Spring/Summer 1983, pp. 49-67.

[198] Luconi, *The Italian American Vote in Providence, p. 211.*

[199] Steele, "No Racials," p.75, and pp. 80-84.

[200] *Il Progresso Italo-Americano*, June 3 and 7, 1942.

[201] LaGumina, *Vito Marcantonio, The Peoples Politician*, Kendall-Hunt Publishers, Dubuque, pp.64-65.

[202] Polenberg, *One Nation Divisible*, p. 55.

[203] *Il Progresso Italo-Americano*, December 19, 1943.

[204] Irvin L. Child, *Italian or American? –The Second Generation in Conflict*, Russell and Russell, New York, 1970, pp. 42-43.

[205] *Il Progresso Italo-Americano,* October 19, 1941.

[206] *Il Progresso Italo-Americano,* March 23, May 17, and September 5, 1942.

[207] Killinger, p. 168.

[208] Fraser M. Ottanelli, "Fascist Informant and Italian-American Labor Leader: The Paradox of Vanni Buscemi Montana," *The Italian American Review*, Vol. 7, No. 1, Spring/Summer 1999, pp. 104-116.

[209] Vanni B. Montana, *Amoristico*, U. Bastogi Editore, Livorno, 1975, pp. 171-178.

[210] John S. Crawford, *Luigi Antonini, His Influence on Italian American Relations*, New York, 1951, p.35.

[211] *Il Progresso Italo-Americano,* June 3, 1943.

[212] *Il Progresso Italo-Americano,* May 29, 1942. LaGumina, "Case Studies of Ethnicity and Italo-American Politicians," *The Italian Experience in the United States*, edit. by Tomasi and Engle, Center For Migration Studies, Staten Island, New York, 1970, p. 151.

[213] LaGumina, "Case Studies of Ethnicity and Italo-American Politicians," The Italian Experience in the United States, (Editors: S.M Tomasi and M. Engel), 1970. pp.143-161, p. 156.

[214] *Il Progresso Italo-Americano,* January 11, 1942.

[215] *Il Progresso Italo-Americano,* October 19, 1941.

[216] *Il Progresso Italo-Americano,* January 16, March 3, April 5, 1942..

[217] Jerre Mangione, *An Ethnic At Large*, G. P. Putnam's Sons, New York, 1978, p. 273.

[218] Mangione, *An Ethnic At Large,* p. 286-287.

[219] Di Stasi, *Una Storia Segreta,* p. xviii. DiStasi refines the figures further

stating that "upwards of 1,500 resident aliens were eventually arrested and given hearings meant to determine how dangerous they were. Some 257 of those deemed most dangerous were then interned for the duration of the war. See p.3.

[220] *Il Progresso Italo-Americano*, May 28, 1942.

[221] *Il Progresso Italo-Americano,* May 28 29, 30, 1942.

[222] Diggins, *Mussolini and Fascism*, p. 351.

[223] *Il Progresso Italo-Americano,* January 4, 1942.

[224] *Il Progresso Italo-Americano,* March 22, 1942.

[225] *Il Progresso Italo-Americano,* May 17, 1942.

[226] *Il Progresso Italo-Americano*, September 3 and 6, 1942.

[227] See LaGumina, *From Steerage to Suburb*, p. 137.

[228] Gilbert Sandler, *The Neighborhood The Story of Baltimore's Little Italy*, Bodine and Associates, Inc., Baltimore, Maryland, 1974, p. 41.

[229] Frank P. Augustine, *La Bella America*, Watertown Daily Times, Watertown, New York, 1989, p. 158.

[230] *Il Progresso Italo-Americano,* February 1, 1942.

[231] *The Golden Lion*, (New York State OSIA monthly) January- February 2002.

[232] *Il Progresso Italo-Americano,* August 9, 1942.

[233] New York *Journal American*, May 14, 1942.

[234] *Il Progresso Italo-Americano*, February 11, 1943; April 19, 1942.

[235] *Il Progresso Italo-Americano*, June 3 and 4, 1942.

[236] *Il Progresso Italo-Americano,* December 11, 1942, October 1, 1945.

[237] *Il Progresso Italo-Americano,* June 20, 1943; December 20, 1944, December 16, 1945.

[238] *Il Progresso Italo-Americano,* April 5, 1942; April 12, 1943.

[239] *Il Progresso Italo-Americano*, December 1, 1943.

[240] New York *Daily News*, April 21, 1942.

[241] Kenneth Paul O'Brien, Lynn Parsons Hudson, ed., *The Home Front War*, Greenwood Press, Westport, Connecticut, 1995, p. 3. See also John Bradley, *Flags of Our Fathers*, Bantam Books, New York 2000, pp. 266-267.

[242] *Il Progresso Italo-Americano,* March 23, 1942.

[243] *Il Progresso Italo-Americano,* May 17, 1942.

[244] *Il Progresso Italo-Americano,* July 26, 1942; September 9 and 20, 1943.

[245] *Il Progresso Italo-Americano,* 9/13/42.

[246] *Il Progresso Italo-Americano,* May 12, 17, September 12, 1942.

[247] Stefano Luconi, "World War II and Italian-American Voters," Italian Americans, *A Retrospective on the Twentieth Century,* edit. by Paola Sensi Isolani and Anthony J. Tamburri, American Italian Historical Association,, 2001, pp. 61-71, p.66.

[248] *Il Progresso Italo-Americano,* September 13, 1942.

[249] *Il Progresso Italo-Americano,* September 30, 1942.

[250] *Il Progresso Italo-Americano,* October 5, 1942.

[251] Mangione, *Ethnic at Large,* p. 287.

[252] *Il Progresso Italo-Americano,* October 18, 1942.

[253] *Il Progresso Italo-Americano,* October 15, 19/42.

[254] *Il Progresso Italo-Americano,* October 16, 1942; April 12, 1943.

Chapter V

[255] Tricarico, *Greenwich Village,* p. 34.

[256] *Il Progresso Italo-Americano,* August 7, 1945.

[257] Octavia Capuzzi Locke, "My Mamma's Letters" *Reader's Digest,* V140 June 1992, pp.125-127. "Mamma's Letter Writing," *Johns Hopkins Magazine,* June 1987, pp. 17-19.

[258] Joseph Bentivegna *Interview,* Nov. 12, 1999.

[259] Guido Tintori, "New Discoveries, Old Prejudices," *Una Storia,* DiStasi, p. 244.

[260] *Il Progresso Italo-Americano,* January 4, 1942.

[261] *Il Progresso Italo-Americano,* November 7, 1943.

[262] *Il Progresso Italo-Americano,* August 27, 1945. The often-quoted figure that more than one million Italian Americans served in the armed forces was stated repeatedly throughout the war and afterward. In April 1944, for instance, newly-appointed Chairman of the Democratic National Committee, Robert Hannegan, profuse in his greetings to Italian Americans, referred to the more than one million in uniform. *Il Progresso Italo-Americano,* April 18, 1944.

[263] *Il Progresso Italo-Americano,* February 2, 1943.

[264] New York *Daily News,* March 21, 1942. *Il Progresso Italo-Americano,* April 19, September 19, 1942; February 23, May 12, 1943.

[265] New York *Sun,* July 7, 1943. *l Progresso Italo-Americano,* March 20, 1943.

[266] *Il Progresso Italo-Americano,* March 23 August 8, 1943; December 17, 1944.

[267] *Il Progresso Italo-Americano,* November 7, 1943.

[268] *Congressional Record,* 79th Cong.,1st sess., Vol. 91, July 24, 1945, p.7995.

[269] *Il Progresso Italo-Americano,* August 27, 1945.

[270] Jonathan James Cavallero, "Redefining Italianita: The Difference Between Mussolini, Italy, Germany, and Japan in Frank Capra's "Why We Fight,'", *Italian Americana* Vol. XXII, Number 1, Winter 2004, pp. 5-16.

[271] Cavallero, "Redefining Italianita: The Difference Between Mussolini, Italy, Germany, and Japan in Frank Capra's "Why We Fight," p. 11.

[272] Cavallero, , "Redefining Italianita: The Difference Between Mussolini, Italy, Germany, and Japan in Frank Capra's "Why We Fight,"p.12.

[273] *Michael S. Shull and David Edward Wilt, Hollywood War Films, 1937-1945,* Macfarland and Co. Publishers, Jefferson, North Carolina, 1996, p. 399. It is especially revealing to note that the descriptive entry in this book fails to mention that this story was based on Toscani's real life experience. The Council of Books in Wartime designated the book on which the film was based as one of the books to promote the good that Americans were performing during the conflict.

[274] *Il Progresso Italo-Americano,* October 21, 1944.

[275] *Il Progresso Italo-Americano,* November 11, 12,23, 1942; June 4, 1943.

[276] *Il Progresso Italo-Americano,* June 28, September 13, October 25, 1942.

[277] .For more on the remarkable transplantation of a culture from Sicily to Middletown, Connecticut see Walter Sangree, *Mel Hyblaeum,* Masters Dissertation, Wesleyan University, May 1952.

[278] An Italian national and member of the Organization for Italian Resistance, Raimondo Craveri, is quite explicit in his praise of Corvo and the work of the Italian Section of the O. S. S., Raimondo Craveri, *La Compagna d'Italia e I Servizi Segreti, La Storia dell'ORI (1943-1945),* La Pietra, Milano, 1980, passim. See also R. Harris Smith, *OSS The Secret History of America's First Central Intelligence Agency,* University of California Press, Berkeley, California, 1972, p. 85.

[279] See Max Corvo, *The O.S.S. in Italy 1942-1945, A Personal Memoir,* Praeger Books, New York, 1990, p. 5. Although there has been some criticism about the effectiveness of Corvo's operation, he nevertheless is credited with understanding the best ways to carry out intelligence activities in Italy. Vittorio Gozzer, "OSS and ORI: the Raimondo Craveri and Max Corvo Partnership," *Journal of Modern Italian Studies,* Vol. 4 Number 1, Fall 1999, pp.32-36.

[280] The Corvo/Donovan relationship was undoubtedly strengthened by Corvo's marriage to Donovan's niece. See letter from Earl Brennan to Martin S. Quigley,

August 27, 1981 "Martin S. Quigley Papers, Box 1, Folder 51, Georgetown University.

[281] Bradley F. Smith *The Shadow Warriors*, Basic Books, Inc. Publishers, New York, 1983, p.xv.

[282] Studs Terkel, *The Good War*, Pantheon Books, New York, p. 459.

[283] Petruzzi, *My War,* p. 48, describes how his experience of reading a Division HQ bulletin board notice ordering anyone who could speak French, Spanish, German, or Italian led to report for schooling and training as a prisoner of war interrogator.

[284] Smith, *The Shadow Warriors,* p. 228. See also Stephen Ambrose, *The Supreme Commander: The War Years of General Dwight D. Eisenhower,* (Doubleday, Garden City, N.Y. 1970), p. 216.

[285].Corvo, *The O.S.S. in Italy 1942-1945, A Personal Memoir,* pp. 42,, 273, 236.

[286] *Letter* from Barney Levantino to author, September 10, 2004.

[287] Corvo, *The O.S.S. in Italy 1942-1945, A Personal Memoir*, p. 63.

[288] Letter from Earl Brennan to Martin S. Quigley, August 27, 1981, "Martin S. Quigley Papers," Box 1, Folder 51, Georgetown University Archives. So extraordinary was the relationship between Brennan and Corvo that when Brennan died, Corvo was designated guardian of his ashes. Letter from Max Corvo to Martin S. Quigley, May 9, 1985, "Martin S. Quigley Papers, Box 1, Folder 65, Georgetown University.

[289] B. F. Smith, *The Shadow Warriors,* p. 229.

[290] *Interview,* Frank J. Tarallo, by Salvatore J. LaGumina, Aug. 2, 1975, Middletown, Connecticut.

[291] B. F. Smith, *The Shadow Warriors,* p.210.

[292] *Interview*, Tarallo.

[293] Ambrose, *Eisenhower,* p.221. See also Marc Antonio Bragadin, *The Italian Navy in World War II,* Annapolis, Md. 1957, p. 253 for information on German troop buildup in the spring of 1943.

[294] Carlo D'Este, *Bitter Victory, Battle for Sicily,* E.P. Dutton, New York, 1988, p 627.

[295] *Interview*, Tarallo.

[296] *Interview,* Tarallo.

[297] Allan M. Winkler, *Home Front U.S.A. –America During World War II,* p. 64. See also Jeffries, *Wartime America,* pp. 114-115.

[298] *Il Progresso Italo-Americano,* August 3, 1943. See also Winkler, *America During World War II,* p.65.

[299] For more insight on this matter see, Pozzetta, "My Children are my Jewels,' 70-1.

[300] *Il Progresso Italo-Americano*, June 6, 1943.

[301] *Il Progresso Italo-Americano,* July 9, 1944.

Chapter VI

[302] *Il Progresso Italo-Americano,* May 23, 1943.

[303] San Diego *Union*, June 25, 1943.

[304] *Il Progresso Italo-Americano,* 9/20/42, 11/6/42

[305] *Il Progresso Italo-Americano,* September 6, 1942.

[306] *Il Progresso Italo-Americano,* July 8, 1945.

[307] *Il Progresso Italo-Americano,* July 18, 1943.

[308] New York *Journal American*, September 3, 1943.

[309] *The New Yorker*, Vol. 19, June 26, 1943, pp. 14-15. See also *Il Progresso Italo-Americano*, July 4, 1943.

[310] New York *Daily Mirror*, as quoted in *Il Progresso Italo-Americano* , June 20, 1943.

[311] A. Russell Buchanan, *The United States and World War II,* Vol. I, Harper & Row Publishers, New York, p.186.

[312] New York *Times*, July 26, 1943.

[313] *Il Progresso Italo-Americano,* September 9, 1943.

[314] New York Times, July 26, 1943. *Il Progresso Italo-Americano*, September 9, 1943.

[315] Winston Churchill, *Closing the Ring*, Houghton Mifflin Company, Boston, 1951, p. 140.

[316] *Il Progresso Italo-Americano*, May 14, 1944.

[317] New York *Times,* June 13, 1944.

[318] Allen V. Martini, "15 Minutes Over Paris," *Saturday Evening Post,* Vol. 216, November 20, 1943, pp.12-15.

[319] *Il Progresso Italo-Americano*, August 1, 1943.

[320] New York *Times*, June 3, 1944.

[321] Mark M. Spagnuolo, *Don S. Gentile, Soldier of God and Country*, College Press, East Lansing, Mi., 1986, p. vii.

[322] Spagnuolo, *Gentile,* p. 125.

[323] For more on Gentile's spirituality see Spaguolo, *Gentile,* passim.

[324] Spagnuolo, *Don S. Gentile,* 287-288,

[325] *Il Progresso Italo-Americano*, April 20, 1944.

[326] *Il Progresso Italo Americano*, April 13 to 24, 1944.

[327] *Il Progresso Italo Americano,* April 21, 1944

[328] Spagnuolo, *Don S. Gentile,* 303- 313.

[329] *Medal of Honor, 1863-1968*, Committee on Labor and Public Welfare, United States Senate, Sub-committee on Veterans Affairs, 90th Cong. 2nd Sess.

[330] Franklin M. Reck, *Beyond the Call of Duty,* Thomas Y. Crowell, New York, 1944, pp. 19-26.

[331] Brokaw, *The Greatest Generation*, p. XXI. Having quit school before he entered the service at the end of the war Merli returned to high school where he completed his courses to obtain his degree. Aware of his fame his younger classmates also sought his autograph. *Il Progresso Italo-Americano*, October 5, 1945.

[332] "Life Goes to a Hero's Homecoming," *Life*, Vol. 15, No. 15,(October 11, 1943), pp.126-129; Daniel Monaco, "Above and Beyond the Call, The John Basilone Story," *Ambassador*, Vol. 24, Winter 1994- 1995, pp. 14-17.

[333] San Diego *Union*, June 25, 1943; New York *Journal-American*, September 5, 1943.

[334] Monaco, "Above and Beyond the Call," p.17.

[335] A fuller account of the actions is to be found in James D. Horan and Gerald Franks, *Out in the Boondocks,* G. P. Putnam's Sons, New York, 1943, pp. 11-19.

[336] *Newsday*, July 23, 1987.

[337] . For more information on this topic see: Deanna Paoli Gumina, *The Italians of San Francisco 1850-1930.* Center for Migration Studies, Staten Island, N.Y., 1978.

[338] *Il Progresso Italo-Americano,* March 21, 1943.

[339] Noel F. Busch, "Joe DiMaggio," *Life*, (May 1, 1939), pp.63-69.

[340] Murray Kempton, "Joltin Joe --Oddly Struck as a Mortal," *Newsday*, February 16, 1987.

[341] Noel F. Busch, "Joe DiMaggio," *Life*, (May 1, 1939,) pp. 63-69.

[342] Maury Allen, *Where Have You Gone Joe DiMaggio*," E. P. Dutton & Co., Inc. New York, 1975, p. 49.

[343] *Current Biography*, 1941, p. 226.

[344] Ken Ringle, "To Be Perfectly Frank," Washington *Post*, December 10, 1995.

[345] Pete Hamill, *Why Sinatra Matters*, Little, Brown &Co., New York, p. 93.

[346] Hamill, *Why Sinatra Matters,* p. 38.

[347] Hamill, *Why Sinatra Matters*, p.38.

[348] Hamill, *Why Sinatra Matters*, p.42.

[349] Boston *Globe,* May 15, 1998.

[350] *Il Progresso Italo-Americano*, October 24, 1945.

[351] Arnold Shaw, *Sinatra Twentieth Century Romantic*, Holt, Rinehart and Winston, New York, 1968, p. 67.

[352] Gay Talese, "Frank Sinatra Has a Cold," *Fame and Obscurity*, World Publishing Co. New York, 1970, pp.-3-40.

[353] *Il Progresso Italo-Americano*, July 16, 1944.

[354] *Il Progresso Italo-Americano*, October 25, 1945.

[355] *Il Progresso Italo-Americano*, November 3 and 8, 1945.

[356] Hamill, *Why Sinatra Matters*, p. 180.

Chapter VII

[357] LaGumina, *Impellitteri*, pp. 28-30.

[358] Jerome Krase, "The Missed Step," *Italians and Irish in America,* ed. Francis X. Femminella, Staten Island, American Italian Historical Association, 1985, pp. 184-187.

[359] Krase and Charles La Cerra, *Ethnicity and Machine Politics*, University Press of America, New York, 1991, p. 10.

[360] Krase and La Cerra, *Ethnicity and Machine Politics,* 77-95.

[361] Krase and La Cerra, *Ethnicity and Machine Politics,* pp. 38-41.

[362] Weld, *Brooklyn in America,* p.146.

[363] Weld *Brooklyn in America,*p.148.

[364] *Marcantonio Papers,* Box 14, Folder: International Relations, Italy General. Letter from Marcantonio to General J.A. Ulio, April 24, 1942. Letter from Alan Cranston to Marcantonio, April 27, 1942. Box 22, Folder Italo-Americans in this War, Speech, August 6, 1943.

[365] *Il Progresso Italo-Americano*, October 11, 1942; June 6, 1943.

[366] LaGumina , "Case Studies of Ethnicity and Italo-American Politicians," *The Italian Experience in the United States*, (S.M. Tomasi, M. H. Engel, eds., Staten Island, 1970, p. 151.

[367] Alfred Connable and Edward Silberfarb, "Carmine DeSapio in the Smokeless Room," *Tigers of Tammany*, Holt Rinehart, and Winston, New York, 1967 pp. 295-333, p. 305.

[368] New York *Times*, July 28, 2004, See also, Connable, Tigers of Tammany;

Warren Moscow, *The Last of the Big Time Bosses,* Stein and Day Publishers, New York, 1971.

[369] *Il Progresso Italo-Americano* August 1, 1943.

[370] Diggins, *Mussolini and Fascism*, p.348.

[371] *Il Progresso Italo-Americano* November 23, 1942.

[372] Diggins, *Mussolini and Fascism*, p. 332.

[373] New York *Times*, February 21 and May 4, 1944.

[374] See Alberto Cupelli, "The U.S. Italian Language Press Dances to the Nazi Tune," *Il Mondo,* Vol. Vii., No. 6, June 1944, pp. 3-8, p.5.

[375] Killinger, "Nazione Unite...," pp.157-195.

[376] Killinger, "Nazione Unite...," p. 165.

[377] Dorothy Gallagher, *All The Right Enemies,* Penguin Books, New York, 1989, p. 195.

[378] Lorraine M. Lees, National Security and Ethnicity: Contrasting Views during World War II," *Diplomatic History*, Vol. 11, No. 2, 1987, pp. 1134-125.

[379] Thomas Kessner, *Fiorello LaGuardia and the Making of Modern New York*, Penguin Books, 1991, 519.

[380] *Il Progresso Italo-Americano,* June 20, 1943.

[381] New York *Daily Mirror*, June 17, 1943, as quoted in *Il Progresso Italo-Americano,* June 20, 1943.

[382] Diggins, *Mussolini and Fascism*, pp.409, 415.

[383] Reginald Rowan Belknap, *American House Building Work in Messina and Reggio*, G.P. Putnam's Sons, New York, 1910, p. 260.

[384] *Il Progresso Italo-Americano* Aug 4, 1943.

[385] Francis Spellman, "Report from Italy," *Colliers*, Vol. 115, January 20, 1945, p. 11. See also: "Revolution Threatens Italy," *American Mercury,* Vol. 59, December 1944, pp.647-657; Hilda Fisher, "The Allies Blunder in Italy," *Current History*, Vol. 8, January 1945, pp. 52-56.

[386] *Il Progresso Italo-Americano,* July 27, August 8, 29, 1943.

[387] *Il Progresso Italo-Americano,* July 2, 1943.

[388] *Il Progresso Italo-Americano,* July 25, 1943.

[389] *Il Progresso Italo-Americano,* August 8, 1943.

[390] Diggins, *Mussolini and Fascism,* p. 417.

[391] *Il Progresso Italo-Americano,* April 26, 1944.

[392] *Il Progresso Italo-Americano,* April 23, 1944.

[393] *Il Progresso Italo-Americano,* April 15, July 4,12, 1945.

[394] *Il Progresso Italo-Americano*, February 2, 1945.

[395] Harry Coles and Albert K. Weinberg, *United States Army in World War II,* Special Studies, *Civil Affairs: Soldiers Become Governors,* Center for Military History, United States Army Washington, D.C. 1992, pp. 166-167.

[396] *Il Progresso Italo-Americano,* June 22, 1944.

[397] New York *Sun*, July 24, 1943.

[398] New York *Times*, March 27, 1944.

[399] New York *Times*, October 2, 1944.

[400] *Il Progresso Italo-Americano* June 22, 1944.

[401] Buchanan, *The United States and World War II,* p. 174.

[402] Musmanno, *The Italians in America*, p.7; Mike Dillon, "La Storia, Michael A. Musmanno," *Primo*, Vol. 3, No. 4, pp. 18-23. *Il Progresso Italo-Americano,* April 5, 1942.

[403] Glenn B. Infield, *Disaster at Bari*, New York: Macmillan, 1971, p. 83.

[404] *Il Progresso Italo-Americano,* June 25, 1944.

[405] New York *Times, April* 27, 1944.

[406] *Il Progresso Italo-Americano* June 25, 1944.

[407] .www: Judge Marchisio, "Memo Robert S. Patterson to Franklin D. Roosevelt, August 31, 1941.

[408] New York *Times*, October 18, December 11, 1944.

[409] *Il Progresso Italo-Americano,* September 20, November 6, 1942.

[410] *Il Progresso Italo- Americano* September 26, 1942.

Chapter VIII

[411] Kennedy, *Freedom From Fear*, p. 600.

[412] DeConde, *Half Bitter, Half Sweet*, p. 250.

[413] *Il Progresso Italo-Americano*, June 4, 1944.

[414] *Il Progresso Italo-Americano,* November 23, 1943.

[415] *Il Progresso Italo-Americano,* June 11, 1944.

[416] *Il Progresso Italo-Americano,* July 18, 1943.

[417] Mormino, Immigrants on the Hill, p. 224.

[418] *Il Progresso Italo-Americano,* August 8,14,23, September 1, December 2, 1943.

[419] Westbury *Times*, February 25, 1944; *Il Progresso Italo-Americano,* June 26, 1944.

⁴²⁰ *Il Progresso Italo-Americano,* August 12, 1943.

⁴²¹ *Interview,* Phil Dario, December 12, 2003.

⁴²² *Interview,* Elmeda Capoferri Deitz, September 12, 2003.

⁴²³ Orsi, *Madonna of 115ᵗʰ Street,* p. 69.

⁴²⁴ Miranda, *The Immigrants Speak,* (Edit. LaGumina), pp. 133-134.

⁴²⁵ Belmonte, *Italian Americans in World War II,* p. 100; *Interview,* Francesca LaGumina June 6,2004.

⁴²⁶ Belmonte, *Italian Americans in World War II,* p. 100.

⁴²⁷ Letter John Brindisi to author , n.d.

⁴²⁸ Richard Aquila, *Home Front Soldier,* State University of New York Press, Albany, 1999, p. 42.

⁴²⁹ *Il Progresso Italo-Americano,* December 16, 1943, June 21, 1945.

⁴³⁰ New York *Sun,* July 17, 1943.

⁴³¹ *Interview,* Albert Romeo, March 7, 1985.

⁴³² Charles Ferroni, "POWS during WWII,"unpublished manuscript, and accompanying letter from Ferroni to LaGumina, April 3, 1995. p.16.

⁴³³ DeConde, *Half Bitter, Half Sweet,* p. 255.

⁴³⁴ Ennio Di Nolfi, "The Italian Americans and American Foreign Policy From World War II To The Cold War (1940-1948)," pp. -107, *The United States and Italy: The First Two Hundred Years,* Humbert S. Nelli, editor, American Italian Historical Association, New York, 1977, p. 99.

⁴³⁵ New York *Times,* May 27, 1944.

⁴³⁶ DeConde, *Half Bitter, Half Sweet,* p. 260, 262.

⁴³⁷ Mary L. DiNinno, "Ethnic and Political Consciousness in the New York Italian Community, 1940-1944," Thesis, San Diego State University, 1980, pp. 160-164.

⁴³⁸ Luconi, "World War II and Italian American Voters," *Italian Americans, A Retrospective on the Twentieth Century,* American Italian Historical Association, 2002, pp. 51-71.

⁴³⁹ OSS-FNB Report No. B-201, 31 May 1944, File 191-210, Box 1960. (Cited by DiNinno, p. 167.)

⁴⁴⁰ DiNolfo. "The Italian-Americans and American Foreign," pp. 92-107, p. 100.

⁴⁴¹ DiNinno, "Ethnic and Political Consciousness," pp. 176-177. DiNinno accused Italian American leaders in 1943 of "paying lip service" to the notion of effecting a true democratic transformation of Italy.

⁴⁴² Frances Perkins, *The Roosevelt I Knew,* Harper and Row, New York, 1946, p. 120.

443 Robert E. Sherwood, Grosset and Dunlap, New York, 1950, p. 822.

444 New York *Times*, October 19, 1944.

445 LaGumina, *Vito Marcantonio*, p. 68.

446 Luconi, *From Paesani to White Ethnics*, p.108.

447 Divine, Foreign Policy, The Illusion p. 145.

448 Arthur M. Schlesinger, Jr., editor, *History of Presidential Elections, 1789*-1968, Vol. IV, McGraw-Hill Publishers, New York, 1971, p. 3090.

449 Jeffries, *Wartime America*, p. 166.

450 DiNinno, "Ethnic and Political Consciousness," pp.179-181.

451 *Il Progresso Italo-Americano*, October 15, 1944. DiNinno, "Ethnic and Political Consciousness," p. 185.

452 New York *Times*, November 9, 1944.

453 Louis L. Gerson, *The Hyphenate in Recent American Politics and Diplomacy*, University of Kansas Press, Lawrence, 1964, p. 127.

454 *Il Progresso Italo-Americano,* February 11, 12, 1944.

455 New York *Times*, May 28, 1944.

456 Mario Macaluso, *Prickly Pears and Oleanders*, 1st Books Press, 2002, p. 43.

457 *Il Progresso Italo-Americano,* January 10, 1944.

458 *Il Progresso Italo-Americano,* April 23, 1944.

459 *Il Progresso Italo-Americano*, October 19, 1945.

460 *Interview,* Nastasi, June 11, 2004.

461 Janet Worrall, "Italian Prisoners of War in the United States: 1943-1945," *Italians Americans in Transition*, Proceedings of the XXI Annual Conference of the American Italian Historical Association, (edit. by Joseph Scelsa, Salvatore J. LaGumina, Lydio Tomasi, 1990, pp.253-261.

462 Nat Brandt, *Harlem at War*, Syracuse University Press 1996, p. 219.

463 Ferroni, "POWS during WWII," p. 40.

464 DeConde, *Half Bitter, Half Sweet*, p. 262.

465 New York *Times* June 18, 1944.

466 Brooklyn *Eagle*, May 10, 1945.

467 Worrall, "World War II, Internment, and Prisoners of War," *The Italian American Experience: An Encyclopedia*, (edit. LaGumina, et. al.), Garland Publishers, New York, 2000, p. 704.

468 *Il Progresso Italo-Americano*, July 10, 1943.

469 Interview Madeline Sutera, June 4, 2003.

[470] Orsi, *The Madonna of 115ᵗʰ Street*, p. 68.

[471] New York *Times,* June 18, 1944)

[472] Augustine, *La Bella America*, 159.

[473] Musmanno, *The Story of the Italians in America*, p. 216.

[474] David Neft, Richard M. Cohen, Michael L. Neft, *The Sports Encyclopedia, Baseball*, St. Martins, New York, pp. 228-229.

[475] Nat Fleischer and Sam Andre, *An Illustrated History of Boxing*, Citadel press, New York, 2001, p. 351. *Il Progresso Italo-Americano,* March 29, 1942.

[476] Curt Samson, "Family Album," *Golf Digest*, Vol. 42, January 2000, p.36+. *Il Progresso Italo-Americano,* December 7, 1942.

Chapter IX

[477] Bradley, *Flags of Our Fathers*, p.294.

[478] *Il Progresso Italo-Americano*, July 4, 1945

[479] Bradley, *Flyboys*, Little, Brown & Co., New York, 2003, p. 6.

[480] *Il Progresso Italo-Americano,* September 18, 1944.

[481] *Il Progresso Italo-Americano,* May 7, 1943.

[482] *The Golden Lion,* Vol. 37, No. 11-12, November-December, 2003.

[483] Henry A. Mucci, "We Swore We'd Die or Do It'" *Saturday Evening Post,* April 7, 1945, pp. 18-19.

[484] New York *Times*, February 2, 1945. See also Henry Mucci, "Rescue at Cabanatuan," *Infantry Journal,* Vol.:56, April 1945, pp. 15-19.

[485] *Il Progresso Italo-Americano*, June 25, 1945.

[486] New York *Post*, May 4, 1943.

[487] Louis Zamperini with David Rensi, *Devil at My Heels*, William Morrow, New York, 2003, p120.

[488] Zamperini, *Devil at My Heels,* p. 284.

[489] Brokaw, *The Greatest Generation*, p. 15.

[490] *Il Progresso Italo-Americano*, March 8, 21, 28, 1943.

[491] *Il Progresso Italo-Americano*, May 12, 1943.

[492] Brooklyn *Eagle*, June 3, 1945.

[493] New York *Sun*, August 6, 1943.

[494] New York *Sun*, July 8, 1943.

[495] Ralph Cindrich, Lessons in Life, Profootball Weekly.com. June 2, 2003.

[496] *Il Progresso Italo-Americano*, January 10, 1944. This was not the first time that Fuoto demonstrated bravery --he earned battlefield commendation for the Tunisian campaign and the landing at Salerno.

[497] *Newsday*, September 3, 1995.

[498] *The Daily Star*, Oneonta, October 12, 1996.

[499] *Newsday*, June 15, 2000.

[500] *Il Progresso Italo-Americano,* December 24, 1944.

[501] *Il Progresso Italo-Americano*, May 23, 1943.

[502] Long Island *Star Journal*, August 24, 1944.

[503] Jeanie Prianti Bongiorno, *Newsday*, November 7, 1995 and August 13, 1998.

[504] *Il Progresso Italo-Americano*, December 6, 1942.

[505] Kearns Goodwin, *No Ordinary Time*, pp.339, 448-449.

[506] *La Vigna,* Vol. XII, Issue 3, Fall Harvest Issue, September 1995.

[507] Jeffries, *Wartime America*, p. 173.

[508] *Il Progresso Italo-Americano*, May 9, 1945.

[509] Jay Maeder, editor, *Big Town, Big Time*, New York *Daily News*, New York, 1999, p. 105.

[510] *Il Progresso Italo-Americano*, August 26, 1945.

[511] Bradley, *Flags of Our Fathers,* p.305.

[512] Tuttle, *Daddy's Gone to War,* pp. 101-102.

[513] Luconi, *The Italian American Vote in Providence,* p. 112.

[514] Pozzetta, "My Children are My Jewels,' p.74; Ferroni, "POWS during WWII," p. 16.

[515] Pozzetta, "My Children are My Jewels,' p. 72.

[516] Mario Puzo, "Choosing a Dream: Italians in Hell's Kitchen," *The Godfather Papers*, Fawcett Publications, Inc., Greenwich, Conn. 1972, p. 26.

[517] Jeffries, *Wartime America,* pp. 186-187.

[518] Jeffries, *Wartime America,* p.188.

[519] Wartime prosperity was evidenced even among Italian Americans engaged in farming as, for example, in the New Paltz, New York area. "The war had caused the price of apples and other agricultural products to skyrocket! Thus the farm prospered even more." Penzato, *Sicilian and Female,* p. 307.

INDEX

LaVergne, TN USA
09 February 2010
172466LV00004B/158/A